Law and Philosophy Library

Volume 135

The Law and Philosophy Library, which has been in existence since 1985, aims to publish cutting edge works in the philosophy of law, and has a special history of publishing books that focus on legal reasoning and argumentation, including those that may involve somewhat formal methodologies. The series has published numerous important books on law and logic, law and artificial intelligence, law and language, and law and rhetoric. While continuing to stress these areas, the series has more recently expanded to include books on the intersection between law and the Continental philosophical tradition, consistent with the traditional openness of the series to books in the Continental jurisprudential tradition. The series is proud of the geographic diversity of its authors, and many have come from Latin America, Spain, Italy, the Netherlands, Germany, and Eastern Europe, as well, more obviously for an English-language series, from the United Kingdom, the United States, Australia and Canada.

More information about this series at http://www.springer.com/series/6210

Pierluigi Chiassoni • Bojan Spaić
Editors

Judges and Adjudication in Constitutional Democracies: A View from Legal Realism

Springer

Editors
Pierluigi Chiassoni
University of Genova
Genova, Italy

Bojan Spaić
University of Belgrade
Belgrade, Serbia

ISSN 1572-4395 ISSN 2215-0315 (electronic)
Law and Philosophy Library
ISBN 978-3-030-58185-5 ISBN 978-3-030-58186-2 (eBook)
https://doi.org/10.1007/978-3-030-58186-2

This Springer imprint is published by the registered company Springer Nature Switzerland AG.
The registered company address is: Gewerbestrasse 11, 6330 Cham, Switzerland

Contents

Editors and Contributors

About the Editors

Pierluigi Chiassoni is Professor of Jurisprudence at the University of Genova School of Law and a permanent fellow of Tarello Institute for Legal Philosophy. His jurisprudential interests span from economic analysis of law to legal interpretation and human rights. His main publications include Positivismo giuridico. Una investigazione analitica (Mucchi Editore, 2013), Tecnica dell'interpretazione giuridica (il Mulino, 2007), El discreto placer del positivismo jurídico (Externado de Colombia, 2016), La tradición analítica en la filosofia del derecho. De Bentham a Kelsen (Palestra, 2017), Ensayos de metajurisprudencia analítica (Olejnik, 2017), and Interpretation Without Truth (Springer, 2019).

Bojan Spaić is Assistant Professor of Jurisprudence at the University of Belgrade Faculty of Law and Alexander von Humboldt Research Fellow of the Institute for Public Law, Constitutional Law and Legal Philosophy of the University of Heidelberg. He has edited books in English and in Serbian including Jurisprudence and Political Philosophy in the 21st Century: Reassessing Legacies (with Miodrag Jovanović, published by Peter Lang, 2012), Fundamental Rights: Justification and Interpretation (with Kenneth Einar Himma, Eleven International Publishing, 2016), and Unpacking Normativity: Conceptual, Normative, and Descriptive Issues (with Kenneth Einar Himma and Miodrag Jovanović, Hart Publishing, 2018). He has published three books in Serbian and papers in Serbian and English regarding legal interpretation, ontological and methodological hermeneutics, and pragmatism.

Contributors

Luka Burazin University of Zagreb, Zagreb, Croatia

Pierluigi Chiassoni University of Genova, Genova, Italy

Riccardo Guastini University of Genova, Tarello Institute for Legal Philosophy, Genova, Italy

Jasminka Hasanbegović University of Belgrade Faculty of Law, Belgrade, Serbia

Brian Leiter Karl N. Llewellyn Professor of Jurisprudence and Director of the Center for Law, Philosophy and Human Values, The University of Chicago Law School, Chicago, IL, USA

Dan Priel York University Osgoode Hall Law School, Toronto, ON, Canada

Giovanni Battista Ratti University of Genoa, Genova, Italy

Bojan Spaić University of Belgrade, Belgrade, Serbia

Michel Troper University Paris Nanterre, Nanterre, France

Introduction

Pierluigi Chiassoni and Bojan Spaić

In the last couple of decades, three topics have gained prominence in the province of jurisprudential inquiries: (1) legal interpretation; (2) legal realism; (3) the role of judges in contemporary constitutional democracies.

The first topic, legal interpretation, has been investigated both in general, and with particular attention being paid to judicial interpretation. The interest for the subject has been spurred by theoretical and practical purposes alike. On the theoretical side, legal interpretation (mostly in the judicial and juristic varieties) has been investigated in order to bring to the fore its nature, purpose, and tools, also by taking stock of philosophy of language and theories of meaning.[1] On the practical side, judicial and juristic interpretation has been investigated as the subject where normative outlooks compete for providing judges and jurists with "the proper theory of interpretation". Here the point was not understanding what legal interpretation is; it was, rather, suggesting how it *should* be performed (to which goals, by which means), in order for it to be "legally correct".[2]

The second topic, legal realism, has been the subject of a widespread revival of interest. This was due to a combination of three jurisprudential concerns. First, the need both to achieve a thorough and deep understanding of the realist legacy (American Legal Realism, Scandinavian Legal Realism, Italian Legal Realism, French Legal Realism), outside of any stereotyped or self-serving picture, and to

[1] See, e.g., Guastini (2011a, b, c), Marmor (2014) and Chiassoni (2019).

[2] See, e.g., Scalia (1997).

P. Chiassoni (✉)
University of Genova, Genova, Italy
e-mail: pierluigi.chiassoni@unige.it

B. Spaić (✉)
University of Belgrade, Belgrade, Serbia
e-mail: bojan.spaic@ius.bg.ac.rs

P. Chiassoni, B. Spaić (eds.), *Judges and Adjudication in Constitutional Democracies: A View from Legal Realism*, Law and Philosophy Library 135,
https://doi.org/10.1007/978-3-030-58186-2_1

cast light upon the import of such a legacy to present theoretical and practical purposes.[3] Second, the need to explore in a dispassionate way the relationships between legal realism and legal positivism—the need, if you like, to solve the legal realism/legal positivism riddle.[4] Third, the need to establish a new theoretical paradigm (the "New Legal Realism"), taking stock of Old Realism's keen on social sciences.[5]

Finally, the third topic, i.e., the role of judges in constitutional democracy, has become a hotly debated issue, surely as an effect of the ideological warfare launched in American jurisprudence against "judicial activism", but also due to the general interest—for jurists and citizens at large—in establishing the "proper" powers and limits of adjudication and judicial review in a constitutional and democratic state: i.e., those powers and limits that would grant full legitimacy to the judiciary as a separate function of government.[6]

The three strands of inquiry—legal interpretation, legal realism, and the role of the judiciary in constitutional democracies—are obviously intertwined. They are seldom brought together in a systematic way, though. The present volume purports to fill that gap. By collecting the contributions of scholars from different legal and philosophical backgrounds, the volume purports to deal with judicial interpretation and the role(s) of judges in contemporary democracies from the standpoint of legal realism as a revisited and sophisticated jurisprudential outlook.

The issues addressed in the volume include determining the ideas making up the core of legal realism, exploring the relation of legal realism to legal positivism (in the conventionalist, Hartian, variety), investigating the effective and desirable role of judges in contemporary constitutional democracies, identifying the boundaries of judicial interpretation as they appear from a realist standpoint, as well as considering some skeptical outlooks on the very positions of contemporary legal realism.

In the essay "The Roles of Judges in Democracies: A Realistic View", Brian Leiter provides a realist account of democracy and a realist account of the "obligations" of the judges working therein. This allows him to proceed to answering the main question by generalizing about the influence of actual functioning democracies on judges and adjudication. In a situation in which interpretative practices in every legal system give judges broad discretion in interpretation and adjudication, and in

[3]On legal realism in general, see, e.g., Guastini (2011a, b, c) and Hanoch (2017). On American legal realism, see, e.g.: Leiter (2007) and Hanoch (2013). The major strand of Italian legal realism is represented by Genoese legal realism. Genoese legal realism originated in the investigations of Giovanni Tarello (1934–1987), as a development of ideas from American and Scandinavian Realism, combined with a generous dose of analytic philosophy (see, e.g., Giovanni 1962, 1974, 1980), and has its present most authoritative contributions in the works of Riccardo Guastini (see., e.g., Guastini 1993, 2004, 2011a, b, c). On Genoese legal realism, see, e.g., Chiassoni (1999) and Ferrer and Ratti (2011). French legal realism has its forefront contributions in the works of Michel Troper: see, e.g., Troper (2001, 2007, 2011).

[4]See, e.g., Leiter (2019).

[5]See, e.g.: Merz et al. (2016a, b) and Klug and Merry (2016).

[6]See, e.g., Barak (2008) and Ferrajoli (2017).

which political and moral preferences heavily influence judicial resolutions of disputes, Leiter distinguishes between three types of judiciary: progressive, status quo, and reactionary.

In the essay "Is Realism at Odds with Constitutional Democracy?" Pierluigi Chiassoni tackles the question of the alleged tension between legal realism and constitutional democracy ("the realism-constitutional democracy puzzle"). How can, after all, a theory that questions the truthfulness of the cognitivist theory of adjudication be reconciled with the ideal of the rule of law, which is an essential feature in contemporary constitutional democracies? Chiassoni singles out four strategies that have been adopted by legal theorists to minimize this tension (namely, the Neutralization Pattern, the Weakening Pattern, the Surrender Pattern, and the Confinement Pattern), bringing to the fore in turn the flaws of each of them. He does not come to the conclusion that the project of constitutional democracy should be abandoned, though. Rather, his take is that realism has a therapeutic effect, pointing to the Surrender Pattern, together with some convenient measures of Confinement, as a successful way-out from the puzzle.

In a detailed overview of the history of ideas about the proper role of the judge, Jasminka Hasanbegović starts her essay "Legal Identity of Judge Transformed: Images of Judge in Early Modern and Contemporary Democracy" with the question about the basic differences between the role of the judge in the pre-modern and in the modern era, respectively. Her core claim is that the conception of the judicial role in society has not changed dramatically through history. Still, in the modern era, Hasanbegović claims, two ideal types of judicial activity have emerged in stark opposition to one another. The first type is best exemplified by the Montesquieu's well-known view that judges merely (have to) pronounce the words of law; the second is best exemplified by the legal-realist notion that the law, at the end of the day, is what judges say that the law is.

The essay by Riccardo Guastini—"An Exercise in Legal Realism"—provides a realist outlook on seven issues in contemporary legal philosophy. Guastini sets forth what, from a realistic standpoint, he considers the proper way of (1) understanding the relation between legal realism and legal positivism, (2) accounting for the concept of validity, (3) providing a theory of interpretation, (4) tackling with the issue of the ontology of law, (5) outlining an epistemology of legal cognition, (6) explaining the nature of the so-called rule of recognition, and, last but not the least, (7) analyzing the concept of obligation. The central theses of Guastini's paper emphasize the role of judges as the agents of authoritative interpretation of normative texts, and they open the way for an analysis of the stipulative nature of legal interpretation and its boundaries.

Michel Troper starts his essay—"A Causal View of Legal Interpretation"—with the problem of consistency and predictability of legal interpretation within a realist account of legal interpretation. If the (radically) skeptical version of the realist account of interpretation is true, if judges always decide what meaning is to be ascribed to a legal text, which are the causal factors that, nonetheless, make legal interpretation mostly uniform and generally predictable? Starting from the distinction between having an obligation and being obliged, Troper answers the question by bringing to the fore the checking pressure of the "systemic" connections inside and outside of the judiciary.

In their essay "Rule of Recognition and Methods of Interpretation", Luka Burazin and Giovanni Battista Ratti analyze the relation between the rule of recognition and methods of interpretation. The rule of recognition, they claim, is best understood as setting the criteria for something to be a source of law, and not as setting the criteria for something to be a legal norm. This move is made possible by distinguishing between normative texts, which are enacted by legislators, on the one hand, and legal norms, which belong to the interpreters' discourse, on the other. This clarification results in the conclusion that the rule of recognition isn't at odds with legal realism and helps furthering the understanding of the disagreement among officials about the interpretation of one and the same legal text.

The essay "Legal Realism and Legal Doctrine" by Dan Priel distinguishes between two versions of legal realism—traditional and scientific—and analyses their relation to legal doctrine and legal scholarship. He pays particular attention to the version of legal realism proposed by Hanoch Dagan, pointing out that it follows the path traced by the traditional version of legal realism, focussed on judge-made law. Priel's preference, however, goes to something close to the scientific version of legal realism, being concerned with (and hospitable to) legal doctrine as the output of legal scholars' daily dealing with law and legal problems.

Finally, in "Epistemic Authority and Legal interpretation" Bojan Spaić tackles the issue of predictability of judicial interpretative decisions from the perspective of realist accounts of legal reasoning. The paper presents an analysis of authority meant to bring to the fore the different kinds of authority that are relevant for legal interpretation and argues that the proper way to understand these authorities is by employing the concept of institutional control of legal interpretation. The analysis substantiates the conclusion that authority is a key component for understanding judicial interpretation as a stipulative enterprise, though without implications of arbitrariness.

A couple of remarks are in order, by way of conclusion.

First, the present volume purports to complement recent publications on ("new") legal realism,[7] while remaining distinctive in content and scope. It focuses on interpretation and adjudication as the main concerns of both classical and contemporary legal realism, and gives pride of place to a realist assessment of the role of judges and adjudication in constitutional democracies. This is meant to set the ground for providing a careful formulation of realist positions regarding the law, interpretation and its limits, adjudication and its limits, as well as for considering a few challenges to realist jurisprudence. In this way, the volume is distinctly jurisprudential.

Second, given the three main topics that are its subject matter, we hope, however, that the book will be of some use not only to the circumscribed auditorium of jurisprudents and legal philosophers. Indeed, the several essays are also meant to

[7]See, in particular, the works cited above, at footnote 4.

be of use to legal practice: especially to judges and jurists, be they working in countries with a stable and developed judiciary, as well as in countries with a developing judicial branch.

References

Barak A (2008) The judge in a Democracy. Princeton University Press, Princeton

Chiassoni P (1999) L'ineluttabile scetticismo della "Scuola genovese". In: Comanducci P, Guastini R (eds) Analisi e diritto 1998. Ricerche di giurisprudenza analitica. Giappichelli, Torino, pp 21–76

Chiassoni P (2019) Interpretation without truth. A realistic enquiry. Springer, Berlin

Ferrajoli L (2017) La democrazia costituzionale. Il Mulino, Bologna

Ferrer J, Ratti GB (eds) (2011) El realismo jurídico genovés. Marcial Pons, Madrid

Guastini R (1993) Le fonti del diritto e l'interpretazione. Giuffrè, Milano

Guastini R (2004) L'interpretazione dei documenti normativi. Giuffrè, Milano

Guastini R (2011a) Interpretare e argomentare. Giuffrè, Milano

Guastini R (2011b) La sintassi del diritto. Giappichelli, Turin

Guastini R (2011c) Rule-scepticism restated. In: Green L, Leiter B (eds) Oxford studies in legal theory. Oxford University Press, Oxford

Hanoch D (2013) Reconstructing American legal realism & rethinking private law theory. Oxford University Press, Oxford

Hanoch D (2017) Contemporary legal realism. In: Sellers M, Kirste S (eds) Encyclopedia for law and social philosophy. Springer, New York

Klug H, Merry SE (eds) (2016) The new legal realism: studying law globally. Cambridge University Press, Cambridge

Leiter B (2007) Naturalizing jurisprudence: essays on American legal realism and naturalism in legal philosophy. Oxford University Press, Oxford

Leiter B (2019) Legal positivism as a realist theory of law. In: Mindus P, Spaak T (eds) The Cambridge companion to legal positivism

Marmor A (2014) The language of law. Oxford University Press, Oxford

Merz E, Macaulay S, Mitchell TW (eds) (2016a) The new legal realism: translating law-and-society for today's legal practice. Cambridge University Press, Cambridge

Merz E, Macaulay S, Mitchell TW (eds) (2016b) Translating the social world for law: linguistic tools for a new legal realism. Oxford University Press, Oxford

Scalia A (1997) A matter of interpretation. Federal Courts and the Law. Princeton University Press, Princeton

Tarello G (1962) Il realismo giuridico americano. Milano, Giuffrè

Tarello G (1974) Diritto, enunciati, usi. Studi di teoria e metateoria del diritto. Il Mulino, Bologna

Tarello G (1980) L'interpretazione della legge. Giuffrè, Milano

Troper M (2001) La théorie du droit, le droit, l'État. Presses universitaires de France, Paris

Troper M (2007) Le gouvernement des juges, mode d'emploi. PU Laval, Quebec City

Troper M (2011) Le droit et la nécessité. Presses universitaires de France, Paris

Pierluigi Chiassoni is Professor of Jurisprudence at the University of Genova School of Law and a permanent fellow of Tarello Institute for Legal Philosophy. His jurisprudential interests span from economic analysis of law to legal interpretation, the history of analytical jurisprudence, and human rights. His main publications include *Positivismo giuridico. Una investigazione analitica* (Mucchi Editore, 2013), *Tecnica dell'interpretazione giuridica* (il Mulino, 2007), *Da Bentham a Kelsen. Sei capitoli per una storia della filosofia analitica del diritto* (Giappichelli, 2016), *Interpretation without Truth* (Springer, 2019).

Bojan Spaić is assistant professor of Jurisprudence at the University of Belgrade Faculty of Law and Alexander von Humboldt Research Fellow on the Institute for Public Law, Constitutional Law and Legal Philosophy of the University of Heidelberg. Spaić has edited multiple books in English and in Serbian including: Jurisprudence and Political Philosophy in the twenty-first Century: Reassessing Legacies (with Miodrag Jovanović, published by Peter Lang, 2012), Fundamental Rights: Justification and Interpretation (with Kenneth Einar Himma, published by Eleven international Publishing, 2016), Unpacking Normativity: Conceptual, Normative and Descriptive Issues (with Kenneth Einar Himma and Miodrag Jovanović, Hart Publishing, forthcoming in 2018), Savremeni problemi pravne i političke filozofije (with Damir Banović, published by Šahinpašić, 2016). He published two books in Serbian and multiple papers in Serbian and English regarding legal interpretation, ontological and methodological hermeneutics, pragmatism.

The Roles of Judges in Democracies: A Realistic View

Brian Leiter

Abstract What are the "obligations" of judges in democracies? An adequate answer requires us to be realistic both about democracies and about law. Realism about democracy demands that we recognize that electoral outcomes are largely, though not entirely, unrelated to concrete policy choices by elected representatives or to the policy preferences of voters, who typically follow their party based on "tribal" loyalties. The latter fact renders irrelevant the classic counter-majoritarian (or counter-democratic) worries about judicial review. Realism about law requires that we recognize that judges, especially on appellate courts, will inevitably have to render moral and political judgments in order to produce authoritative resolutions of disputes, one of the central functions of a legal system in any society. That means it is impossible to discuss the "obligations" of judges without regard to their actual

The contribution was initially published in volume 6, number 2 (2020) of Revista Estudos Institucionala published by Federal University of Rio de Janeiro (ISSN 2447-5467) under CC-BY licence.

The earliest version of this essay was presented as the keynote address at an international conference on "Interpreting Law: The Role of Judges in Contemporary Democracies" at the University of Belgrade in Serbia on October 14, 2016. I am grateful for comments and questions on that occasion, especially from Michel Troper. A later version was presented at the University of Chicago Law School work-in-progress luncheon, and elicited many helpful questions and comments; I recall with gratitude those from Omri Ben-Shahar, Dhammika Dharmapala, Lee Fennell, Todd Henderson, William Hubbard, Jennifer Nou, Eric Posner, Julie Roin, and David Weisbach. Later versions benefitted from questions and comments, both before and after, at a workshop at Syracuse University College of Law (thanks especially to Keith Bybee, David Driesen, and Cora True-Frost, with apologies again to those I forgot) and at the University of Surrey Centre for Law and Philosophy (thanks especially to Stephen Bero, Ken Ehrenberg, Diana Richards, and Alex Sarch, with the same apologies). I also thank Taylor Coles, University of Chicago Law School Class of 2018, and Aaron Graham, a PhD student here at Chicago, for valuable research assistance. I am grateful for support from the Alumni Faculty Fund of the Law School.

B. Leiter (✉)
Karl N. Llewellyn Professor of Jurisprudence and Director of the Center for Law, Philosophy and Human Values, The University of Chicago Law School, Chicago, IL, USA
e-mail: bleiter@uchicago.edu

P. Chiassoni, B. Spaić (eds.), *Judges and Adjudication in Constitutional Democracies: A View from Legal Realism*, Law and Philosophy Library 135,
https://doi.org/10.1007/978-3-030-58186-2_2

moral and political views, as well as the moral and political ends we believe ought to be achieved.

1 Introduction

What should the role of a judge be in contemporary democracies? That is our topic, but it has two important component parts that we should examine separately: a judge's role and democracy. Let us begin with a few introductory words about the former.

On one sensible view, succinctly articulated by Professor Leslie Green of Oxford University (2016, p. 323), judges "settle disputes by applying pre-existing standards." Pre-existing standards need not be codified, and they need not be legally authoritative, though most will be. The central thought is that a judge in a legal system assesses disputed conduct relative to a norm that (usually) pre-dates the conduct and thus was not created by the judge. Sometimes, of course, those denominated judges make retroactive decisions, holding actors accountable to standards that they never would have (or even could have) recognized at the time, and sometimes the judges themselves create the standard, but these are not the normal cases for the judicial role, though they may be among the most important roles: authoritative resolution of disputes is central to civic peace. In any case, let us call making decisions according to pre-existing standards the *Minimal Role* of a judge.

Green (ibid., 334–335) proposes three further "obligations" of judges, following H.L.A. Hart:

(1) "Judges have an obligation to apply valid law in making rulings, and. . .to make correct findings of fact, to know what the law is, to keep their knowledge of the law up to date. . . .";
(2) "Judges have an obligation to keep the law 'legally in good shape'" (quoting John Finnis, and meaning judges should resolve unclarity and conflicts);
(3) "Judges have obligations to regulate their own processes and the conduct in their courts, and to protect the rule of law and the integrity of their jurisdiction from those who would attack it. . . ."

I shall call these the *Minimal-Plus Roles*. Probably judges should do all these things too, though no legal positivist, including Green, thinks that judges have a non-defeasible moral obligation to apply valid law (per #1). The hard issues about the role of judges in democracies are threefold: what are the obligations of judges in determining what the applicable pre-existing standards are and their meaning; when should judges not apply valid law, per their *Minimal-Plus Role*?; and what further "obligations" do judges have beyond the Minimal and Minimal-Plus roles?

In the realistic spirit suggested by my title, let me be clear at the start that "obligations"—understood as *moral* obligations—do not really exist:[1] when we speak of moral "obligations" (or "rights" or "duties") we are expressing certain attitudes, often very intense and insistent attitudes, about what we feel other people should or should not do.[2] Expressing such attitudes is central to human life: as Nietzsche ([1883] 1976, II.13) put it, "all of life is a dispute over taste and tasting," and there is value in distinguishing between the strength and character of different tastes, as talk of "obligation" nicely does. Like other people who are products of the post-Enlightenment, post-WWII consensus, my "tastes" run towards individual rights and freedom and the rule of law, in which judges can play a crucial role in constraining behavior by other state actors, since such institutional practices seem to enhance aggregate human well-being.[3]

Not having illusions about obligation talk, however, is not simply a matter of fussiness about philosophical distinctions: imagine if theorists who said judges have "obligations" to do X said, instead, judges are "required by God" to do X? Recognizing that the latter is false—God does not exist, and so, unsurprisingly, has no views about anything, let alone the obligations of judges—means it is possible to express contrary attitudes without violating any moral or rational norm. The conceptual and practical space is open for contrary recommendations. This is a more important point, I think, than is usually recognized in recent academic writing. Assumptions *about what is the case* exercise a powerful normative force on human behavior and thought—sometimes for very good reason, to be sure. For example, *that it is the case that the door is closed and locked* gives me a very powerful prudential reason not to try to march straight through the doorway. Let us call this *the normativity of fact*: that something is taken to be factual or real, *to be the case*, influences, sometimes quite profoundly, what people think is possible, permissible, and so on.[4] Sometimes, as in the case of locked doors, that's a good thing, but other times, it is not. So when we deny, in a realistic spirit, that moral obligations are metaphysical facts, we are making both a true metaphysical claim (the ontology of the world includes no moral obligations[5] even if it includes some locked doors)

[1] *Legal* obligations, rights and duties do exist: they are certain kinds of social artifacts (like "money" and "stocks"), produced by legal systems, and whether or not they obtain depends on whether they satisfy the existence-conditions for such legal norms in that system (see Leiter 2018).

[2] See esp. Stevenson (1944).

[3] Talk of "taste" like the economists' talk of "preferences" runs the risk of flattening the important differences between our attitudes about what others ought to do. I "prefer" chocolate to vanilla, but I do not simply "prefer" toleration to genocide: those who "prefer" vanilla are not my mortal enemies, those who "prefer" genocide are.

[4] This is related to what Marxists call "reification," where some contingent and optional practice is treated as natural and necessary.

[5] See Leiter (2001, 2015a).

and, at the same time, we are defeating the normativity of fact where its normativity has no real justification.[6]

When humans speak of moral "obligations" they are speaking of what they *really want or expect* others to do, perhaps *no matter what,* or subject to only *stringent excuses*. This is certainly revealing about the feelings of those engaged in such talk, and perhaps also revealing about their social and economic circumstances: Nazis, for example, thought of their actions in terms of obligations,[7] and this included judges—not surprising, since, as Hart argued a half-century ago ([1961] 2012, 116), where there is a legal system, judges take themselves to have "obligations" (or something obligation-like) to apply the valid legal norms, even when others might reasonably deem them catastrophically wrong to feel that way. What this should remind us of is that talk of "obligation" is an important feature of human social existence, but it is also compatible with a radical revision of human attitudes and thus a different set of attitudes about what our "obligations" are. Suitably deflating the idea of "obligation" is important if we are to think clearly about the roles of judges: for example, even in cases where judges "promise" through an oath of office to do certain things, it may be that they should sometimes act otherwise.[8] We return to that issue, also, below.

So can we generalize about the "role of judges in democracies"? We can, though subject to some constraints, since judges and democracies seem to differ along various dimensions. For example, there are "civil service" judiciaries in which appointment and promotion depends on evaluation by other judges, as in Britain; there are "political" judiciaries in which appointment depends on political connections and affiliation, as in the United States; and there are mixed models in which, for example, purportedly "peer" evaluation of judges for appointment and promotion is, in fact, influenced by political partisanship (I am told Italy is such a case). Democracies differ in some respects as well: some are plutocracies masquerading as democracies (for example, the United States); some are incipient authoritarian societies masquerading as democracies (for example, Hungary and Poland); and some are more conventional representative democracies with all their pathologies of class conflicts and political personalities (for example, the current United Kingdom).

A serious discussion about the roles of judges in democracies has to be *realistic* both about judges and about democracies. It has to acknowledge what judges really do and how democracies actually function, and it has to be clear about what judges can do against those backgrounds. It also has to be explicit about our normative aspirations and ideals (and also whether judges can realize them). Normative aspirations and ideals tend to be inchoate and not wholly consistent, though in their broad outline in the present historical moment they are clear: no one needs a

[6]Of course, "justification" itself is normative, but normativity has a "justification" in my deflated sense when it comports with instrumental desires like not walking into closed doors.

[7]See Pauer-Studer and David Velleman (2015).

[8]A promise might be thought to generate a *moral obligation* to fulfill certain functions in an institutional role. Whether those functions are obligations of the role is separate from the question whether there is a real moral obligation to fulfill those functions simply because of a promise.

moral *theory*, after all, to know whether they are against racism or in favor of racial equality, against chattel slavery or in favor of human freedom, against cruelty or in favor of treating people in a dignified way, against human misery or in favor of human happiness. (The problem, after all, with academic friends of Jobbik in Hungary, the National Front in France, or Donald Trump in America is not that they failed to appreciate the correct moral theory![9]) I suppose throughout that judges, like other regular post-Enlightenment folk, should try to promote human well-being on some reasonable understanding (the theoretical differences between extant accounts rarely matter given the constraints imposed in practice on judicial power)—though the role of judges in helping to promote human well-being will vary quite a bit depending on the nature of the judiciary and the nature of the democracy. My main topic will be the kinds of realistic variations and constraints on exercise of this judicial role. I thus hope this essay will be a contribution to the on-going revival of realist political and legal theory against the moralizing fantasies of so much academic writing about these matters over the last half-century.[10] *Theory* will be important in what follows—for example, empirical theories about voting behavior in democracies, as well as philosophical claims about the nature of law—but *normative* theory will not be.[11]

I start with a realistic view of democracies, and then turn to judges.

2 A Realistic View of Democracy

Democracies typically have two features in common: individuals have *the right to vote* for some number of those who hold political power and they also enjoy *rights to certain individual freedoms*. So, on the one hand, democracies hold elections in

[9]Remember that normative theory delivers no decisive conclusions about what ought to be done, being hostage to "intuitive" starting points that themselves can never be defended. See generally, Leiter (2016a).

[10]For examples of the realist revival, see Posner (1999, 2008), Geuss (2008), perhaps Williams (2005), and also Leiter (2012, 2015b).

[11]Realists deny the priority of theorizing about moral truth to theorizing about how political and legal actors should behave, that is, they deny that we should treat political and legal theory as simply "applied ethics," without regard to the strategic questions peculiar to each domain. The central idea is that realists "should theorize about the distinctive forces that shape real politics" and judicial behavior (Rossi and Sleat 2014, p. 689). Realism, in this sense, is partly about attention to feasibility constraints (ibid., 690–691), though not wholly. (An example of realist feasibility constraints in operation is the debate between the moralist Stephen Gardiner and the realist David Weisbach in *Debating Climate Ethics* (Gardiner and Weisbach 2016)). But feasibility does not exhaust the realist approach to questions about what political and legal actors should do. There are normative considerations peculiar to both the political and legal domains: in the former, stability and security; in the latter, authoritative resolution of disputes that arise in any human community. But realism in recent political theory is characterized by neglect of the characteristic of classical realism in Thucydides, Machiavelli, and Nietzsche, namely, attention to *what human beings are really like.* See Leiter (2019).

which some significant portion of the citizenry can vote for some range of candidates or parties (perhaps two or three or four), the elections are fair and incumbents can actually be voted out of office: this is the crux of the democratic ideal that "the people rule." On the other hand, democracies also typically, in the post-World War II era, protect some range of individual rights—rights to expression, privacy, and fair legal process most prominently—though again to varying degrees.[12] Call the combination of electoral rights and rights to individual freedom "Democratic Values." Debates about the role of judicial review of legislation in democracies typically focus on the electoral aspect, and how that is consistent with judicial invalidation of legislation when it violates individual rights: in the United States, this is called the "counter-majoritarian" difficulty (Bickel 1962), though in parliamentary systems, it could also be called the "counter-democratic" difficulty, since judges, once again, defy the will of a democratic legislature, though less often a majoritarian one.[13] A realistic view of democracy should help us see why this latter concern is without merit, and why the real question for judges who embrace "Democratic Values" should be whether laws really protect the individual rights that are equally central to Democratic Values.[14]

The reason we should disregard the supposed counter-majoritarian or counter-democratic difficulty is because there is almost never a plausible sense in which the particular laws passed by a legislature represent the views of an electorate, whose will is then thwarted. That laws reflect the view of the electorate would be true only if two further claims were true:

(1) The majority of the legislature intended the legislation to achieve purpose X.
(2) The majority (or plurality) of people who elected the legislature (the "electorate") wanted them to pass legislation which achieved purpose X.

The first claim has been subjected to various kinds of critique by economists and public choice theorists, who emphasize that collective intentionality in a legislature is a fiction, and a misleading one.[15] But the more serious problems arise for the second claim, which presupposes something doubtful: that law-makers are elected

---

[12]The protection of the individual freedoms is typically dependent on allegiance to the family of "rule of law" virtues, such as an independent judiciary, the principle that no one is above the law, the requirement to treat like cases alike, the publicity of legal standards, etc. It is not wholly dependent—contra Lon Fuller and other anti-positivists—since the *substantive content* of the law matters crucially, even if all the other virtues are honored.

[13]The United States Congress is not a majoritarian institution either as it happens—its Senate is obviously not, and its House of Representatives, due to gerrymandering, is not either. The United Kingdom is a special case, since the courts cannot invalidate acts of Parliament on grounds of violating individual rights, but they can declare them incompatible with such rights, and thus prompt a legislative reevaluation.

[14]I assume, with Mill among others, that protection of individual rights generally promotes human flourishing and well-being. Perhaps this is false, but as of now, we have no reason to think it is.

[15]See Easterbrook (1983, pp. 547–548) and Easterbrook (1994, p. 68); but cf. Ekins (2012). But even the defenses of intention do not really establish the requisite level of specificity of intention that would make the counter-majoritarian difficulty meaningful.

because of commitments to pass particular kinds of legislation to achieve particular goals. Even in its most plausible form, known as the "spatial theory of voting" in the empirical political science literature, it supposes only that people vote for the party that is closest (in ideological space, as it were) to their ideological "preferences." But even if voters really did that, this would rarely license the conclusion that any particular piece of legislation that achieved purpose X reflects the will of the voters. There are, of course, the fundamental theoretical difficulties with this view due to Arrow's Theorem (Achen and Bartels 2016, pp. 23–30),[16] but even more worrisome for the spatial theory is the overwhelming evidence that voters do not have clear ideologies. For example, in the 1980s—the height of the reactionary Reagan Era in the United States, when the social welfare state was under sustained attack—nearly 65% of Americans thought the government was spending too little on "assistance to the poor," but at the same time only 25% thought too little was spent on "welfare" (ibid., 30), a term that had been demonized by Reagan, even though it means "assistance to the poor"![17] What this shows is that expressions of purported "ideology" by the population are sometimes nothing of the kind, unless by "ideology" one does not mean what voters actually believe about concrete policy questions!

This is surprising to university professors, of course, who are disproportionately "ideologues" in the sense defined by the American political scientist Philip Converse in 1964, namely, those who have well-defined views about policy questions (such that, e.g., they realize that "assistance to the poor" is the same as "welfare," and either favor or oppose both). In Professor Converse's study, these "ideologues" were 3% of the population, while 85% of the voting population "seemed to think about parties and candidates in terms of group interests or the 'nature of the times' or in ways that conveyed 'no shred of policy significance whatever'" (Achen and Bartels 2016, p. 32).[18] Ironically, academic interest in the United States in the "counter-majoritarian" difficulty about judicial review of legislation flourished precisely after the period studied by Professor Converse.

---

[16]Achen and Bartels reprise, with new evidence, arguments first made by Elmer Schattschneider (1960). Spatial voting theorists, in turn, have produced new evidence in the last decade to try to resist the realist conclusions. An important example is Jessee (2009). The problem with this literature is that its results are compatible with the realist hypotheses about the role of group identity in driving party identification, and the way in which voters conform their views to the party leaders rather than the other way around. I acknowledge that the argument of the paper is hostage to the soundness of the realist picture, but since realism in every domain I know of—international relations, political theory, legal theory, historical explanation—is always the most explanatorily successful approach, I am willing to rest my argument on the Achen and Bartels version.

[17]We don't know how clarification about the terms would have shifted preferences, of course, but it is easy to see how it could have gone either way: some of the anti-welfare folks would have realized that "assistance to the poor" was meant to incorporate all the putatively bad aspects of welfare; similarly, some of the pro-"assistance to the poor" folks might have been horrified to learn that what they favored really had the putatively bad aspects of welfare. And, of course, we can imagine the converse.

[18]See Kinder and Kalmoe (2017) for an updated and concurring investigation of ideological identificationin the American public.

If the spatial theory of voting fares poorly in showing why we should worry about judicial invalidation of democratically enacted laws that violate individual rights, the alternatives fare even worse. The "retrospective theory" of democracy suggests that voters express their judgment of the past performance of those they vote for (or against). That sounds somewhat promising, but in fact voters primarily respond to economic events only in the several months preceding an election (ibid., 148–158) and, more importantly, they do not discriminate between events for which elected officials bear some plausible causal responsibility and those events which are basically natural disasters: floods, droughts, even shark attacks (on one occasion) have all influenced voters in past elections (118–135).[19] Simply put: if voters are miserable in the months before an election, often regardless of the cause of the misery (122–137),[20] they generally take out their unhappiness in their voting

[19]Achen and Bartels' shark attack claim has been challenged in Fowler and Hall (2018). The first half of Fowler and Hall is irrelevant, since it tests an hypothesis that Achen and Bartels do not defend, namely, that shark attacks influence presidential elections. Achen and Bartels focus on a rather singular case—the multiple shark attacks in 1916 along the New Jersey coast, which attracted national and international attention, and which were utterly unprecedented. Their finding was that in the coastal counties closest to the site of the widely covered attacks, Woodrow Wilson's share of the vote declined markedly by comparison to both his 1912 results *and* his results in New Jersey counties farther removed.

The relevant part of the Fowler and Hall critique centers on disputing choices by Achen and Bartels about the various comparison classes, and most of those critiques simply show that, if you redraw the comparison classes, the statistical effect on election outcomes of the shark attacks is reduced. The notion of "statistical significance" is epistemically vexed, to put it mildly, but what is missing from the Fowler and Hall critique is any serious attention to the question of "mechanism," that is, the causal processes by which a certain event X brought about an outcome Y. Only with a plausible story about mechanism can we really rule out or in "statistically significant" or "statistically insignificant" correlations, since the P value of greater than 95% is both arbitrary and largely meaningless (Colquhoun 2014). (The basic problem is that 95% confidence that an effect is not random compared to the null hypothesis does not guarantee it is a *real* effect (a real cause-effect relationship). What we need to know *in addition* is how good our test is for detecting *real effects* and how many real effects there are in the sample studied (the latter, of course, is hard to estimate). But consider: even with the standard $p = 0.05$ standard of statistical significance, if our measures only capture 80% of *real effects*, and real effects are only 10% of our sample, then one-third of our positive results will turn out to be false positives even with the standard P value. Cf. ibid., 4–5.).

Achen and Bartels are aware of the need for a story about causal mechanisms (cf. their discussion of narratives at 138–142), and the shark attack case, while amusing and memorable, is only one small data point for their general hypothesis that voters are terrible at assigning causal responsibility for events that affect them adversely. If the underlying causal mechanism in their explanatory story is that ordinary voters have little understanding of causal responsibility, and yet adverse experiences influence their voting behavior, then they have a story about mechanism which Fowler and Hall lack.

[20]Caveat: sometimes voters need a narrative before assigning blame. Achen and Bartels discuss the case of the catastrophic Spanish influenza pandemic of 1918, which felled half a million Americans yet didn't translate to losses at the polls for incumbents: "[N]o thread of elite rhetoric or popular discourse seems to have suggested any attribution of responsibility to President Wilson or other public officials. As long as no one supplied a convincing argument that the government did control or should have controlled the spread of the pandemic or its horrific consequences, the pain of millions failed to have any electoral impact" (142).

behavior. If there are reasons for judges committed to individual rights and human well-being to hesitate to invalidate legislation produced by such a process, those reasons can have nothing to do with the moral importance of democratic voting.

I should pause here to emphasize that there may well be other reasons for judges to hesitate.[21] Most importantly, settled law creates settled expectations, and unsettling those have costs that judges must consider. In addition, and as we will return to below, invalidating legislation may affect the legitimacy of the courts, and it may also provoke backlash from other branches of government. But what is important to notice is that both these reasons for judicial restraint have nothing to do with the moral significance of how the population voted.

An alternative account of voting behavior recently defended most vigorously by self-described "realists" about democracy, Professors Christopher Achen and Larry Bartels, does nothing to restore the moral importance of democratic voting. On their view, it is "group identity" that best explains voting behavior in democracies.[22] By group identity, they mean the religious, racial, ethnic, occupational and cultural identities[23] that are important to people: their "tribes" for short. On their "group theory of politics—the powerful tendency of people to form groups, the ensuing construction of 'us' and 'them,' and the powerful role of emotion rather than reason in directing group activity"—"group attachments are easily generated and profoundly felt" (Achen and Bartels 2016, p. 215).[24] What Achen and Bartels argue is that the group identity largely explains the political party with which individuals identify, and we know that, as Professor Converse put it, "expressions of party identification were much more stable" over time than ideological convictions (ibid., 34). In other words, for most voters, their *tribal loyalties* drive party identification, and party identification then drives voting behavior.[25]

In some measure, popular commentary on the political process in America has registered this fact: we all know that African-Americans vote Democratic by overwhelming majorities, and that white men do not. But this also explains another important empirical finding, namely, that voters typically adjust their views to fit the ideology of their party (or its most visible representatives), rather than choosing parties based on how well they fit the voter's own views (ibid., 41–45, 258–264,

---

[21]This is important to emphasize because many of my ultimate recommendations could apply to other official actors, albeit in slightly different terms. But there are aspects of institutional role and public expectations that caution restraint in all cases, including the judicial, but they vary with institutional role.

[22]Caveat: their evidence comes largely, but not exclusively, from the U.S.

[23]The "cultural" identities are often geographically bounded: cf. Achen and Bartels (2016, chap. 9).

[24]Note that there is no reason that voting in accordance with one's group identity means voting in accordance with one's "interests" or well-being. Achen and Bartels do not claim otherwise. On any plausible view of human interests or well-being, voting in the pattern described by Achen and Bartels would stand in only an accidental relationship to the interests or well-being of the voters.

[25]Crucially, tribal loyalty does not drive party identification based on party ideology, except at the margins.

chap. 10)![26] That fact helps make sense of the peculiarity of the Trump phenomenon in the United States, since he, in fact, rejected many staples of the "Republican brand" since the Reagan Revolution of the 1980s, though he won an overwhelming percentage of Republican voters in the end (I return to Trump below).

Ideology of a party can matter at the margins, of course: at some point a particular "tribe" registers that a particular party is clearly friendly or hostile to the tribe. African-Americans in the United States supported Republicans from the end of the Civil War through the 1920s (at least when they could vote) since, after all, it was a Republican President who freed them from chattel slavery. (Unsurprisingly, a group freed from slavery noticed that fact.) Although Roosevelt began capturing a large share of the African-American vote in the 1930s, it was not until Truman desegregated the armed services in 1948 that a majority of African-Americans began to identify as Democrats (though Republicans still got a third or more of the African-American vote throughout the 1950s). But then it was a Democratic President, Lyndon Johnson, who ended *de jure* segregation in America in 1964, winning 94% of the African-American vote that year, and since then African-Americans have voted overwhelmingly for Democrats (Bositis 2012, p. 9) (though, strikingly, as Achen and Bartels (2016, pp. 246–258) document, Southern Whites were moving to the Republicans before the 1960s). But ideological considerations only go so far. African-Americans continued to support Democrats, including the Clintons (Bill and Hillary), despite the evidence that they were not very good for the African-American community.[27] Of course, it will be fairly noted that the Clintons were always less hostile to interests of the African-American community than the Republicans, but even so, it hardly explains the failure of African-Americans to rally to Senator Bernie Sanders, a Roosevelt New Dealer, in the 2016 Democratic primaries. Reflexive loyalties do seem to explain it.

Ironically, in the end, the absence of a member of their tribe on the ticket also helps explain the fact that African-American turnout was depressed in the 2016 Presidential election compared to elections when Obama was the candidate (Cohn 2016):[28] African-Americans, highly motivated to turn out to vote when one of their own was a candidate, were not nearly as enthusiastic about voting for a white woman and a white man in 2016. At the same time, some modest number of white working-class voters (not more than 100,000 in the three crucial states of Pennsylvania, Michigan, and Wisconsin), some of whom had supported Obama in 2012, flipped to

---

[26]This was true in the case of Hitler too: for one of the most chilling discussions in the book, see pp. 314–316, which argues that the 1932 electoral success of the Nazis was almost entirely due to Protestant voters switching from the traditional Protestant parties (discredited by the crisis of capitalism beginning in 1929) to the National Socialists, while Catholics continued to vote as before. As Achen and Bartels note, the National Socialists did not emphasize anti-semitism at all in the 1932 campaign.

[27]See, e.g., Alexander (2012).

[28]Note that the decline in African-American turnout was consistent across states that had enacted new voter suppression rules and those that had not.

Trump in 2016 (ibid.).[29] This indicates that at least some *highly salient* parts of *expressed* ideology are relevant to some voters (Achens and Bartels do not deny this, but they are, conceptually, sloppy, which is typical of this literature—but they *de facto* acknowledge the point with their endless hedging about what "mostly" or "often" explains voting behavior). As the rabble-rousing filmmaker Michael Moore observed, when Trump came to Detroit and threatened auto executives that they had better not move their plants outside the U.S. *or else*, he did something no other candidate of the two ruling class parties in the U.S. had done in living memory (Moore 2016). "Free trade" has become a mantra of the ruling class and its intellectual apologists like Paul Krugman in America, but when a Presidential candidate repudiated it in the Mafioso terms in which Trump specializes, some number of voters took note, perhaps contributing to his victory in states with lots of industrial working-class voters like Pennsylvania, Michigan, and Ohio. And yet this result still confirms the main point of the realist theory of democracy. The working-class voters who flipped to Trump were largely union members,[30] their loyalty to their class as defined by union membership (an increasingly uncommon loyalty in America) having an effect on their votes. If we are realists about democracy, then we need to acknowledge, as Achen and Bartels document, that tribal loyalties explain a frightening amount about voting behavior, while moral or ideological commitment generally does not, except in the extreme cases or among a small segment of the electorate.[31]

It is worth quoting at some length Achen and Bartels' own summary of their findings, since it makes clear the extent to which the popular, and theoretical, conceptions of democracy bear little relationship to any reality. In the summary that follows, they presuppose that party identification drives most voting behavior, and then focus on the case of the "pure" independent voters[32] in the American context, those who do not lean to either the Democrats or Republicans:

---

[29]See also Cohn (2017).

[30]See, e.g., Bump (2016) and Weigel (2016).

[31]Achen and Bartels are particularly critical of "highly idealistic models of *participatory* or *deliberative* democracy" (301). They write: "These models of democracy emphasize—indeed, they often simply assume—rationality, mutual consideration, and the patient exchange of publicly justified reasons for supporting specific policies. Thus, they rest on essentially the same unrealistic expectations about human nature embodied in the folk theory [of democracy]" (ibid.). Although I think Achen and Bartels are right to be dismissive of deliberative democracy theories, their reification of "human nature" cannot go unchallenged: none of the evidence supports the claim that the unrealistic character of deliberative democracy has anything to do with essential biological and psychological facts about human beings. The evidence they adduce only supports the view that *under the conditions in which most people live*, they have neither the time nor the interest to engage in deliberative democracy fantasies.

[32]They here mean to exclude the "independents" who in fact, on further questioning, lean to one party or the other. They also mean to exclude quite clearly a category they don't mention, namely, "academic independents," who, as ideologues, have such well-defined views on policy questions that no existing party could be adequate to their excruciatingly "nuanced" conception of what

While they, too, have group ties and social identities, they are often quite unclear about which groups "belong" in which party. Typically less-informed, they may fail to grasp what is at stake in the choice of one party or another, much less where their overall interests lie. Thus, they are often swept along by the familiarity of an incumbent, the charisma of a fresh challenger, or a sense that it is "time for a change," even when the government did not cause the current unsatisfactory situation and cannot greatly alter it. When the party balance is close. . .election outcomes turn on how these "swing voters" happen to feel when they go to the polls. As Philip Converse [citation omitted] put it, "Not only is the electorate as a whole quite uninformed, but it is the least informed members within the electorate who seem to hold the critical balance of power, in the sense that alternations in governing party depend disproportionately on shifts in their sentiment."

The result is that, from the viewpoint of governmental representativeness and accountability, election outcomes are essentially random choices among the available parties—musical chairs. Elections that "throw the bums out" typically do not produce genuine policy mandates, not even when they are landslides. *They simply put a different elite coalition in charge* [emphasis added]. This bloodless change of government is a great deal better than bloody revolution, but it is not deliberate policy change. The parties have policy views and they carry them out when in office, but most voters are not listening, or are simply thinking what their party tells them they should be thinking. This is what an honest view of electoral democracy looks like. (Achen and Bartels 2016, p. 312)

The topic unaddressed by Achen and Bartels is the mechanism by which a particular "elite coalition" emerges from the "musical chairs" electoral process. Marx had an account of how elite consensus emerges, but an adequate account of the emergence of a particular "elite coalition" would no doubt turn on the mechanisms by which control of extant political parties can be seized. On this Achen and Bartels are silent, but it is the really crucial research question suggested by their realism about democracy.

But back to our main topic: given realism about democracies, what does it mean to say, as I said earlier, that some democracies are merely "masquerading" as such, concealing in reality plutocracies or incipient authoritarian societies? The answer, I believe, is, in one sense, rather simple. It means that the tribal loyalties operate in such a way that actual decisions about policy are taken either by (a) economically dominant groups in accord with their interests, not the interests of the tribal groups that support them; or (b) authoritarian groups in accord with their interests, and not the interest of those tribal groups that support them.[33] The former was true in the Clinton Administration of the 1990s, and the incipient Trump Administration is already beginning to fit both models, with tax cuts for the rich as well as demonization of minorities and immigrants in the name of "jobs" and "national security." How that came to be the case in the United States is the hard question, but beyond the scope of this paper.[34] But the descriptive generalization still stands.

should be done. As Nietzsche ([1886] 1989, II.26) would say, "the rule is more interesting than the exception."

[33]The interests of authoritarian elites often track those of economic elites, but not always.

[34]A useful documentation of the fact that it is the case is Gilens and Page (2014). The standard Marxist theory of the state under capitalism—as the committee that organizes the affairs of the ruling class—would have predicted as much. Two peculiar factors in the American case are the

So if electoral democracy is, as the realists portray it, a matter of tribal loyalties translating into party identification, and then electing representatives, who may or may not even represent the views of the tribes that elected them, how should that affect our conception of the roles of judges?

3 A Realistic View of the Judicial Role

Everywhere judges—consistent with what I dubbed earlier their familiar "Minimal Role"—are expected to apply pre-existing standards, meaning usually "the law," though as judicial oaths of office reveal, they are sometimes expected to do more, and often in terms that are not obviously consistent with the Minimal Role. Whether judges should keep those promises is an open question, but before we get to that, let us look at the promises they are actually asked to make when taking office in a variety of modern legal systems. These promises display some striking ambiguities, and also reveal the extent to which even judicial promises leave much of the judge's role open.

In Serbia, for example, judges take the following (rather typical) oath: "I solemnly swear on my honour that I will perform my duties in compliance with the Constitution and the law, according to the best of my knowledge and ability and in the service of only truth and justice."[35] The promise of Serbian judges embodies the ambiguity in many such promises: namely, between loyalty to the law, and then loyalty to "truth and justice." But how does one serve "truth and justice" if one is supposed to comply with laws that are unjust or contain actual falsehoods? It is unclear from the Serbian oath, though this oath is hardly atypical in this regard.

The German oath, pursuant to the German Judiciary Act,[36] is similar: "I swear to exercise judicial office in conformity with the Basic Law of the Federal Republic of Germany and with the law, to adjudicate to the best of my knowledge and belief, without distinction of person, and to serve the cause of truth and justice alone—so help me God." German jurists, who perhaps know better than most that God does not exist, are allowed to omit the "so help me God" bit at the end. The German oath also adds the interesting demand, one that is otiose on the Basic Law, namely, adjudication "without distinction of person," but that again perhaps reflects the special history of Germany in the last century. Like the Serbian oath, it poses the puzzle how fealty to false or unjust law is compatible with serving only "the cause of truth and justice."

---

huge size of the country, which favors those with resources who can access the mass media, and the high level of religiosity, which capitalism usually destroys more effectively than it has in the U.S. The latter complicates the economic elite story.

[35]Law on Judges, *Official Gazette of the Republic of Serbia*, No. 116, 2008, Art. 54.

[36]Deutsches Richtergesetz [German Judiciary Act], Apr. 19, 1972, BGBL. I at 713 as amended.

An Egyptian judge must swear "by God Almighty that I shall adjudicate between people according to justice and respect the laws,"[37] which poses the same puzzle about how to resolve conflicts between justice and fealty to the positive law (unless justice is just a different way of saying "fealty to law," in which case it is otiose). Judges in Israel must pledge "allegiance to the State of Israel and its laws" and swear "to dispense true justice, not to pervert the law or to show favor."[38] This promise arguably implies that if "true justice" is at stake, then ignoring positive law would not be a "perversion" of such law, but a requirement. In South Africa, judges of the Constitutional Court and Supreme Court promise to be "faithful to the Republic of South Africa," as well as "uphold and protect the Constitution and the human rights entrenched in it, and will administer justice to all persons alike without fear, favour or prejudice, in accordance with the Constitution and the law."[39] This oath has in it an interesting additional ambiguity: is it the duty of judges to protect *actual* human rights or only the "human rights entrenched in" the Constitution? The latter is the more natural reading, but at the same time, it would seem an odd oath if it were rewritten to make that explicit ("I promise to uphold and protect the Constitution and only those human rights recognized by it, but other human rights—well, they get no protection").[40]

Perhaps the most interesting oath in the ones I surveyed is the one from Hungary:

[37]See Shahine (2007) for evidence of this oath being administered.

[38]See State of Israel Judicial Authority (n.d.).

[39]S. Afr. Const., sched. 2 §6(2) as amended by Sixth Amendment Act of 2001 §18.

[40]South African judges frequently rule on whether or not a particular law or practice is consistent with "human rights," appealing to the principles underlying the Constitution. S v Makwanyane and Another (CCT 3/94), for example, struck down the use of the death penalty as inconsistent with the commitment to human rights enshrined in the South African Constitution. (Thanks to Cora True-Frost for calling this case to my attention.) Indeed, the South African Constitution refers to "human rights" without qualification, even though the requirements of human rights under the South African Constitution are not coextensive with those of international human rights law. S v Makwanyane says this directly, as it notes that international human rights law does not ban the death penalty, but holds that the South African Constitution requires otherwise. As the Court stated:

> Our Constitution expresses the right to life in an unqualified form, and prescribes the criteria that have to be met for the limitation of entrenched rights, including the prohibition of legislation that negates the essential content of an entrenched right. In dealing with comparative law, we must bear in mind that we are required to construe the South African Constitution, and not an international instrument or the constitution of some foreign country, and that this has to be done with due regard to our legal system, our history and circumstances, and the structure and language of our own Constitution. We can derive assistance from public international law and foreign case law, but we are in no way bound to follow it.

S v Makwanyane and Another (CCT 3/94) section 39. http://www.saflii.org/za/cases/ZACC/1995/3.html.

> I hereby do solemnly swear that I shall assess the cases entrusted to me in fair proceedings, without bias, conscientiously, solely in accordance with the rules of law; in the fulfilment of my duties, I shall be driven by the desire to uphold justice and equity.[41]

In Hungary, judicial fealty is not to the country, its constitution or legal system, but to impartiality in adjudication "in accordance with the rules of law" and to "justice and equity." This would appear to give a Hungarian judge ample grounds for going beyond the positive law—assuming they had the requisite desire "to uphold justice and equity"—something such a desire is likely to require under Viktor Orban, let alone Jobbik, although there is little sign Hungarian judges are fulfilling their promise.

As the preceding examples make plain, judicial oaths leave it uncertain how judges should resolve conflicts between positive law, truth, and justice. But now, with our realist hats on again, we should remember that the idea that promises *actually bind* has the same status as the idea of "obligation" generally: certainly many people, especially those who have been reading too much Kant, feel very strongly that promises create binding moral obligations. But the promises judges make, as the examples above illustrate, are various and at times vague about the relationship between judicial obligations and obligations to justice and truth. Should one feel that promissory obligations defeat the general "obligations" to do what is just, especially in cases where the promise is ambiguous about how to resolve the conflict between justice and law? Legal philosophers typically note that judges are also human, and insofar as we feel that humans ought to behave morally, then judges should too. From this it follows, as every legal positivist I know believes, that promises to uphold the law notwithstanding, sometimes judges ought to do what is "morally right" even if that is in violation of the Minimal and Minimal-Plus Roles of judges. When we remember what democracy is really like, that judges should sometimes do that should seem less worrisome (though it depends, of course, on the judiciary, a point to which we return below).

The central theoretical constraint in thinking about judicial roles has to do with the nature of law itself, since we would not otherwise know how to interpret the command to apply or follow "the law," so central to the various judicial oaths. There is a superficial if popular view according to which law is created by legislators, and judges are the mere mechanical appliers of the law. Whether the society is authoritarian or democratic, this view is a gross simplification, as all lawyers and scholars know. Even if one agrees that norms are legally valid only in virtue of their source (e.g., legislative or judicial enactment), and even if one agrees that where there is a legal system, there exists Hart's naturalized version of a Kelsenian *Grundnorm*, namely, a practice of officials of treating certain criteria as obligatory criteria of legal validity, that still does not tell us the role of a judge, even on the assumption that judges should "apply the law." Statements of the law, whether by legislatures or

[41] See *Opinion on Act CLXII of 2011 on the Legal Status and Remuneration of Judges and Act CLXI of 2011 on the Organisation and Administration of Courts of Hungary*, European Commission for Democracy through Law, Op. 66 (Mar. 19, 2012).

courts or any other lawmaker, must be *interpreted* so that their import with respect to particular facts is clear. Every serious scholar who has written about legal interpretation over the last century—from the American Karl Llewellyn to the Englishman H.L.A. Hart to the Italian Riccardo Guastini to the Frenchman Michel Troper, among many others—has recognized that interpretive norms in a given legal system accord judges latitude, perhaps great latitude, in saying what the law is. Even the most fantastical sophist and moralist of the last century's legal philosophy, Ronald Dworkin, admitted that no one may really *know* what the right interpretation of the law is (though he, of course, believed there was one and he happened to know what it was). Dworkin's main focus was, ironically, the American constitutional order, in which its highest court is rather clearly—to realists—a super-legislature (Leiter 2015c). What that means, of course, is that judicial decisions interpreting the other sources of positive law can be crucial sources of legally valid norms themselves—and not just for the parties before the court, at least in any legal system that treats judicial precedent as a valid source of law.

So what legal constraints are there on interpretation? Here there is little of a general nature we can say, since norms of legal interpretation vary with legal systems just as Hartian rules of recognition do. Since rules of recognition are social rules in Hart's sense—that is, psycho-social artifacts arising from the actual interpretive practices of the judges that they endorse from an internal point of view—it follows that norms of interpretation can evolve and will vary with the nature of the judiciary and its interpretive practices: for example, civil service systems, where judges are promoted by peer evaluation, create more pressure towards adhering to the prevailing interpretive norms, while systems, like the American, which are political, do not.[42] If there are generalizations available about viable norms of interpretation, I suspect they derive more from sociological facts about how law interacts with society and human interests, and the practical constraints that then emerge on interpretive practices, rather than from any true philosophical thesis about the nature of law. I consider only one example.

In the United States, a small number of judges, and many more legal scholars, have argued that the Constitution should be interpreted according to its "original" meaning. Bear in mind that the U.S. Constitution was written in 1789, though amended in significant part after our Civil War in the 1860s. Originalism in America has come in two varieties. One version is that constitutional provisions should be interpreted in accordance with the *intentions* of those who wrote the provisions. The other version, popularized especially by the late Justice Antonin Scalia of our Supreme Court, is that constitutional provisions should be interpreted in accordance with the original "public meaning" of the provisions, the latter determined not by historical inquiry into the intentions of framers of the provisions, but by old

[42]Cf. Gilmore's (1961) "explanation" of legal realism and Posner (1996) on the American vs. British judiciary.

dictionaries and historical evidence about the circumstances and problems to which the provision was responsive.[43]

The first version of originalism famously confronted the problem of identifying meaningful *intentions* of collective bodies, especially about matters they never could have anticipated.[44] The second version was also afflicted by disputes about how one fixes the initial "public" meaning.[45] But there is a deeper practical problem afflicting both versions: the real problem is *not* that there is never any fact about the original intent or meaning of a constitutional provision (sometimes there is), but that serious commitment to original intentions or meanings will inevitably undermine *constitutionalism* altogether, that is, *the idea that political power should be constrained by a piece of legislation that no one living participated in enacting and that cannot be repealed or overridden in the manner of ordinary legislation*. "Originalism" makes for good rhetoric, but usually awful politics, something that all jurists in the U.S. recognize, whether explicitly or not.[46] Let us call this *the Real Problem of Constitutional Interpretation*.

The *Real Problem* is that constitutional restrictions on what current polities want to do always make current polities deeply unhappy. Now we must remember that, given realism about democracy, this is not the same as saying that constitutional restrictions are restrictions on democratic majorities. That is false, since elected officials who might find themselves constrained by a constitution do not represent the moral and political views of current democratic majorities (except sometimes by accident), for the reasons already discussed. That being said, there is a limit to how much political elites and perhaps even voters will tolerate frustration of their

---

[43]See, e.g. Justice Antonin Scalia's originalist opinion in *Crawford v. Washington*, 541 U.S. 36 (2004) reinterpreting the "Confrontation Clause" of the U.S. Constiution as prohibiting the admission of certain kinds of "hearsay" statements against criminal defendants, statements that would otherwise have been admissible under traditional exceptions to the rule excluding hearsay. Because Justice Scalia's approach has created so many burdens for prosecutors, the one former prosecutor on the Supreme Court, Justice Sonia Sotomayor, has been doing her best to weaken the rule: e.g., *Michigan v. Bryant*, 562 U.S. 344 (2011).

[44]See, e.g., Brest (1980). In the U.S., a new originalist literature, inspired by the work of Keith Whittington, tries to dodge this problem by distinguishing "interpretation" (determining the ordinary, communicative meaning of the provision) and "construction" (determining its legal effect). The distinction is dubious, since in every legal jurisdiction I am aware of, there are rules of legal interpretation that make ordinary, communicative meaning irrelevant. (Take the U.S.: is it "cruel and unusual" and thus unconstitutional to execute juveniles? As a matter of ordinary meaning, who knows? But it is clearly unconstitutional now given the rules of legal interpretation in the U.S.) Proponents of the distinction, of course, think this is the way interpretation *ought* to be pursued, but most of them fail to articulate a normative reason for doing so; an exception is Randy Barnett, who thinks the *original* Constitution is morally superior from a moral and political point of view. See Barnett (2004). If that were remotely plausible, then this would be a good argument.

[45]See Zlotnick (1999), esp. pp. 1407–1410 and accompanying notes.

[46]There could, of course, be circumstances where originalist rhetoric is the preferred interpretive device of progressives, a point we should not lose sight of. (Thanks to William Hubbard for pressing me on this point.).

objectives by an old piece of legislation, that is, the constitution.[47] And constitutions are, as we all know, just old pieces of legislation with special prohibitions on their repeal by later legislators, often a degree of generality about political aspirations, and a certain positive moral valence attached to them. One need not be an historical materialist to recognize that the world changes continuously as its economic and productive power evolves, and that these changes affect the values, aspirations, and goals of human beings and their political associations.[48] (Historical materialists do have the theoretical advantage of explaining this!) What that means, of course, is that serious originalism, of either variety (intentionalist or public meaning), endangers the idea of constitutionalism, of the attractiveness of being bound by old pieces of legislation. Constitutionalism as an ideal survives only because incremental adjustments to constitutions by courts are possible in every jurisdiction I am aware of, and so the most offensive aspects of being bound by the will of long-dead people—sometimes rather unappealing long-dead people!—are removed or mitigated. Perhaps constitutionalism has no value, though on the limited evidence we have (after all, only the U.S. and Sweden have constitutions that span four centuries), it seems that constitutions may exercise a human welfare-maximizing constraint on current polities.

Canada, the more European-leaning neighbor of my country, is an interesting case study in this regard. The Canadian Charter, or "constitution," was adopted only in 1982, but the courts moved quickly to repudiate the idea that the intentions of its framers controlled its interpretation. In 1985, the Supreme Court of Canada in *Re B.C. Motor Vehicle Act*[49] made clear that the intention of the framers did not control how the "principles of fundamental justice" should be interpreted. A bit of realistic context is important. The United States Supreme Court claimed authority for itself to settle the meaning of the U.S. Constitution some two hundred years ago,[50] a point that could not have been lost on the Canadian High Court. Also not lost on them was the fact that the framers of the 1982 Canadian Charter were quite alive, and would be for a long time. In order not to have its authority usurped, it was important to make clear, and make clear quickly, that having written the Charter, the authors were done. What that Charter meant was now in the hands of the courts and the polity. But this

[47]In the age of Trump, one might expect that the limit is reached very quickly!.

[48]Cf. not only Marx's corpus, but more recently Ian Morris (2015) and, a bit longer ago, Harris (1974). While Marx treated the level of development of a society's productive powers as a whole as the crucial explanatory variable, Morris (a classical archaeologist) focuses specifically on the degree of energy extraction from nature, while Harris (an anthropologist) looks at short-term material incentives, such as the ability to have enough food to eat in the year ahead. Morris and Harris are, as it were, "micro"-Marxists, accepting the basic Marxist thesis that how people produce the conditions of their material existence determines their beliefs, but filling in the micro-mechanisms that explain the patterns we find. Harris is better than Morris in this regard, since Harris is more alert to what would motivate individuals to act as they do, while Morris operates largely at the level of striking correlations, without sufficient attention to psychological mechanism.

[49][1985] 2 SCR 486.

[50]*Marbury v. Madison*, 5 U.S. 137 (1803).

was not simply a "power-grab," but a clear-headed recognition of the fundamental fact of "constitutionalism": namely, that a polity (e.g., its political elites) will not tolerate being (at least somewhat) bound by its predecessors unless there is substantial room for adjustment. This is why America's most notorious originalist, the late Justice Antonin Scalia, attracted almost no judicial adherents for his radical originalism over nearly 40 years. Most American lawyers and judges are tacit realists, whatever their public ideology.

4 The Roles of Judges in Democracies

So if we are realistic about democracies and about judges, what conclusions can we draw from the preceding observations?[51] I am not interested in the banal "obligations" partly captured by the *Minimal* and *Minimal-Plus* views. I want to focus only on the key issues, as stated earlier: what are the obligations of judges in determining the existence and meaning of the pre-existing standards, when they have latitude within the rule of recognition about how to determine it; and what are the obligations of judges when the meaning of the pre-existing standards are determinate? Since on a realistic view of the judicial role, it involves inherently moral and political judgment (Leiter 2015c), I see no way to answer these questions about the "obligations" of judges without regard to their moral and political views.

Let me introduce some categories that will help us conceptualize the options. The categories are admittedly crude, but their crudity may highlight what is at stake. I use the terms "progressive," "reactionary" and "status quo" in descriptive senses in what follows, though the terms often have moral valences. "Progressive" may seem the least descriptive of the three, but I use it here in what we can call the descriptive "Hegelian sense." Hegel, a deeply religious philosopher,[52] thought that the history of humanity was a matter of recognizing (with the help of Hegel's philosophy, of course) God's intentions for His creation. Divine intentions to one side, what was striking, and which Hegel noticed, is that there has been a general tendency in human history of expanding the domain of "freedom."[53] Think only of democratic voting rights in America: first, it was only propertied white men; then men without property, then women, then non-whites, and so on. The history of humanity, for Hegel, is the

---

[51]I think the view I defend, below, is not that far away from the view articulated by Judge Posner originally in Posner (1999), though I eschew his terminology about "pragmatism" which conceals more than it explains.

[52]Hegel's religiosity had much to do with the pernicious influence he had on Marx, who despite his own atheism, retained allegiance to nonsense like the teleological structure of history.

[53]Cf. my Meador Lecture (Leiter 2013).

history of human recognition of God's plan for the expansion of freedom.[54] *Progressive* means—as a shorthand for its clearly Hegelian background[55]—*increasing the range* of people who enjoy freedom and/or increasing the kind of freedom enjoyed. (Many "progressives," of course, think the range should extend to non-human animals and even non-animal nature. Other "progressives"—I think I am one—are more skeptical.) The boundaries of such freedom are contestable, but the basic pattern is crystal clear: more and more humans (and maybe even non-humans) are entitled to the same moral concern, and the same moral rights, as others. This is the central ideology of post-Enlightenment modernity—shared by Kant and Marx, as well as Rawls and Hayek—and one opposed only by Nazis, fascists, reactionaries, and religious traditionalists of all stripes.[56] One might, of course, insist that the real metric of progress is improvement in "well-being," but that is compatible with the point just made: freedom, in the relevant sense here, stands in a constitutive relationship with "well-being"—you cannot be well-off unless free, and vice versa—so for ease of discussion I will speak strictly in the former terms.

The other two terms again have descriptive content, though also normative connotations, depending on who is using the terms. Those who favor the "status quo" are those who favor, obviously, the way things are. This can have a pejorative connotation when the status quo isn't very attractive by the lights of the speaker, but it need not have such a connotation, since sometimes the status quo is morally preferable to the available alternatives, even by the speaker's lights. Those who are "reactionary" would like to return society to an earlier state of affairs, especially in terms of the legal and political status of citizens: a reactionary opposes the expansion of the freedom the progressive favors.

It is important to note that many debates between so-called "conservatives" and "liberals" are not necessarily debates between reactionaries and progressives in my sense, but rather intramural debates between progressives in the Hegelian sense, that is, those who disagree either about *the means* or about *the extension* of the relevant concepts of freedom. This is one reason that in American scholarly discourse it seems perplexing to put libertarians on the right ("the conservatives"). Libertarians contest the kind of freedom that modernity should progress towards, and so are often at odds with actual reactionaries. From the left progressive point of view, libertarians are reactionaries because of their naivete about how so-called "economic freedom" operates in practice, but that, of course, is precisely what is disputed. (To be sure, to the extent Hegel is right about the progressive tendency of modernity, we should hardly be surprised to find actual reactionaries trying to obscure their position by framing it, for rhetorical reasons, in "progressive" terms.)

[54]Hegel, rather notoriously, seemed to think this expansion reached its perfection with the Prussian state circa 1820, but that tells us more about the parochialism of philosophy than about freedom.

[55]I see no way to understand talk of "progress" except against the Hegelian/Christian background and its normative assumptions.

[56]On "traditionalism," see the twentieth-century Italian fascist philosopher Julius Evola, cited favorably by Trump's former advisor Stephen Bannon.

In talking about the roles of judges in democracies, I assume—without argument, since there is no useful argument that can be given—that judges should facilitate progress, rather than protect the status quo unreflectively or move us backwards. If the reader grants me that assumption, then the question about the roles of judges in democracies becomes clearer, though it has to be relativized to the background facts about the judiciary and the democracy. Here are, I believe, the relevant parameters.

A *Progressive Judiciary* is one that wants to expand freedom, and so exercises its interpretive latitude in service of that end.[57] A *Status Quo Judiciary* takes its promise to uphold the positive law very seriously, and even where there is interpretive latitude, interprets it in favor of the status quo. A *Reactionary Judiciary* is anti-progressive, looking to restrict freedom to the elite classes or races or sects who had enjoyed its exclusive prerogatives in the past.

A *Progressive Democracy* is one in which tribal loyalties have converged upon legislation that expands freedom. Canada and Germany are arguably examples today. A *Middling Democracy* is one in which tribal loyalties entrench a status quo that is neither progressive nor reactionary. The United States is arguably an example today, though perhaps we are about to enter a reactionary era. Finally, a *Reactionary Democracy* is one in which the tribal loyalties have converged upon legislation that restricts freedom, aiming to bestow its benefits only on select elites or groups. Hungary and Poland are arguably examples today.

Finally, we need some way of characterizing the effect of judicial invalidation (or reinterpretation) of legislation in different systems.[58] Let us call a *Judge-Centered System* one in which judicial decisions invalidating legislation are generally accepted and are absorbed with little resistance by political elites and popular constituencies. Let us call a *Legislature-Centered System* one in which legislation has *prima facie* popular and elite legitimacy, and judicial invalidation of such legislation is typically met with skepticism or resistance by elites and perhaps popular constituencies. *Mixed Systems* are ones in which judicial invalidation of legislation sometimes looks like a Judge-Centered system, sometimes like a Legislature-Centered system.

Given these rough categorizations, here is how I suggest we think of the "obligations" of judges in contemporary democracies.

Progressive Judiciaries in Progressive Democracies should exercise minimal interpretive latitude with respect to positive law, and should honor the Minimal Role of judges, scrupulously in Legislature-Centered Systems, since this will both promote progressive ends and honor public expectations and sustain the legitimacy of judicial review. Progressive Judiciaries in Middling Democracies should exercise

---

[57]Note that I assume that a progressive *judiciary* can only promote freedom and equality within the constraints of its institutional role. Other progressives will, of course, pursue progressive ends within the parameters of their roles. (Thanks to Omri Ben-Shahar for pressing me on this issue.)

[58]Of course, there are legal systems in which courts officially lack the power to *invalidate* legislation—Britain, with its doctrine of parliamentary sovereignty may be the most important case, though there is a clear tradition of parliament revisiting legislation when the courts find an "inconsistency" with fundamental rights.

their interpretive latitude in order to move the law in a progressive direction—aggressively in a Judge-Centered System, less aggressively in a Legislature-Centered system. Progressive Judiciaries in Reactionary Democracies should exercise their interpretive latitude aggressively, even in a Legislature-Centered system. The loss of legitimacy for the judiciary in aggressive judicial review is worth the risk given the morally defective character of a Reactionary Democracy.

Now the preceding admittedly simplifies how a progressive judiciary should think about its obligations, especially in Middling and Reactionary Democracies. A judge who thinks she has an obligation to exercise interpretive latitude in the service of progress (perhaps even to disregard settled law in the service of progress) must also take into account the ramifications of doing so—for example, the likelihood of provoking a reactionary legislature to revisit a question where the judge has ruled in a different direction. The pursuit of progress must of course be strategic, within the parameters in which an agent of progress can operate. A progressive judge who disregards the "backlash" effect of her decisions is not a reliable friend of progress.

With that important caveat in mind, we can proceed to the other cases. A Status Quo Judiciary should honor the positive law, and exercise minimal interpretive latitude in a Progressive Democracy, whether its culture is Legislature-Centered or Judge-Centered. In a Middling Democracy, a Status Quo Judiciary in a Legislature-Centered System, should probably act similarly, since it is unlikely to exercise interpretive latitude for progressive ends, and even if it did so, little good would likely result. If the Middling Democracy is Judge-Centered, then a Status Quo Judiciary should exercise its interpretive freedom in progressive directions, to the extent it is able to do so. In a Reactionary Democracy, the obligation of a Status Quo Judiciary is to try to be Progressive!

You can infer from the preceding how my account of obligations will go in the other cases. But let me address one case explicitly, namely, that of Reactionary Judiciaries in Reactionary Democracies. These judges have only one obligation in my view: to resign their position or, equally unlikely, reform their moral views.

The preceding has focused only on the judicial role vis-à-vis legislation, but a similar set of recommendations could be generated for the judicial role in interpreting prior court decisions or constitutional provisions or the edicts of administrative agencies.[59] A Progressive Judiciary will generally produce progressive precedents, though judiciaries are not univocal and there may be outliers of course. In that case Progressive Judges should utilize their interpretive latitude in much the same ways as they do with respect to non-progressive legislation. Here the risks are likely to be different than in the legislation case: that is, the risk is not provoking legislative backlash, but judicial backlash from less progressive colleagues. Once again, the same kinds of considerations apply as in the legislation case: progressive lower courts need to be mindful of their status quo or reactionary higher courts, and

[59]Thanks to Jennifer Nou for pressing me on this point.

so on. But the basic idea is the same: progressive judges ought to pursue, strategically, progressive outcomes, with due attention to context and ultimate outcome.[60]

Now to some all the preceding will sound too facile: surely, the *obligations* of judges should not depend on the quality of their moral views, or the moral quality of the legislation they must review? It is true that the question is typically approached without regard to these kinds of distinctions, but such an approach is unrealistic both about the judicial role and about democracies in my view. Judges should generally honor their *Minimal Role*, but not always. And their *Minimal Role* affords them considerable latitude, and how that latitude should be utilized has to depend on the quality of the judges, i.e., the quality of their moral and political judgment. Insofar as moral and political judgment is essential to exercise of the judicial role, especially at the highest levels of appellate review, and insofar as democracies differ in their moral and political character (as they obviously do), I see no way of discussing what judges should do without regard to their moral and political judgment and the nature of the democracy in which they serve.

To another kind of skeptic this way of thinking about the judicial role will seem to presuppose that we really know what kinds of decisions protect and expand freedom and well-being. Clearly we do not know with certainty what state of affairs would actually maximize real human freedom and well-being. But within the horizons of actual judgment, we often do know, even allowing that there will be contested cases. Decisions that protect the freedom of individual choice, within the limits set by some reasonable understanding of the Millian Harm Principle, and decisions which support social-economic policies that protect people from misfortune and encourage productive activity within capitalist relations of production (the current benchmark, of course) are good decisions. All complications to one side, the preceding basically describes the neoliberal consensus of the past half-century.[61] There may be hard cases, of course, where it is unclear, and so the obligation of judges will be less clear.

[60]A nice example of strategic thinking by progressive judges comes from cases in Ohio in the 1840s and 1850s, in which judges were confronted with the question of whether to return escaped slaves to the slave-holding American South. Considerations of comity first dominated, but by the 1850s receded. Compare *Birney v. State*, 8 Ohio 230, 238 (Ohio 1837) (holding the indictment for harboring an escaped slave defective for not charging scienter, thus not reaching the question whether a slave who escaped while in transit through Ohio was free ("it thus becomes unnecessary to decide upon the other points,... of a character too important in their bearing upon the whole country to be adjudicated upon without necessity")), and *State v. Hoppess*, 2 West.L.J. 279 (Ohio 1845) (holding a slave escaped from a boat docked to the Ohio shore of the Ohio River was a fugitive and thus subject to recaption under federal law, but noting that a slave brought voluntarily into Ohio would be emancipated), with *Anderson v. Poindexter*, 6 Ohio St. 622, 630–631 (Ohio 1856) ("There has never been a period during our state government, when a slave could for one single moment, by the consent and act of its owner, be placed and continued in bondage here.... Kentucky can not, by the law of comity, demand of this state an abrogation of its constitution and municipal laws, to promote any of its own peculiar institutions...."). For a thorough account of the Ohio slave transit and fugitive slave cases of this period, see Finkelman (1981, chap. 6). (Thanks to Todd Henderson for calling my attention to these cases.).

[61]The neoliberal consensus may be wholly wrong (as I think it is), in which case interpret "progressive" etc. accordingly.

But the only theory of judicial obligation that avoids such problems is one that would be morally ridiculous (e.g., judges should defer to whatever the legislature or executive says, regardless).

In any case, the genuinely hard cases, from a progressive point of view, are few and far between. The Affordable Care Act honored the Hegelian impulse to maximize freedom by extending access to healthcare—essential to well-being—and the U.S. Supreme Court correctly upheld it,[62] albeit in a way designed to appease the ideological deformities of the current moment in American political life. If there is an argument against the ACA, it has to be that its means were inadequate to its objective—and to the extent they were, it seems to have been because of the need for political compromise in its passage. Legalizing same-sex marriage[63] obviously expanded freedom, with the arguments against it turning on religious and metaphysical fantasies about the alleged "nature" of marriage[64] that bore no relation to the role of marital union in the capitalist West. American free speech doctrine is a notorious moral catastrophe,[65] shielding Nazi sociopaths and pathological defamers, in a way no other democracy does. That the U.S. Supreme Court has gone so wrong in the latter cases, as it has on its campaign financing decisions,[66] is easily explicable by the pathologies of American plutocracy (people with money to burn that amplifies their voice over other citizens think such amplification is central to free speech).[67] But the important point is that these kinds of decisions are pretty obviously wrong from the standpoint of progressive judges. The disagreements on these issues between progressive judges and others who are not explicitly reactionaries are disputes about the empirical facts. If the facts were otherwise, progressive judges should yield, of course.

In this regard, I should emphasize that my proposed template for thinking about judicial obligations is easily applicable as well by jurists and theorists who dispute the empirical facts. A libertarian—that is, someone who disputes the extension of "freedom" and especially the facts about state regimes that maximize it—can accept the preceding framework, but maintain that, for example, the ACA should have been invalidated, since it did not *really* maximize human well-being. On this interpretation, invalidation of the ACA is the "progressive" decision, because of a dispute about the nature of freedom and facts about the legislation in application. This view is wrong, but at least we have now located the dispute in the right place, rather than in nonsense about the act/omission distinction as the U.S. Supreme Court did. So, too, an actual reactionary, one who does not think human freedom and well-being without regard to rank or status matters, can also think the ACA should be invalidated, since maximizing the freedom of *all* human beings has no value—not

[62]*National Federation of Independent Business v. Sebelius*, 567 U.S. 519 (2012).

[63]*Obergefell v. Hodges*, 135 S.Ct. 2584 (2015).

[64]See, e.g., Girgis et al. (2012).

[65]For doubts, see Waldron (2012) and Leiter (2016b) (2013 Julius Stone Address in Jurisprudence).

[66]See, e.g., *Citizens United v. Federal Election Commission*, 558 U.S. 310 (2010).

[67]Cf. Leiter (2016b).

because such a decision is progressive, but because a reactionary decision is preferable. Obviously, in both cases, it is dubious that the interpretive latitude afforded judges, even in America, would have licensed that outcome *on those reasons,* but that might not matter if judges at the highest appellate levels choose outcomes that are legally permissible on the basis of their moral and political views, and the boundaries of permissibility are fluid and wide.[68]

In short, I think it is a virtue of my account that it locates the dispute at the right place: not about some putatively "generic" judicial obligation, but at the level of substantive disputes about the facts about how particular policies affect human beings. Counting against my approach, however, is the fiction that judges are morally and politically neutral appliers of the law. I do not want to deny that this fiction is taken very seriously in most societies that honor Democratic Values and that it may turn out to be of crucial importance to human freedom and well-being in some circumstances: realism demands as much. But I am not aware of a legal system that has really tested the relevant hypothesis about the fiction. In that system, the polity would actually understand that pre-existing legal standards can never be adequate to the array of problems that courts are asked to address and would, with H.L.A. Hart, renounce the desire for it to be otherwise:

> [W]e should not cherish, even as an ideal, the conception of a rule so detailed that the question whether it applied or not to a particular case was always settled in advance, and never involved, at the point of actual application, a fresh choice between open alternatives. . . .[T]he reason is that necessity for such choice is thrust upon us because we are men, not gods. It is a feature of the human predicament (and so of the legislative one) that we labour under two connected handicaps whenever we seek to regulate, unambiguously and in advance, some sphere of conduct by means of general standards to be used without further official direction on particular occasions. The first handicap is our relative ignorance of fact: the second is our relative indeterminacy of aim. . . .[H]uman legislators can have no such knowledge of all the possible combinations of circumstances which the future may bring. This inability to anticipate brings with it a relative indeterminacy of aim. When we are bold enough to frame some general rule of conduct (e.g. a rule that no vehicle may be taken into the park), the language used in this context fixes necessary conditions which anything must satisfy if it is to be within its scope, and certain clear examples of what is certainly within its scope may be present to our minds. They are the paradigm, clear cases (the motor-car, the bus, the motor-cycle). . . .We have initially settled the question that peace and quiet in the park is to be maintained at the cost, at any rate, of the exclusion of these things. . . .[But] [w]e have not settled, because we have not anticipated, the question which will be raised by the unenvisaged case when it occurs. . . .[W]hen [it]. . .does arise, we confront the issues at stake and can then settle the question by choosing between the competing interests in the way which best satisfies us. . . (Hart [1961] 2012, pp. 128–129)

If there were a legal system that embraced Hart's realism, and then produced catastrophic results for human well-being, we should all pause. We can put the point more starkly: if the fiction is really essential to maximizing human well-being, then this paper should be suppressed. But if the fiction is what I and Hart suspect it is, and

[68]I am skeptical they are wide enough for the reactionary, but if, following Karl Llewellyn, the boundaries of legitimate interpretation are defined by a sociological fact—current opinion among lawyers and jurists—then we can hardly be confident.

recognizing it as such would be salutary, then our public discourse about judges in democracies must change accordingly.

References

Achen CH, Bartels LM (2016) Democracy for realists: why elections do not produce responsive Government. Princeton University Press, Princeton
Alexander M (2012) The new Jim crow: mass incarceration in the age of colorblindness. The New Press, New York
Barnett RE (2004) Restoring the lost constitution: the presumption of liberty. Princeton University Press, Princeton
Bickel AM (1962) The least dangerous branch: the supreme court at the bar of politics. The Bobbs-Merrill Company, Inc., New York
Bositis DA (2012) Blacks and the 2012 Democratic National Convention. Joint Center for Political and Economic Studies, Washington, D.C. https://jointcenter.org/sites/default/files/Blacks%20and%20the%202012%20Democratic%20National%20Convention.pdf. Accessed 7 Jan 2019
Brest P (1980) The misconceived quest for the original understanding. Boston Univ Law Rev 60:204–238
Bump P (2016) Donald Trump got Reagan-like support from union households. Washington Post, November 10. https://www.washingtonpost.com/news/the-fix/wp/2016/11/10/donald-trump-got-reagan-like-support-from-union-households/?utm_term=.201cdd53fd28
Cohn N (2016) How the Obama coalition crumbled, Leaving an Opening for Trump. New York Times, December 23. http://www.nytimes.com/2016/12/23/upshot/how-the-obama-coalition-crumbled-leaving-an-opening-for-trump.html
Cohn N (2017) The Obama-Trump voters are real. Here's what they think. New York Times, August 15. https://www.nytimes.com/2017/08/15/upshot/the-obama-trump-voters-are-real-heres-what-they-think.html
Colquhoun D (2014) An investigation of the false discovery rate and the misinterpretation of *p*-values. Royal Soc Open Sci 1(3 (November)):140216. https://doi.org/10.1098/rsos.140216
Easterbrook FH (1983) Statutes' domains. Univ Chicago Law Rev 50(2(Spring)):533–552
Easterbrook FH (1994) Text, history, and structure in statutory interpretation. Harv J Law Public Policy 17(1 (Winter)):61–70
Ekins R (2012) The nature of legislative intent. Oxford University Press, Oxford
Finkelman P (1981) An imperfect union: slavery, federalism, and comity. The University of North Carolina Press, Chapel Hill
Fowler A, Hall AB (2018) Do shark attacks influence presidential elections? Reassessing a prominent finding on voter competence. J Politics 80(4 (October)):1423–1437. https://doi.org/10.1086/699244
Gardiner SM, Weisbach DA (2016) Debating climate ethics. Oxford University Press, Oxford
Geuss R (2008) Philosophy and real politics. Princeton University Press, Princeton
Gilens M, Page BI (2014) Testing theories of American politics: elites, interest groups, and average citizens. Perspect Politics 12(3 (September)):564–581. https://doi.org/10.1017/S1537592714001595
Gilmore G (1961) Legal realism: its cause and cure. Yale Law J 70(7 (June)):1037–1048
Girgis S, Anderson RT, George RP (2012) What is marriage? Man and woman: a defense. Encounter Books, New York
Green L (2016) Law and the role of a judge. In: Ferzan KK, Morse SJ (eds) Legal, moral, and metaphysical truths: the philosophy of Michael S. Moore. Oxford University Press, Oxford, pp 323–341
Harris M (1974) Cows, pigs, wars and witches: the riddles of culture. Random House, New York

Hart HLA (1961) 2012. The concept of law, 3rd edn. Oxford University Press, Oxford
Jessee SA (2009) Spatial voting in the 2004 presidential election. Am Polit Sci Rev 103 (1 (February)):59–81. https://doi.org/10.1017/S000305540909008X
Kinder DR, Kalmoe NP (2017) Neither liberal nor conservative: ideological innocence in the American public. University of Chicago Press, Chicago
Leiter B (2001) Moral facts and best explanations. Soc Philos Policy 18(2 (Summer)):79–101. https://doi.org/10.1017/S0265052500002910
Leiter B (2012) In praise of realism (and against "Nonsense" Jurisprudence). Georgetown Law J 100(3 (March)):865–893
Leiter B (2013) The boundaries of the moral (and Legal) community. Alabama Law Rev 64 (3):511–531
Leiter B (2015a) Normativity for naturalists. Philos Iss Suppl Noûs 25(1 (October)):64–79. https://doi.org/10.1111/phis.12046
Leiter B (2015b) Why Marxism still does not need normative theory. Analyse und Kritik 37(1–2 (November)):23–50. https://doi.org/10.1515/auk-2015-1-204
Leiter B (2015c) Constitutional law, moral judgment, and the supreme court as super-legislature. Hastings Law J 66(6 (August)):1601–1616
Leiter B (2016a) The paradoxes of public philosophy. Indian J Legal Theory 1(1 (May)):51–64
Leiter B (2016b) The case against free speech. Sydney Law Rev 38(4 (December)):407–439
Leiter B (2018) Legal positivism about the artifact law: a retrospective assessment. In: Burazin L, Himma KE, Roversi C (eds) Law as an artifact. Oxford University Press, Oxford, pp 3–28
Leiter B (2019) Realism and moralism in political thought. In: Andina T, Condell A (eds) Post-truth, philosophy and law. Routledge, London
Moore M (2016) Michael Moore in TrumpLand. Directed by Michael Moore. Produced by Dog Eat Dog Films and IMG Films
Morris I (2015) Forages, farmers, and fossil fuels: how human values evolve. Princeton University Press, Princeton
Nietzsche F (1883) 1976. Thus Spoke Zarathustra. In: The Portable Nietzsche (trans: Walter Kaufmann). Penguin Books, New York
Nietzsche F (1886) 1989. Beyond good and evil: prelude to a philosophy of the future (trans: Walter Kaufmann). Vintage Books, New York
Pauer-Studer H, David Velleman J (2015) Konrad Morgen: the conscience of a Nazi Judge. Palgrave Macmillan, London
Posner RA (1996) Law and legal theory in England and America. Oxford University Press, Oxford
Posner RA (1999) The problematics of moral and legal theory. Harvard University Press, Cambridge
Posner RA (2008) How judges think. Harvard University Press, Cambridge
Rossi E, Sleat M (2014) Realism in normative political theory. Philosophy Compass 9 (10 (October)):689–701. https://doi.org/10.1111/phc3.12148
Schattschneider EE (1960) The semisovereign people: a realist's view of democracy in America. Holt, Rinehart and Winston, New York
Shahine A (2007) Egypt women sworn in as judges despite opposition. Reuters, April 10. http://uk.reuters.com/article/uk-egypt-women-judges-idUKL1047186020070410. Accessed 3 Jan 2019
State of Israel Judicial Authority (n.d.) The judges: declaration of allegiance. http://elyon1.court.gov.il/eng/system/index.html. Accessed 27 Jan 2019
Stevenson CL (1944) Ethics and language. Yale University Press, New Haven
Waldron J (2012) The harm in hate speech. Harvard University Press, Cambridge
Weigel D (2016) How voters who heavily supported Obama switched over to Trump. Washington Post, November 10. https://www.washingtonpost.com/politics/how-voters-who-heavily-supported-obama-switched-over-to-trump/2016/11/10/65019658-a77a-11e6-ba59-a7d93165c6d4_story.html?utm_term=.92c3dd91729f

Williams B (2005) Realism and moralism in political theory. In: Hawthorn G (ed) In the beginning was the deed: realism and moralism in political argument. Princeton University Press, Princeton, pp 1–17

Zlotnick DM (1999) Justice Scalia and his critics: an exploration of Scalia's fidelity to his constitutional methodology. Emory Law J 48(4 (Fall)):1377–1429

Brian Leiter is Karl N. Llewellyn Professor of Jurisprudence at the University of Chicago Law School. His books include *Nietzsche on Morality* (Routledge, 2002; 2nd ed., 2015), *Naturalizing Jurisprudence* (Oxford University Press, 2007), *Why Tolerate Religion?* (Princeton University Press, 2013), and *Moral Psychology with Nietzsch*e (Oxford University Press, 2019). His most influential jurisprudential work is a seminal reinterpretation of the tradition of American legal realism, which connected the realist view of legal adjudication with naturalist positions in philosophy and philosophy of law.

Is Realism at Odds with Constitutional Democracy?

Pierluigi Chiassoni

Abstract The paper is devoted to the realism-constitutional democracy puzzle. On the one hand, constitutional democracy is committed to rule of law values like the "government of laws" (and not "of men"), legality, certainty, and separation of powers. On the other hand, legal realism sets forth a theory of adjudication that casts doubts upon the viability of rule of law values. After a preliminary part on judicial discretion and the realistic theory of adjudication, four strategies for solving the puzzle are analysed in turn: the Neutralization Pattern, the Weakening Pattern, the Surrender Pattern, and, finally, the Confinement Pattern. Apparently, only the Surrender Pattern, together with some wise measures of Confinement, seems apt to providing a successful way-out.

1 The Realism-Constitutional Democracy Puzzle

Constitutional democracy, as we all know, is a form of government committed to rule of law values of "government by laws" (and not "by men"), legality, certainty, separation of powers, hierarchy of legal sources, subjection of legislation to the constitution, subjection of jurisdiction to the constitution and legislation.[1]

Paper presented at the International Conference "Interpreting Law—The Role of Judges in Contemporary Democracies", Faculty of Law, University of Belgrade, Belgrade, October 14, 2016.

---

[1]See e.g. Raz (1977), Bobbio (1985), Celano (2013), Ruiz Manero (2014a, c), Pino and Villa (2016) and Ferrajoli (2013, 2016a, b, 2017). Barberis (2016b) accounts for a sceptical view about the ideal of the "rule of laws". "Laws"—the sceptics claim—, being a human product, *cannot* rule; only men *can* rule. This is pure good sense. Indeed, the issue is, precisely, *how* men, provided they *must* rule, *should* rule. In this connection, the ideal of the "rule of laws" is usually understood, more mundanely, as the ideal of the rule by general laws ("normativism"), as opposed to the rule by

---

P. Chiassoni (✉)
University of Genova, Genova, Italy
e-mail: pierluigi.chiassoni@unige.it

P. Chiassoni, B. Spaić (eds.), *Judges and Adjudication in Constitutional Democracies: A View from Legal Realism*, Law and Philosophy Library 135,
https://doi.org/10.1007/978-3-030-58186-2_3

Legal realism, as we all know, endorses a "sceptical", non-cognitivist, theory of judicial interpretation and application of law. It claims judicial discretion and judicial creation of law to be pervasive legal phenomena, and defends such a view as the sole true theory, against any variety of "formalist", or cognitivist, theory.[2]

It is clear, then, why legal realism appears to be at odds with constitutional democracy; why, in other words, there is a realism-constitutional democracy puzzle.

To begin with, legal realism undermines one of the basic theoretical presuppositions of constitutional democracy. It casts the light of doubt on the empirical possibility of effectively carrying out the rule of law values to which constitutional democracy is committed. Indeed, if judges are discretionary agents that "create" the very law they are going to apply to individual cases, what comes of legality, certainty, separation of powers, hierarchy of sources, etc.?

Furthermore, as a consequence of that theoretical undermining, legal realism poses a challenge to the ability of constitutional theory (the philosophical and juristic theory of constitutional democracy) to cope with the apparently recalcitrant reality of adjudication, by way of adequate institutional engineering.

From a logical point of view, three forms of way-out from the realism-constitutional democracy puzzle are conceivable.

The first form of way-out consists in adopting (what I dub) a *bilateral accommodation strategy*. This strategy involves solving the realism-constitutional democracy puzzle by revisiting both the (normative) theory of constitutional rule of law, on the one hand, and the (descriptive) theory of judicial discretion and lawmaking, on the other hand, in such a way that, in the end, they come to refer to compatible, harmonious, social phenomena.

The second form of way-out consists in adopting (what I dub) a *unilateral accommodation strategy*, where the direction of fit goes from the (purportedly descriptive) theory of adjudication to the (normative) theory of constitutional rule of law. This strategy involves solving the realism-constitutional democracy puzzle by revisiting the theory of judicial discretion in such a way that it comes to refer to a social phenomenon compatible (or not "in tension") with the carrying out of the rule of law values of constitutional democracy, as they are currently understood in constitutional theory.

The third form of way-out consists, finally, in adopting a *unilateral accommodation strategy*, where the direction of fit goes, instead, from the (normative) theory of constitutional rule of law to the (descriptive) theory of adjudication, as outlined by realism. This strategy involves solving the realism-constitutional democracy puzzle

---

case-by-case, *ad hoc*, individual decisions ("decisionism"). The tension between ("radical") realism, on the one hand, and liberalism and democracy, on the other, is also explored in Martí (2002), pp. 259–282. Martí claims that, as matter of pragmatic consistency, a radical realist cannot consistently be a supporter of liberal and democratic political institutions; he also suggests that, from the point of view of (radical) realism, we should "abandon whatever claim to liberalism and democracy [. . .] provided there is no possibility of successfully carrying them out" (p. 279). I will come back to this (dismal) claim at the end of the paper.

[2]See e.g. Tarello (1962), Twining (1973), Leiter (2007), Guastini (2011) and Chiassoni (2014).

by revisiting the theory of constitutional rule of law so as to make it capable of coping with the phenomena brought to the light by the realist theory of adjudication. It must be noticed that three varieties of the third accommodation strategy are available. Indeed, one can cope with the reality of adjudication, as depicted by realism, first, by loosening the requirements of constitutional rule of law; secondly, by strengthening them; thirdly, by resorting to some combination of loosening and strengthening. In the loosening case, the theory of constitutional rule of law is being adapted to fit to the (assumedly) untameable reality of adjudication. This involves giving up too exigent, unrealistic, "propaganda" requirements (like, e.g., the requirement of "absolute" or "mechanical" legality of jurisdiction, the requirement of "perfect" specialization of government functions, the requirement of an "absolute" or "mechanical" "rule of laws"), and turning them in as many regulative ideals. In the strengthening case, the theory of constitutional rule of law is improved by designing measures for affecting, contrasting, reducing and taming, so far as possible, the reality of adjudication, as realism depicts it and we see it everyday in our constitutional systems. In the mixed case, both ways are pursued at once.

A glance on the literature reveals that, in recent years, constitutional theorists have in fact taken up the challenge of legal realism. It reveals furthermore that, among the jurists and legal philosophers playing as constitutional theorists, all the three strategies, in their above-mentioned varieties, have been put to work.

If we pause to consider the outcomes of their individual efforts—I am referring, of course, to a (hopefully fair but) very limited sample out of a large literary whole—we may see that four distinct patterns for coping with the realism-constitutional democracy puzzle have been adopted.

From the vantage point of their way of dealing with judicial discretion, these are the Neutralization Pattern, the Surrender Pattern, the Weakening Pattern, and the Confinement Pattern. The *Neutralization Pattern* adopts a bilateral accommodation strategy. The *Surrender Pattern* adopts a unilateral accommodation strategy that emphasizes the need for loosening the (normative) theory of constitutional democracy to make it fit to the (descriptive) realistic theory of adjudication. The *Weakening Pattern* adopts a unilateral accommodation strategy that emphasizes the possibility of revisiting the (descriptive) realistic theory of adjudication to make it fit to the (normative) theory of constitutional democracy. Finally, the *Confinement Pattern* adopts a unilateral accommodation strategy that emphasizes the need for strengthening the (normative) theory of constitutional democracy in view of coping reactively with the (descriptive) realistic theory of adjudication.

I will proceed as follows. In the first part of my paper, I will offer a nutshell account of judicial discretion (Sect. 2) and legal realism's theory of adjudication (Sect. 3). This will provide the necessary theoretical background. In the second part, I will consider briefly each of the four patterns above, as they are instanced, and argued for, in essays written by influential contemporary civil law scholars (Sects. 4–6). The analysis, as we shall see (Sect. 7), suggests the following conclusions—valid, but for the last one, just in relation to the samples considered. One, the Neutralization Pattern is too good to be true. Two, the Weakening Pattern is self-deluding wishful thinking. Three, the Confinement Pattern requires a revolution in legal culture that looks like a highly utopian "regulative ideal". Four, the Surrender Pattern with some dose of Confinement measures is, apparently, the only way-out so far immune from objections. Five, by way of generalization, it seems reasonable to suppose that constitutional theory will never be able to meet the realistic challenge, except by a wise mixture of surrendering and confinement.

2 Judicial Discretion

Judicial discretion is no easy bird to catch. If we take into account the several definitions that are afoot in jurisprudential writings, judicial discretion may be characterized either as the *legally conferred power* (competence, authorization), or as the *de facto liberty*, for a judge, of *choosing between alternative courses of action* (in the broadest sense of "courses of action") *bearing on the decision of a case* (controversy, lawsuit) *at hand.*[3]

Judicial discretion as a *de facto* liberty is a naturalistic notion. It is tantamount to the empirical possibility, for a judge, of choosing to do, or abstain from doing, something relevant for deciding a case.[4] Two different varieties of liberty-discretion are to be singled out: *law-breaking discretion* and *reflective-selection discretion.*

Law-breaking discretion consists in the natural liberty, for a judge having the duty to decide a case, of choosing between following the law or departing from it, such a liberty being the effect of the absence of (compelling) physical or psychological restrictions (the latter including diverse factors ranging from sympathy to practical convenience to the allegiance to social, moral or legal standards). Law-breaking discretion—it is claimed—is a necessary feature in any positive

[3]The literature on judicial discretion is immense. To the present purpose, I have profited from Caracciolo (2001), pp. 252–254; Barak (1989), p. 7; Dworkin (1963), pp. 624–638; Dworkin (1967), pp. 32–40; Easterbrook (2004), pp. 1–20; Hart (1956), pp. 658, 665; Hart (1994), "Postscript", pp. 273–276; Iglesias Vila (2000), pp. 134–173; Lifante Vidal (1989), pp. 3–62. Caracciolo considers a general feature of judicial discretion that the choice be done "according to the judge's *own* criteria" (Caracciolo 2001, p. 253). I find the clause puzzling. A criterion of choice may be "a judge's own" in two different ways: by selection, i.e., because the judge has selected it, though it is an established criterion among culturally accepted or acceptable others; or, rather, by invention, i.e., because the judge has created it, in an exercise of practical autonomy. In the former case, the judge is applying an autonomously selected heteronomous criterion (for instance, a principle of a given social or critical morality), because she thinks that criterion to be the "best"; in the latter case, the judge is applying an autonomously selected autonomous criterion, always because she thinks it to be the "best". The heteronomous reading seems closer, here and now, to widespread social expectations.

[4]Generally speaking, saying that an agent A has the *de facto* liberty of doing something (say, *f*) in an individual situation S, means that (1) A is capable of doing *f*, and (2) there are no compulsive factors, in S, that deprive A of the possibility of choosing between doing *f* or not doing *f*. On human liberty, see von Wright (1984), pp. 107–170, especially, to the present purpose, pp. 116–119.

legal order, for no legal order can ever, at least so far,[5] completely rule out the possibility for judges to decide "against the law".[6]

Reflective-selection discretion consists in the natural liberty, for a judge having the duty to decide a case, of choosing between two or more alternative courses of action, within a set of reasonable, *prima facie* lawful or right, alternatives, such a liberty being the effect of the absence of normative standards pointing to, and converging upon, one determinate solution for the case at hand.

I think the notion of judicial discretion as *de facto* liberty should be ruled out from jurisprudential discourse, and power-discretion be used instead as the sole theoretically worthwhile notion. It seems weird regarding the natural liberty of a judge to depart from the law, to break her duty of being a loyal law-applying agent, as being a form of "discretion". To be sure, we do not consider the natural liberty of an ordinary citizen to break a traffic law as a form of "discretion": we would not say that Mr. John F. Smith, a gourmets-celebrated City butcher, "has the discretion of passing red lights in Regent Street"; we would not talk of "citizens' discretion" in connection with law-oriented behaviours like paying taxes and omit murders. "Discretion", as used in legal discourse, carries an institutional meaning: refers to an institutional, norm-conferred, position. The same considerations apply to the notion, I have just singled-out for argument's sake, of reflective-selection discretion.[7] Accordingly, in what follows, I will focus on power-discretion only. As a consequence, as we shall see, from the vantage point of the realism-constitutional democracy puzzle, the problem becomes whether, and to what extent, the working of "our" legal orders necessarily involves *discretion-situations*: i.e., situations where judges have to exercise discretionary powers. With these caveats in mind, let's move to power-discretion.

As a power (competence, authorization), judicial discretion is, by definition, always conferred, expressly or tacitly, by some (explicit or implicit) norm of a legal system concerning jurisdiction. Four varieties of power-discretion

---

[5]What about implanting a device inside of judges' skulls controlling their mental behaviours, and inflicting horrible headaches (to begin with, of course) any time a "wrong" decision is being adopted? Caracciolo, by the way, also offers a conceptual argument: norms are, by definition, entities that are apt for being violated. An un-breakable law is no law (Caracciolo 2001, p. 253).

[6]Caracciolo (2001), p. 253. By the way, Kelsen's (1960, pp. 242–251, 271–274) doctrine of the tacit alternative clause may be seen as a tool for accommodating judicial decisions "contrary to statutory law" to the dynamics of legal systems and a positivist theory of validity "as existence".

[7]Indeed, even a superficial consideration suggests the notion of "*de facto* discretion", as applied to judges, to be the output of a confusion between two theoretical perspectives that should be carefully kept apart: namely, the psychological and the normative one. Such confusion, to be sure, is favoured by the ambiguity of the word "discretion". Indeed, the term may refer either, in ordinary language, to individuals' *psychological capacity for judgment* (ability of discernment), or, in technical-legal language, to the *power, vested upon appointed legal organs, of making binding decisions* based not on the mechanical application of pre-existing plain and exact rules, but on a considered, judicious, specification and concretization of broad and vague standards.

(discretion-as-power) may be considered: *picking-out discretion*, *delegation discretion*, *fixing-up discretion*, and *correction discretion*.[8]

Picking-out discretion is the power (competence, authorization), for a judge, of *choosing one alternative out of a closed, pre-established, set of alternatives*, according to criteria the judge herself is entitled to select.[9] By assumption, any alternative in the set represents a legally correct answer, so that the law is indifferent as to the one that will finally be chosen and carried out in an individual case.[10]

Delegation discretion is the power (competence, authorization), for a judge, of choosing the content of their decisions on a particularist, case-by-case way. Were it to concern every judicial decision in a legal order, this form of discretion would have the effect of "eliminating whatever general rule or norm, but the one that establishes such a faculty for judges".[11] Delegation discretion is, in other terms, the typical mark of cadi law: a form of "rule of (wise?) men" totally at odds with the "rule of laws".

Fixing-up discretion is the power (competence, authorization), for a judge, of *fixing-up defective laws and establishing the legally correct answer for the cases at hand*. Its exercise is typically required in situations where, because of gaps or semantic indeterminacy ("open texture"), pre-existing legal norms have run out and the judge, in order to decide the case, has to make up (to "create") the very standard she is going to apply.[12] Unlike picking-out discretion, fixing-up discretion requires judges to do something more than choosing among a given set of alternatives, and this amounts to some piece of interstitial lawmaking. Unlike delegation discretion, fixing-up discretion is not particularist lawmaking, though: it concerns

---

[8]According to Barak (1989, p. 7) judicial discretion is: "the power the law gives the judge to choose among several alternatives, *each of them being lawful*". Which sort of lawfulness may be at stake here? Two candidates can be considered: *ex ante lawfulness by content* and *ex post lawfulness by delegation*. In the former case, it is lawful by content because, as in the case of picking-out discretion (Caracciolo 2001, p. 253), the judge is given the power to choose among the alternatives of a closed and pre-determined set; in such situations, whatever the judge decides, it is lawful *ex ante* by content, if her decision falls inside of the set. Contrariwise, in the latter case, which corresponds to delegation discretion (Caracciolo 2001, p. 253), the decision is lawful *ex post* by delegation: whatever the judges decides is, by institutional design, lawful. Notice that "strong discretion" *à la* Dworkin corresponds to something like delegated discretion; there are only *ex post* right answers, provided some minimum requirements of no-preposterousness are satisfied. Instead, "weak discretion" *à la* Dworkin corresponds, as we shall see in a moment, to controversial issue discretion.

[9]On this notion, see the remarks I make in footnote 3.

[10]Caracciolo (2001), p. 253. Picking-out discretion is typically exercised when judges select one out of the several possible meanings of a given legal provisions. This idea, having Kelsen's notion of norms as frames of alternative meanings in mind, I have elaborated a little bit more in Chiassoni (2016b, 2019, ch. 2).

[11]Caracciolo (2001), p. 253.

[12]See Caracciolo (2001), pp. 253–254, who, by the way, leaves open whether this kind of judicial discretion is normative, that is to say, a decision-making *power* conferred by the law, or empirical, that is to say, an instance of judicial *de facto* liberty. As I said in the text, to the present purpose, and in the light of how our legal systems work, the normative reading of fixing-up discretion is preferable.

the establishment of legally (and rationally) justified general standards, likely to be applied in future controversies.

Correction discretion, finally, is the power (competence, authorization), for a judge, of departing from an established, clear, and determinate "bad law", and replacing it with a "good law", presented as the all-things considered legally correct answer for the case at hand.

Sometimes analysts consider a further notion of judicial discretion. This is *controversial issue discretion*, namely, the power (competence, authorization), for a judge, of *identifying the legally correct answer for a case at hand, where there is reasonable controversy over which such a right answer is, where*, in other words, *"mechanical" application of law is not viable.*[13] A moment's reflection, however, suggests controversial issue discretion to be a notion that captures a property likely to be present where there is room for the exercise either of fixing-up or of correction discretion.

The preceding analysis of judicial discretion in general can be put to work for defining a notion that plays a central role in the realistic theory of adjudication: this is the notion of interpretive discretion. In very rough, and very broad, terms, *interpretive discretion* can be understood as the legally conferred power (competence, authorization), for judges having the duty to decide a case, to choose among alternatives bearing on the interpretation of law.

If, out of analytical convenience, we take the pain of distinguishing between *textual interpretation*, or *interpretation proper*, on the one hand, and *normative integration*, on the other hand, as referring to two groups of activities jointly embraced by ordinary usage of the phrase "interpretation of law", it may be worthwhile distinguishing two sorts of interpretive discretion: namely, interpretive discretion proper and normative integration discretion.

Interpretive discretion proper is the power (competence, authorization), for a judge, in relation to the interpretation of a previously identified set of legal provisions (source-sentences, normative-clauses), of *choosing between two or more reasonable alternatives concerning the legally correct translation of those source-sentences into one or more explicit norms.*[14]

Normative integration discretion, contrariwise, is the power (competence, authorization), for a judge, of *choosing among two or more reasonable alternatives concerning the legally correct enrichment of a previously identified normative set* (i.e., a set made of explicit norms, implicit norms, or components of both sorts).

---

[13] Caracciolo (2001), p. 254.

[14] It seems necessary defining interpretive discretion in terms of reasonable alternatives, if we wish to account for a basic aspect of judicial interpretation in our legal culture: that is to say, its being an argumentative game, belonging to the realm of rhetoric. From the standpoint of judicial interpretation and integration, the law can in fact be considered as a rhetorical normative system. As a system, to wit, that consists, at any given time, of the totality of the rhetorical consequences of a given set of source-sentences. I have offered a short presentation of this view in Chiassoni (2016b, 2019, ch. 2).

Normative integration discretion concerns, accordingly, the identification of the *implicit components* of normative sets: it concerns adding to a given normative set some implicit principle,[15] norm of detail,[16] priority rule,[17] or statement about the correct institutional status of source-sentences and norms.[18]

If we pause to consider the objects or entities the discretionary choices of judges may fall upon, these appear to be of two different sorts: *methodological directives* and the *materials* or *resources* required to put such directives to work. It seems worthwhile distinguishing, accordingly, between methodological discretion and materials (or resources) discretion.

Methodological discretion is the power (competence, authorization) of selecting directives (rules, canons) concerning textual interpretation or normative integration. It concerns, more precisely, the selection of the methodological code the judge is going to use in view of identifying and justifying some interpretive or integrative conclusion bearing on the decision of a case.

Materials discretion is the power (competence, authorization) of selecting the relevant interpretive or integrative resources: that is to say, the set of data—sources-sentences, principles, precedents, legislative history, juristic constructions, linguistic uses, philosophical outlooks, political theories, moral principles, scientific theories, etc.—which, in combination with methodological directives, serve to identify (*ex ante*), and justify (*ex post*), interpretive or integrative conclusions.

Armed with this portable theory of judicial discretion, we may now cast a (fugitive) glance on the realistic theory of adjudication.

3 Realism on Adjudication

To the present purpose, the realistic theory of adjudication can be rehearsed in the form of eleven claims. I will present them in an apodictic, or quasi-apodictic, form.

1. *Authoritative texts* (constitutional clauses, statutory provisions, etc.) *are not self-interpreting entities*. There must always be some interpreter to pour meaning into the otherwise dead letter of their words and phrases.
2. *Authoritative texts, and previous juristic and judicial interpretations and normative integrations thereof, if any, are not self-applying entities*. There must always be some interpreter who takes into account texts and the previous interpretations and integrations thereof, and, upon a judgment that may involve selecting,

[15]Like, e.g., "No man may profit from his own wrong".

[16]Like, e.g., "Car producers are liable to customers for design defects".

[17]Like, e.g., "Principle P1 ought to prevail over principle P2 in cases C1".

[18]Like, e.g., "Norm N1 is a supreme constitutional principle". I have briefly considered this and other "interpretive" sentences typically recurring in judicial and juristic discourse in Chiassoni (2016b, 2019, ch. 2).

modifying, and refining such previous interpretations and integrations, applies them to individual cases.

3. *Authoritative texts are methodologically ambiguous*. From a strictly methodological standpoint, that is to say, from the vantage point of the interpretive techniques (canons, directives, maxims) that are available "here and now" in our legal cultures, authoritative texts are always capable of a plurality of alternative meanings. Indeed, any authoritative sentence whatsoever is open, technically speaking, to three alternative forms of reading: a literal reading (or according to linguistic conventions), an extended reading, or a restricted reading. For lovers of clear and distinct ideas, realism characterizes here for making an empirical claim about (what may be called) the *universal methodological ambiguity* of source-sentences.
4. *Authoritative texts are axiologically ambiguous*. Legal cultures are typically rife with ethical pluralism and practical disagreements. Judges, jurists and people-at-large—even in apparently monolithic societies—typically entertain different views about the "proper" way to see the constitution, judicial review, the role of parliament, judicial interpretation, etc. Accordingly, the same source-sentences are likely to receive competing, mutually exclusive, interpretations, when they turn out as battlefields for ideological warfare. Likewise, to be sure, they can be the points where an overlapping consensus about their "proper meaning" obtains. In such cases, they are, so to speak, the "parts of the (law-)boat" nobody, at least during a certain time-span, wishes to fight upon.[19] And the cases they regulate turn out to be inter-ideological easy cases.
5. *Judicial and juristic interpretation of authoritative texts and normative integration are reflective undertakings*. From a psychological point of view, these activities belong to the reflective working of the mind, not to its automatic working. They are part of so-called "System 2", not of so-called "System 1".[20] Accordingly, so far as judicial interpretation is concerned, any view purporting to draw a line between mere understanding, which would be immediate, unreflective, and afoot in "easy cases", and interpretation proper, which would take place, instead, in case of doubt ("hard cases"), provides a misleading, impoverished, picture of the phenomenon.
6. *Judicial and juristic interpretation of authoritative texts and normative integration are holistic undertakings*. No authoritative clause, even when a judge applies it in its clear literal or conventional meaning, is ever interpreted "by itself": namely, as an isolated legal sentence that emits a linguistic stimulus perceived by automatically reacting judicial readers. Rather, it is always interpreted within the background, and as a particle, of a larger set of rules and principles, which, for

[19]From a conceptual standpoint, I account for this phenomenon by means of the notion of conjectural axiological interpretation. See Chiassoni (2016b, 2019, ch. 2).

[20]For this distinction, see Kahneman (2011), pp. 20–24. I have argued for the reflective character of juristic interpretation in Chiassoni (2016b, 2019, ch. 2), under the headings of juristic textual, meta-textual and conjectural interpretation.

example, may justify its literal interpretation and application as systemically correct. The same considerations apply, mutatis mutandis, concerning normative integration.

7. *Judicial interpretation of authoritative texts or normative integration never is a purely cognitive undertaking (never is a pure "act of cognition")*. Rather, it always includes some "act of will" and involves some piece of practical commitment.[21] To begin with, any interpretation whatsoever necessarily depends on the previous selection of interpretive directives (criteria) and interpretive resources (materials) by the acting interpreter; this involves volition and decision-making. Furthermore, interpretive directives and interpretive resources are usually selected out of allegiance to some definite legal axiology (ideology of positive law), which sets the "proper" goals interpretation must carry out. Accordingly, any view purporting to depict judicial interpretation as a cognitive enterprise, either universally, or in some sort of situations (the notorious "easy cases"), provides an impoverished, false picture of the phenomenon. The same considerations apply, mutatis mutandis, concerning normative integration.

To be sure, interpretive volition may sometimes be of a purely conformist sort: the interpreter decides to follow an established, majoritarian, interpretive practice, considering it to be the only course of action viable to her—though, while doing so, she may deem such a way of proceeding to be unreasonable, unjust, or seriously inconvenient. A conformist decision, however, is still a decision.

8. *Judicial interpretation of authoritative texts and normative integration are discretionary enterprises*. So far as textual interpretation and normative integration are concerned, judges are expressly or tacitly endowed with two basic discretionary powers, which are both required in order for them to decide individual cases. To begin with, there is the power of making binding decisions, if only for the individual case at hand, concerning the "correct" set of methodological directives to be used in order to identify and justify their interpretive or integrative outputs

[21]Guastini (2011, pp. 45–54) claims that judicial and most of juristic interpretation is never purely cognitive in character (never purely a matter of "knowledge"), but always involves some decision (always a matter of "will"), because legal texts, or rule-formulations (like, e.g., a constitutional provision), are indeterminate, and they are indeterminate both at the level of "abstract interpretation", due to the ambiguity of rule-formulations, and at the level of "concrete interpretation", due to the vagueness of the predicate terms used in rule-formulations. In other words, Guastini grounds (what we may call) his "universal decisional character" thesis about the nature of legal interpretation on a "universal indeterminacy thesis": universal indeterminacy makes decision-making necessary, when interpreting a rule-formulation to any practical purpose. Guastini, however, affirms that rule-formulations are "often ambiguous"; furthermore, as we all know, vagueness is an intermittent phenomenon: any predicate term can be vague, but is never vague all the time, as regards to any individual case whatsoever. Such points, clearly, are to the effect of undermining the universal decisional character thesis. Accordingly, if we want to rescue it, the universal indeterminacy thesis must be rephrased in terms of universal *methodological* indeterminacy, and supplemented with further argument, coping with situations where methodological indeterminacy is reduced (overcome) by an on-going cultural (and ideological) convergence upon "one" reasonable method and result. This is what I have done above in the text.

(methodological discretion). Furthermore, there is the power of making binding decisions, if only for the individual case at hand, concerning the "correct" set of interpretive materials, or resources, to be used in applying the methodological directives that have been previously selected (materials discretion).

Upon consideration, there would be no room, in a legal culture, for exercising interpretive discretion (in the wide sense including interpretive discretion proper and integration discretion: see Sect. 2 above), if the legal culture were characterized by the existence of an ideally-working methodological code: that is to say, by the presence of a code characterized by the joint properties of being objective, endowed with strict normativity, complete, exclusive, and efficient. Where a code is *objective*, when it is an evident datum to every judge and jurist: something "out there", which can just be known by any competent lawyer; it is *endowed with strict normativity*, when, to any competent lawyer, it is undefeasibly binding on textual interpretation and normative integration; it is *complete*, when it exhausts the set of methodological directives available for correctly interpreting the source-sentences or integrating them; it is *exclusive*, when no alternative objective code exists; and, finally, it is *efficient*, when the directives of the objective code always point to definite sets of resources (which are, as we have said, the data necessary to apply them), and, in relation to such sets of resources, always point to (just) one definite conclusion for any case at hand—be it the translation of a legal provision (a source-sentence) into some explicit norm, the identification of the implicit norm relevant for the case, etc.

Unfortunately, such an objective, strictly normative, exclusive, complete, and efficient code was never seen in our legal experiences,[22] and, due to the set of properties that characterizes it, it is very unlikely it can ever be seen. Furthermore, even if it existed, being a set of directives in a natural language, it would be neither self-interpreting, nor self-applying: How should interpreters proceed in interpreting the objective methodological code? Perhaps, only a comprehensive and successful training process of psychological internalization—one that turns the use of the code into a set of "quasi-natural" behaviours, one that makes the use of its directives something like a "second nature" for interpreters—would do.[23] A legal experience with a methodological code working in that naturalized way, however, would be a reality very far away from our legal experiences. Besides, it would be something extremely weird. At the point that we could even doubt whether, in such situation, there would be law, as we are used of thinking about it.

It may happen of course that, in a given legal culture, in relation to a certain kind of source-sentences (say, criminal law statutes), a certain interpretive code comes to be widely regarded by judges and jurists as the only "correct" methodological code, and acquires in that way a (contingent) social objectivity and (something very close to) strict normativity. Also in those situations, however, interpreters will typically have occasions for exercising methodological discretion. They will fatally be called

[22]Think, for a telling instance, at the French Exegetical School (Chiassoni 2016a, Chap. IV).

[23]On these phenomena, see e.g. Celano (2016a), pp. 2–16.

to making reasoned choices about precisifying, putting into hierarchical order, and enriching the directives of the "objective" code.

9. *Judicial interpretation of authoritative texts is a creative enterprise.* It does "create law", it does "make law", in view of the decision of the individual cases at hand. How can that be? How can we make sense of this opaque creationist metaphor? From a realistic vantage point, there are apparently (not least than) five different ways for judicial interpretation to be a "creative" undertaking: namely, by selection, by repair, by correction, by interpretive enrichment, and by methodological innovation.[24]

First, judicial interpretation may "create law" by selection. This occurs when judges choose one meaning out of the several, alternative, determinate, meanings that, for a given authoritative text (say, a given statutory provision), can be justified on the basis of current interpretive methods and current legal axiologies. The creative contribution of judicial interpretation, here, consists in overcoming the methodological and axiological ambiguity of authoritative texts, if only for the individual case at hand. This occurs by an act of semantic reduction that constitutively establishes a one-to-one relationship between the text and one determinate meaning thereof. The reduction results, in turn, from a methodological choice in favour of some set of interpretive directives and interpretive resources, which sets are being treated as paramount as to the individual piece of interpretation to be performed, in force of their coherence with the axiological outlook the interpreter adopts.

Second, judicial interpretation may "create law" by repair. This occurs when judges fix up some (assumed) defect of an authoritative text, which prevents it from expressing a complete, determinate meaning in relation to the individual case at hand. An authoritative text can be defective either by syntactic, semantic, or pragmatic ambiguity, or due to the vagueness of its descriptive terms. In all these cases, the text presents loose ends that need repairing. The creative contribution of judicial interpretation consists, here, in sewing up such loose ends by means of disambiguation and precisification.

Third, judicial interpretation may "create law" by correction. This occurs when judges consider the established meaning of an authoritative text—its culturally rooted literal, customary, juristic, or case-law meaning—as substantially un-correct (wrong): usually, by being either "over"-inclusive, or "under"-inclusive, as to the individual case at hand. The creative contribution of judicial interpretation, here, consists in rectifying the un-correct established meaning: that is to say, in replacing it with a different meaning that judges regard as the proper and legally correct one.

[24]On judicial creation of law, the most illuminating essays are, to my knowledge, Carrió (1965), Bulygin (1966) and Wroblewski (1992). The account I provide in the text takes a different stance, though.

This, by way, is what happens when judges overrule some established interpretation of a source-sentence.

Fourth, judicial interpretation may "create law" by interpretive enrichment. This occurs when judges provide an "extensive interpretation" of an authoritative text: i.e., one by means of which they add some further explicit norm to the set of explicit norms corresponding to the established meaning of that text.[25] Unlike creation by correction, creation by interpretive enrichment does not involve the criticism, and discarding, of the established meaning of an authoritative text. Unlike creation by normative integration, which is a form of enrichment the outputs of which are implicit norms, creation by interpretive enrichment points to some further explicit norm. It must be noticed, however, that interpretive enrichment and normative integration are often performed by way of the same rhetorical forms of reasoning (from analogy, *a contrario*, *a fortiori*, from the nature of things, from principles, from juristic concepts, from juristic theories of legal institutes, etc.). Furthermore, they usually work as means for coping with gaps, concretizing legal principles, bringing to the light the complete micro normative system concerning a certain matter.

Fifth, judicial interpretation may "create law" by methodological innovation. This occurs when judges provide a new meaning for the relevant legal provision at hand, on the basis of some new, so far never employed, interpretive method. The creative contribution of judicial interpretation, here, consists in deciding a case at hand on the basis of a norm, presented as the meaning of an authoritative text, which is different from the ones previously "in stock". This makes creation by methodological innovation different from creation by selection. Creation by methodological innovation may combine, and conspire, with creation by repair, correction or interpretive enrichment.

I am conscious that the above theory of judicial creation of law may look puzzling. We may wonder about the actual occurrence and the degrees of creative intensity that characterize the five sorts of interpretive creation above. The repair, correction, methodological innovation and interpretive enrichment varieties of interpretive creation show up in some cases only. They are a "local" phenomenon, the statistical relevance of which is purely contingent, and display a high (sometimes even very high) degree of creative intensity. Contrariwise, the selection variety of interpretive creation shows up in every case (remember, authoritative texts are not self-interpretive entities and are methodologically ambiguous): it is, in other words, a

[25]When I talk of *explicit* norms being created by enrichment, I have in mind the situations where a given source-sentence, say $S\text{-}S_1$, which is usually taken to express a certain norm, N_1, is made to express *also* a further norm, N_2 ($S\text{-}S_1 = N_1 \& N_2$). On the phenomenon of "complexity" in the meaning of source-sentences, see Guastini (2011), pp. 41–42. According to Eugenio Bulygin, judges make law whenever the general norm they apply to an individual case at hand is neither identical to any already existing norm, nor a logical derivation from already existing norms (Bulygin 1966, pp. 75–87). This is a normativist approach, deliberately opaque to interpretation (and, by the way, dubious as to the no-deducibility condition). Contrariwise, the five notions of judicial lawmaking I consider in the text are interpretation-transparent.

"global" phenomenon. Its degree of creative intensity may be very low. It depends, in fact, on whether the choice of methods and outputs is conformist, or not: i.e., on whether, or not, the interpreter, by her choice about method and output, just follows the herd.

10. *Playing with facts*. When the desired result—what the judge regards as the legally correct solution to the case at hand—cannot be reached by ordinary interpretive techniques, judges can, and do usually, proceed by playing with the facts of the case. This way of proceeding, emphasized by the "facts-skepticism" variety of legal realism, is sometimes also called "equitable understanding of facts", or "equitable balancing of facts".[26] As the Roman Law and Common Law traditions show, the judicial playing with facts may even reach the point of resorting to fiction.[27]
11. *Lawmaking as a collective enterprise*. From the standpoint of the practice of interpretation, the whole process of lawmaking appears a complex collective venture, where the legislature provides authoritative texts (source-sentences) and the interpreters—judges and jurists—provide the explicit and implicit meaning-contents of those texts. They both "make law", though in different guises and at different stages of the lawmaking process. The legislature "makes law" as a set of authoritative words and sentences. Judges—and, by way of proposal, jurists—"make law" as a set of rules and principles that are the interpretive, rhetorical "consequences" of those authoritative words and sentences.[28]

4 The Neutralization Pattern

As you may recall (Sect. 1 above), the Neutralization Pattern is the result of adopting what I have called a *bilateral accommodation strategy* for solving the realism-constitutional democracy puzzle.

A clear example of this pattern can be found in an essay of Mauro Barberis.[29] There, he sets to the task of identifying some "possible solutions" to what he presents as a "fundamental contradiction" in the Western legal culture of the last two centuries.[30] On the one side, according to the principle of separation of powers,

---

[26]Ferrajoli (1989), pp. 135–156; Ferrajoli (2012), pp. 216–221.

[27]I provide a survey of theories of judicial fiction in Chiassoni (2019, ch. 7).

[28]The literature on legal realism is boundless. Here I have proceeded by my own reading of the realistic theory of adjudication. A short companion of the main theses of realism (from ontology to interpretation) can be found in the essay contributed by Guastini for the present conference (Guastini 2016). On legislation from a realistic viewpoint, see, e.g., Chiassoni (2015, 2019, ch. 11).

[29]Barberis (2004), pp. 1–21; see also Barberis (2016a), pp.13–35.

[30]Barberis (2004), p. 1.

and, particularly, of separation between the legislative and the judiciary branches of government, judges ought not to make any law, but always ought to apply the laws made by the legislature. On the other side, according to the realistic theory of interpretation, judges cannot avoid making law, when they decide cases. The "fundamental contradiction at the heart of contemporary legal culture" consists precisely in this: judges ought not to create law, but they cannot avoid creating it.[31]

Being an analytical jurist, Barberis looks for a way-out by performing a three-steps investigation, where a careful, historical and theoretical, analysis of the terms involved is carried out.

In the *first step* of his investigation, Barberis brings to the fore three different "theses" that, in his view, would travel under the encompassing, ambiguous, "separation of powers" label. These are the thesis of "separation of powers" as distinction between different government functions, the thesis of "separation of powers" as balancing of powers, and, finally, the thesis of "separation of powers" as specialization of powers, or separation of powers in a strict sense.

The first thesis—"separation of powers" as distinction of powers—is tantamount to a "cognitive" claim. It belongs to the descriptive—not justificatory, not normative—theory that, following Montesquieu, identifies three basic functions in the working of any (developed) form of government whatsoever: the legislative function, the executive function, and the judiciary function.

Contrariwise, the second thesis—"separation of powers" as balancing of powers—is tantamount to a "normative" claim. It belongs to the normative theory according to which, if we wish to pursue the goal of political liberty, the competences in the exercise of the three functions of government must be mixed up in such a way that each branch of government interferes with the others, working as a check, or as a counter-power, to the other branches' eventual abuses.

The third thesis—"separation of powers" as specialization of powers—is, again, "normative" in character. It belongs to the normative theory according to which, if we want to give pride of place to the democratically elected legislature, and protect the political and civil liberties of the subjects, the three functions of government must be exactly vested in as many specialized branches, in such a way that to each branch corresponds, roughly, one, and only one, governmental function, and no interferences take place.[32]

In the *second step* of his investigation, Barberis singles out, symmetrically (symmetry is a golden, though tacit, rule of analysis), three different "theses" concerning jurisdiction, that would travel under the encompassing, ambiguous, name of "legal realism". These are "the free law doctrine", "radical realism", and "moderate realism".

The free law doctrine is a "normative" variety of legal realism. It advocates the ascription to the judges of an explicit lawmaking power, complementary to the

[31]Barberis (2004), p. 1.

[32]Barberis (2004), pp. 2–8.

lawmaking power of the legislature, in order to ensure that justice be done in deciding individual cases.

Radical realism represents, contrariwise, a (purportedly) "cognitive" thesis. It claims that legal (constitutional, statutory, etc.) clauses "do not have any meaning" *before* judicial interpretation. Consequently, all law is, properly speaking, judge-made law, for it is judges who create it, though under the guise of interpretation (broadly understood).

Finally, moderate realism represents, again, a "cognitive" thesis. It is moderate, since it does not deny that legal (constitutional, statutory, etc.) clauses have any meaning before judicial interpretation. It claims, rather, that authoritative texts, before judicial interpretation, have several different and alternative meanings, so that judicial interpretation "creates law", at least, in the weak sense of reducing—by selection—their structural indeterminacy (ambiguity).[33]

In the *third*, and last, *step* of his investigations, Barberis brings to the fore that the "fundamental contradiction" is to be regarded, more precisely, as the "contradiction" between the principle of separation of powers, in its strict, specialization, reading, on the one side, and legal realism, as a cognitive theory of adjudication, on the other side. It is at this point that, in order to suggest a possible way-out, Barberis adopts a Neutralization Pattern.

Is there any possibility of reconciling the strict doctrine of separation of powers with realism as a cognitive theory of judicial interpretation? The answer, according to Barberis, can be positive. To get to it, however, realism and the doctrine of strict separation of powers must be mutually accommodated. On the one hand, realism must be understood as moderate realism, leaving aside the dubious pretences of radical realism. On the other hand, the doctrine of strict separation of powers, insofar as it concerns the relationship between legislature and judges, must be understood as requiring, properly, that the legislature should be the sole, exclusive, holder of the power to create laws endowed with universal validity: i.e., laws that apply in general (*erga omnes*), that are binding for abstract classes of subjects. This requires, in turn, that judges should have no power of making laws endowed with universal validity.[34]

Notice that the strict principle of separation of powers, in this reading, does not concern at all the judicial creation of law as considered by moderate realism. Indeed, such creation of law, by itself, does not amount to the creation of general legal rules endowed with universal validity. It consists, rather, in "creating" norms that are valid only between the parties of each individual controversy. Therefore, from the standpoint of strict separation of powers, if understood in the way we have just mentioned, such a creation of law by judges is an innocuous, and therefore irrelevant, legal phenomenon.[35] This conclusion would apply, it must be noticed, even if we adopt a more robust variety of moderate realism: one that encompasses not only judicial

[33]Barberis (2004), pp. 8–15.

[34]By the way, this is positive law, for instance, in France (see art. 5 of the "Preliminary title" to the Civil Code) and Italy (see art. 101 of the Italian Constitution).

[35]Barberis (2004), pp. 15–21.

creation by selection, but also judicial creation by repair, interpretive enrichment, correction, methodological innovation, and normative integration (see Sect. 3 above).

The solution Barberis proposes for the realism-constitutional democracy puzzle is, apparently, portentous: You *can* have the cake (strict separation of powers), *and* eat it (judicial creation of law). From our vantage point, it represents, as I said, a clear instance of the Neutralization Pattern. Due to a "proper" understanding, *both* of the principle of separation of powers, which is one of the fundamentals of constitutional democracy, *and* of the realistic theory of judicial interpretation, in a way that makes it to be tantamount to moderate realism, the tension between realism and constitutional democracy is apparently neutralized. It just fades away.

There is a problem, however. As I said at the outset, the neutralization way of solving the realism-constitutional theory puzzle (at least in the version I am considering here) may appear too good to be true.

To begin with, Barberis's picture of moderate realism may look moderate at the point of excess. Leaving (unpalatable) radical realism aside, moderate realism, if we wish to be fair to it, should rather be conceived as encompassing all the different forms of judicial creation of law I have just recalled (and illustrated in some detail at Sect. 3 above): namely, besides creation by selection, also creation by repair, interpretive enrichment, correction, methodological innovation, and normative integration.

Furthermore, there is a thesis, advanced by Luigi Ferrajoli—perhaps, the staunchest defender of a "positivist" variety of constitutionalism, against the "principles", "post-positivist", or "natural law" constitutionalism at present so popular among legal scholars—, that cannot be overlooked.

Ferrajoli accepts as true a descriptive theory according to which any positive legal order is made of two components. The first component is the "law in force" or "binding law"; it is "posited or produced by authorities competent to produce it"; it is made of authoritative "signs and normative sentences", and is identified as such from the standpoint of the "normativistic principle".[36] The second component is the "living law"; it is tantamount to "the plurality of normative interpretations that can be associated" to the signs and normative sentences of binding law, and is identified as such from the standpoint of the "realistic principle".[37]

Now, taking into account this distinction, Ferrajoli claims that the rule of law values ought to obtain not only insofar as the "binding law" (the "law in force", the "law in books") is concerned, but also in relation to the "living law" (the "law in action").[38]

The Neutralization Pattern suggests, as we have seen, that the law in force (created by the legislature) and the living law (created by judges) dwell, so to

[36]Ferrajoli (2012), p. 225.

[37]Ferrajoli (2012), p. 225.

[38]See Ferrajoli (2012), pp. 221–234; Ferrajoli (2013), pp. 285–290; Ferrajoli (2016a, b), pp. 154–178, 211–226.

speak, on two different, noncommunicating, floors of the legal building. It presupposes that the interstitial, case-by-case, individual-case binding judicial creation of law does not affect the universally binding law made by legislative sentences.

Ferrajoli maintains, however, such a view to be unsound—and a piece of self-delusion, if you want. Judicial creation of law may go beyond the "normal" or "physiological" level compatible with the tenets of constitutional rule of law. When this occurs, the living law, insofar as it is the output of a jurisdiction that violates the borders of the "ordinary" powers of interpretation and equitable connotation of facts (insofar as, for instance, it indulges in the balancing of constitutional rights), trespasses into the province of the law in force: upsets the hierarchy of legal sources and flies in the face of the rule of law values of separation of powers, legality, and the subjection of jurisdiction to the constitution and legislation.[39]

If Ferrajoli is right, the challenge of realism to constitutional democracy and constitutional theory cannot be met by manipulating (accommodating) the positions at stake in the way Barberis considers. In fact, even a moderate (but robust) realistic theory of adjudication—one that encompasses the several ways of judicial creation of law I have identified (see Sect. 3 above)—poses a serious challenge, for it points to a phenomenon that is, at least potentially, dangerous to rule of law values. Any (bookish) constitutional design notwithstanding, the judicial creation of law—in the fixing-up, correction, interpretive enrichment, and normative integration varieties—may become a very important factor in the legal system, substantially prevailing upon the "law in force".

Ferrajoli, it must be noticed, thinks that the challenge of realism *can* be met; that the realism-constitutional democracy puzzle *can* be solved, and in a way preserving rule of law values. That, however, can happen only on the condition of adopting (what I have called) a Confinement Pattern, along the lines he himself sets forth. I will consider later whether Ferrajoli's proposal is sound. Meanwhile, let us cast a glance upon the Surrender Pattern and the Weakening Pattern.

5 The Surrender and the Weakening Patterns

The Surrender Pattern copes with the realism-constitutional democracy puzzle by adopting the first variety of a unilateral accommodation strategy. This is characterized, as you may recall, by revisiting the theory of constitutional rule of law in order to make it fit to the reality of adjudication, as depicted by realism. The leading idea is simple: judicial discretion and judicial lawmaking are structural features of legal orders; they belong, so to speak, to the physiology of positive law; they are a necessary furniture of our legal world. Accordingly, there is only one way of meeting

[39] Ferrajoli (2012), pp. 229–230, 233, 234.

the challenge of realism. This way consists in accepting the realistic theory of adjudication as true, and modifying—by loosening—the requirements of constitutional rule of law in such a way as to make them viable in view of such an uncompressible reality.

A clear example of Surrender Pattern can be found in an essay of Ricardo Caracciolo.[40] While developing his argument, as we shall see in a moment, Caracciolo also takes into account (what I have called) the Weakening Pattern, and lays down a radical critique of it. For this reason, in what follows I will provide an intertwined account of the Surrender and the Weakening Pattern.

Caracciolo sets to the task of inquiring whether "judicial discretion" is compatible with "the minimum", formal and substantive "requirements" of a democratic rule of law.[41]

Being, like Barberis, an analytical jurist, he takes pain at providing a careful elucidation of the key terms at stake, namely, "democratic rule of law" and "judicial discretion". Again, a three-steps inquiry is deployed.

In the *first step* of his inquiry, Caracciolo brings to the fore the four ingredients that, in his view, make up the "basic idea" of "the Rule of Law" in our present culture. These are: (*1*) the ascription and protection of fundamental rights—among which liberty rights, the pillars of individual autonomy, have pride of place; (*2*) the guarantee of legal certainty, i.e., of the possibility for individuals to make reasonably accurate predictions about the legal consequences of their conduct and the content of judicial decisions about their rights and duties; (*3*) the guarantee of the legality of jurisdiction; and, finally, (*4*) the guarantee of the right of defence, which is the "constitutional right" of every citizen to present arguments in front of a court, whenever her rights and duties are at stake.[42]

The guarantee of legal certainty requires the legality of jurisdiction. The legality of jurisdiction requires, in turn, that "*every* judicial decision be determined by pre-existing law": that the law provides, beforehand, "a right answer" to any individual case that may be brought to a court, so that judges can always "find", and never "make", it.

Caracciolo makes clear, though, that two alternative ways of conceiving the requirement of legality of jurisdiction are available.

According to a strict reading, the legality of jurisdiction requires every judicial decision to be determined by some *pre-existing legal rule*. Every judicial decision must be directly justifiable by pre-existing law; it must be the outcome of a subsumption of the individual case at hand within some previous and applicable legal rule. This notion of legality, notice, requires the law to be a complete normative

---

[40]Caracciolo (2001), pp. 251–260. By the way, a similar unilateral accommodation strategy is adopted also by Endicott (2014, pp. 311–342), who analyses the compatibility between constitutional rule of law and proportionality, and by Celano (2016b, pp. 237–285), who considers the compatibility between constitutional rule of law and ethical particularism.

[41]Caracciolo (2001), p. 251.

[42]Caracciolo (2001), pp. 252–253.

order *at the level of legal rules*. Any incompleteness—in the form of gaps or semantic indeterminacy of the existing rules—opens the gate to judicial lawmaking, if only for the individual cases at hand, and undermines the legality of jurisdiction.[43]

Contrariwise, according to a loose reading, the legality of jurisdiction requires every judicial decision to be determined, if not by some pre-existing legal rule, at least by some *pre-existing legal principle* providing the right answer to the individual case at hand. Notice that, in such cases, legality requires every judicial decision to be only indirectly justifiable by pre-existing law. Indeed, as we know, legal principles apply to individual cases not directly, as rules do (when they are clear and determinate), but through a reflective (and rhetorical) reasoning that typically involves *ordering*—putting competing principles into a hierarchical order, be it either by balancing, or by resorting to the (assumed) permanent "structure" of the set of principles—and *concretization*.

In the *second step* of his inquiry, Caracciolo singles out five varieties of judicial discretion. These correspond to what I have previously identified as law-breaking discretion, picking-out discretion, delegation discretion, fixing-up discretion, and controversial issue discretion (see Sect. 2 above).

In the *third*, and last *step*, of his inquiry, Caracciolo considers which sort of relationship obtains between each of the five varieties of judicial discretion, on the one side, and the requirements of democratic rule of law, on the other side. He comes to the following conclusions:

1. *Law-breaking discretion*, being a pathological phenomenon, does not pose any serious threat to rule of law values—in particular, to legal certainty and the legality of jurisdiction—provided it is controlled, and reduced to a physiological minimum, by social "convention".
2. *Picking-out discretion* is compatible with rule of law values, insofar as the set of alternative courses of actions among which judges can choose is really closed and pre-established, in such a way that individuals can make reasonably sound predictions about the contents of judicial decisions, and any unfair surprise is being ruled out—but for the pathological interferences of law-breaking discretion.
3. *Delegation discretion* is, contrariwise, incompatible with rule of law values. This is so because, as we have seen, it replaces the government of laws (and substantive legality of jurisdiction), with the government by men (the judiciary). However, being the contingent output of apposite delegation laws, it can be ruled out altogether from the positive law of constitutional states—or, in any case, kept within the limits desired by democratic parliaments.
4. *Fixing-up discretion* is, likewise, at odds with rule of law values of legal certainty and the legality of jurisdiction. Indeed, when it shows up, judges do not "find", but "make", the law; they do not apply some pre-established right answer, but, rather, they create the right answer for the cases at hand. Unlike delegation discretion, however, fixing-up discretion cannot be ruled out, unless judges are

[43]Provided, as it is usually the case in modern legal systems, judges have the obligation to decide every case brought to their attention.

forbidden to decide lawsuits any time pre-existing legal rules prove to be gappy or indeterminate. As a consequence, insofar as judges have the duty to decide cases, fixing-up discretion is a necessary feature of positive law. This makes ("absolute") legal certainty and ("absolute") legality of jurisdiction impossible: be it only in part, and at the margins, as it is the case if we think Hart to be right about the proper limits of "judicial discretion"; or as a whole, as it is the case if we think "radical rule scepticism" to be right.[44]

5. *Controversial issue discretion* is, likewise, at odds with the rule of law values of legal certainty and legality of jurisdiction. It presupposes the existence of an open set of competing reasonable solutions for a case at hand, and it cannot be predicted neither which set of reasonable solutions the judges will consider, nor which solution, out of them, they will choose. This, again, turns ("absolute") legal certainty and ("absolute") legality of jurisdiction into as many un-viable institutional goals.[45]

This conclusion by Caracciolo is, however, disputed. The sponsors of controversial issue discretion—Ronald Dworkin and contemporary representatives of principles constitutionalism—deny that to be the case. They claim that legal principles do provide right answers to the individual cases at hand, which pre-exist to judicial decisions, since *there is law*, even *where there is controversy*. They claim that the existence of legal principles rules out any need for fixing-up, strong, judicial discretion. They claim, accordingly, that the application of legal principles to individual cases only requires the exercise of a "weak" form of discretion, that is not a law-creating activity, as the radical realists and Hart (as to marginal cases) maintain, but is, in a sense, still a law-applying activity.[46] These are, in a nutshell, the claims that identify the Weakening Pattern for coping with the realism-constitutional democracy puzzle. Such Pattern—as you may recall and you can see now—adopts a unilateral accommodation strategy, where the theory of judicial discretion is modified in order to present it as a phenomenon wholly compatible with, and not obnoxious to, rule of law values.

The unavoidable question, the question that naturally arises here, is whether the idyllic picture the Weakening Pattern provides is indeed true, or is, rather, the outcome of self-deluding wishful thinking.

Caracciolo stands for the second possibility. He suggests the Weakening Pattern's theory of judicial discretion to be a piece of wishful thinking. He comes, therefore, to seeing the Surrender Pattern—with a dose of Confinement Pattern, as we shall see—,

---

[44]Caracciolo (2001), p. 256.

[45]Caracciolo (2001), pp. 258–259. By the way, the same sceptical claim is made by Hart in the "Postscript" to *The Concept of Law* (Hart 1994, pp. 272–275).

[46]I say "in a sense", since both Dworkin and contemporary principles constitutionalists do not claim the application of principles, and the identification of the right answer they set forth, to be a matter of pure "discovery", as a naïf formalist would have claimed. This, of course, makes the case for the Weakening Pattern even weaker. But let's see Caracciolo's—and Ferrajoli's—critique.

as the only viable way for coping with the realism-constitutional democracy puzzle. Here you are, in a very rough form, the gist of his argument.

1. Supporters of the Weakening Pattern maintain, as we have seen, that legal principles provide, beforehand, right answers to individual cases, making rule of law values viable.
2. Principles, however, work as *prima facie* norms, that is to say, as norms that only provide *prima facie* right answers.
3. There are two different ways of understanding the *prima facie* property of legal principles.

On a first understanding, principles are *prima facie* norms because, by themselves, they only provide *incomplete* right answers, needing to be complemented by other pieces of information. In other words, principles are *prima facie* norms in the sense that, in order to be applied to individual cases, they must be *concretized*: i.e., it is necessary to identify the rule that corresponds to them and applies to the individual case at hand.

On a second understanding, principles are *prima facie* norms because the right answers they provide are *not conclusive*. Principles tend to conflict with one another; in order to be applied to a case at hand (through concretization, as we have just seen), they need to be weighted or balanced: the weightier principle prevails, and provides the all things considered right answer to the case at hand.[47]

4. Now—so Caracciolo's argument proceeds—both ways of understanding the *prima facie* character of legal principles lead to unwelcome consequences from the standpoint of the rule of law.

If we regard legal principles as *prima facie* norms in the first sense (namely, as norms that need concretization), their application requires turning them into rules. But rules are fatally accompanied by strong discretion, which, when needed, makes legal certainty and the legality of jurisdiction unattainable.

Contrariwise, if we regard legal principles as *prima facie* norms in the second sense (namely, as norms that need to be weighed or balanced), they surely do provide right answers beforehand for the individual cases at hand; such answers, however, are troublesome. If, on the one hand, we regard the right answers provided by principles as holding for classes of like cases, we end up by treating them as if they were rules, and so we open the gate to strong judicial discretion, which undermines both legal certainty and the legality of jurisdiction. If, on the other hand, we regard the right answers provided by principles as being particularistic in character, that is to say, as holding *only* for the individual case at hand, such answers become, by definition, unpredictable, and so the exercise of weak discretion, which

[47]Caracciolo (2001), pp. 258–259.

is necessary to balancing principles, proves incompatible with the rule of law value of legal certainty.[48]

5. To sum up. Caracciolo suggests that judicial discretion (in the realist, strong variety) is a necessary furniture of the legal world: both if we consider the law as made of rules (because rules are always indeterminate, at least "at the margins"), and if we consider it as made of rules and principles (because principles are typically indeterminate). Either way, judicial discretion interferes with rule of the law values of legality of jurisdiction (when it shows up in the form of fixing-up discretion) and legal certainty (when it shows up in the forms either of fixing-up discretion, or of controversial issue discretion). This brings to the fore that those values are in fact viable *only in part*.[49] Such a rule of law failure, according to Caracciolo, cannot be avoided. It only can, and should, be compensated—and counter-balanced—by upholding the working of constitutional tribunals as the ideal places where people can exercise their constitutional right of defence in view of getting a legally right answer to the controversies where their rights are at stake.[50] These conclusions make of Caracciolo the defender, as I said, of a Surrender Pattern (the goals of the "absolute" certainty and "absolute" legality of jurisdiction must be given up as unrealistic), with a dose of Confinement Pattern (the right of individuals to argue in courts for their rights must be effectively guaranteed).

It is worthwhile taking stock, before proceeding. The Neutralization Pattern for coping with the realism-constitutional democracy puzzle fails—at least if we consider Barberis's experiment in the light of Ferrajoli's critique. The Weakening Pattern—sponsored by Dworkin and representatives of principles constitutionalism—fails too, as it appears from Caracciolo's critique.[51] Only the Surrender Pattern—with some dose of Confinement Pattern—appears to provide, so far, a reasonable, successful way-out.

---

[48]Caracciolo (2001), pp. 258–259.

[49]Caracciolo (2001), pp. 257–259. Taking side with principles constitutionalism and the Weakening Pattern, Juan Ruiz Manero contests the particularistic character of right answers provided through the balancing of principles, since they would consist in rules of priority applicable to classes of cases, and so making reasonable predictions possible, in tune with the rule of law value of legal certainty (Ruiz Manero 2012, pp. 49–51). However, from the standpoint of Caracciolo, such a claim sounds as an avowal of failure. Being rules, they are open to strong discretion and incompatible with legal certainty and the legality of jurisdiction. Ruiz Manero would insist that they are "relatively stable rule". But, again, that would be an avowal of the ("relative") uncertainty and judicial lawmaking tied to the balancing of legal principles.

[50]The "ideal [of certainty] of the Rule of Law cannot be satisfied in a generalized form, but at least it strengthens the need of preserving another dimension" of such a normative model: the guarantee of the right to defence in front of a constitutional court, since "only a judicial controversy affords ideally to those affected by similar conflicts the opportunity to intervene with their arguments in the search of the legally right answer" (Caracciolo 2001, p. 260).

[51]The Weakening Pattern would fails also if we think that the indeterminacy of rules could be cured by resorting to principles, provided that principles are, in turn, affected by indeterminacy.

This conclusion gets further support from the view adopted by Ferrajoli. One point must be emphasized, however. Ferrajoli is no keen supporter of the Surrender Pattern. From his vantage point, surrendering looks like the output of a lazy reason, too hasty in giving up to the (supposed) reality of judicial discretion and judicial lawmaking. From his vantage point, judicial discretion and judicial lawmaking are not untameable phenomena, as many theorists are used to think; rather, they can be reduced to dimensions compatible with a realistically loosened conception of the rule of law values of a constitutional democracy. This is the kernel of the articulated Confinement Pattern Ferrajoli defends, as we are going to see now.

6 The Confinement Pattern

The Confinement Pattern is the result of adopting the second variety of the unilateral accommodation strategy from constitutional theory to the realistic theory of adjudication. This characterizes, as you may recall, by strengthening the theory of constitutional rule of law in order to cope with the reality of adjudication, as depicted by realism. The leading idea is simple: judicial discretion and judicial lawmaking, in the dimensions they are afoot in nowadays constitutional states, represent a pathological phenomenon which, like any ordinary disease, can and must be cured. The solution to the realism-constitutional democracy puzzle is not, accordingly, just surrendering to judicial discretion and lawmaking as in front of fatal, unavoidable, features of positive law. The solution requires, instead, fighting back: up to the confinement of judicial discretion and judicial lawmaking within minimal, proper, limits.

As I said, one (perhaps, the strongest) advocate of the Confinement Pattern is Luigi Ferrajoli.[52] In what follows, I will provide, first, a very swift glance at Ferrajoli's theory. Then, I will consider whether the theory can stand to criticism and succeed.

The tenets of Ferrajoli's theory may be recounted as follows.

1. Judicial discretion and judicial lawmaking are not necessarily at odds with the rule of law values to which constitutional democracy is committed. This is so, since they are contingent phenomena, the scope of which is a dependent variable of theories about law, legal reasoning, and the judicial function.
2. Principles constitutionalism, the most powerful variety of constitutional theory presently afoot, maintains that:

   Constitutional rights norms (the norms that ascribe fundamental rights) are (to be regarded) not (as) rules, but (as) principles;

   Constitutional principles do usually conflict—for instance, the principle of free speech frequently conflicts with and the principles protecting individual honour and the intimacy of private life;

[52]See, e.g., Ferrajoli (1989, 2012, 2013, 2016a, b, 2017).

When constitutional principles conflict, for instance, in a lawsuit at the constitutional court, the only way to solve the conflict is by means of balancing: i.e., by weighing the conflicting principles;

Judges must be regarded as entrusted with the power both of balancing and of developing the fundamental rights of people, also by identifying implicit, unwritten, constitutional principles.

3. Paradoxically, principles constitutionalism, insofar as it presents constitutional rights norms as principles, and considers balancing to be a necessary feature of constitutional democracy, promotes the destruction of constitutional democracy. This is so, because "balancing contradicts the logic of the rule of law state": it transforms the judicial function "in a source of law", and, in so doing, it destroys "the hierarchy of legal sources", undermines "the separation of powers" between legislation and adjudication, undermines "the principle of the subjection of judges to the law", and brings about "a consequent distortion of the principle of legality as the sole rule of recognition of valid law in our civil law orders".[53]
4. To rescue constitutional rule of law from destruction, it is necessary throwing away balancing, together with the balancing theory of constitutional law, and replacing it with a guarentist theory upholding the following, basic ideas, instead.

Constitutional rights norms can, and must, be considered as *rules*, not as *principles*, insofar as their application to individual cases is concerned.[54]

Being rules, they can enter into two different types of conflicts: "abstract conflicts" ("conflicts in the abstract") and "concrete conflicts" ("conflicts in the concrete").

Abstract conflicts arise at the level of the abstract constitution, i.e., of the constitution as the paramount source of law, considered without paying attention to its application for deciding individual lawsuits. Abstract conflicts can be settled by means of "fixed hierarchies" and the accurate specification of the "limits" of each constitutional rule. Fixed hierarchies are constant relationships of superiority between different types of constitutional rights norms (e.g., between norms ascribing fundamental liberties and social rights, and norms about the private capacities of individuals). Specification of limits is the interpretive process by means of which the antecedent of each constitutional right rule of a certain type is exactly identified in a way that fits perfectly with the exactly identified antecedent of other constitutional rules of that type. The identification of fixed hierarchies among constitutional rules and the specification of the antecedents of constitutional rules are a proper task for constitutional scholarship: it is, perhaps, the most important contribution it can make to the working of constitutional democracies.

---

[53]Ferrajoli (2012), pp. 209–210.

[54]Indeed, Ferrajoli claims such norms to be, at the same time, though from different perspectives, both rules and principles. Rules when they must be applied by judges to individual cases; principles insofar as they serve to build arguments justifying legal decisions (Ferrajoli 2012, 2013).

Concrete conflicts arise at the level of individual lawsuits. They arise when, by hypothesis, the facts of a case at hand can be subsumed under two different, and conflicting, constitutional rights rules. Being subsumption problems, the only way to settle them is by the "appropriate" identification of the facts of the cases, with their peculiarities. Here, according to Ferrajoli, the tool to resolve the competition among constitutional rights rules consists in an "equitable balancing" of the circumstances. This consists, more precisely, in "the understanding and evaluation of the concrete and unrepeatable circumstances and connotations that make of each fact something different from all others, though they belong to the same legally relevant class of cases", and makes possible "the identification of the most adequate norms" to be applied.[55] The judge, accordingly, does not balance, say, the norms about freedom of the press and intimacy of private life. Neither she derives the applicable rules from balancing the different competing principles underneath. Rather, she "balances" whether the facts of the case are, or amount to, a legitimate exercise of freedom of the press, or, contrariwise, amount to a violation of somebody else's privacy. In other terms, to the balancing *à la* Alexy and C. it must be opposed the old equitable balancing of the facts of the case, which is nothing but exercising qualificatory or subsumption discretion, i.e., the power to establish the facts of the individual case and their legally correct (legally proper) normative qualification.

The change of paradigm, consisting in replacing the principles theory of constitutional rule of law with the guarentist theory, requires a change in the legal professionals' beliefs and attitudes about the constitution and constitutional rights norms in a constitutional rule of law state. Such change of paradigm requires, among other things, that realistic theories of jurisdiction, that provide a creationist account of the judicial application of law, be replaced by a "cognitive" theory, urging judges to consider themselves, at least by way of a regulative ideal, as committed to law-applying, and not to law-making, tasks.[56]

The Confinement Pattern represents, to be sure, a powerful attempt to fight judicial discretion and judicial lawmaking back.

From a realistic vantage point, however, Ferrajoli's proposal appears troublesome.

1. The process of identifying fixed hierarchies among constitutional norms is liable both to be rife with uncertainties, and to result in a variety of contrasting proposals, mirroring the variety of axiological allegiances of the several jurists

---

[55]Ferrajoli (2012), pp. 219–220.

[56]To "affirm that the judges create law [as realists and principles-freaks alike are fond of affirming, ndr] is tantamount to confuse interpretation and innovation, application and production, jurisdiction and legis-lation, ascertainment of the meaning of the laws and legislative will, living law and binding law. Because of that, the peculiar, but not casual, convergence of principles-freak constitutionalism, legal realism, and neo-pandecticism", is undermining "the very source of the legitimacy and independence of jurisdiction", "the normativity of constitutions", "the hierarchy of legal sources" (Ferrajoli 2012, pp. 233, 234; see also pp. 229–230; Ferrajoli 2016b, pp. 53–61).

involved. Accordingly, it is likely to result in a plurality of competing hierarchical models among which judges will have to choose.
2. The process of identifying the abstract limits of each fundamental right rule is, likewise, likely to result in a plurality of competing solutions, each one fatally affected by indeterminacy; so that, again, there will be room for judicial discretion and judicial law-making.
3. The judge-binding effect of resorting to the "equitable balancing" of facts, instead of resorting to the balancing of constitutional principles, is dubious. Indeed, it is giving judges the means to get rid of rules—to play with rules, we may say—, by appealing to the unrepeatable, absolutely peculiar, properties of the individual facts at hand. Such a particularistic move, however, as we may gather from Caracciolo (and others[57]), is at odds with the rule of law values of legal certainty and legality of jurisdiction.

To the latter remark, Ferrajoli would reply that, in a properly designed constitutional order, the room for judicial "equitable balancing" of facts would be very limited: indeed, limited to the point of the physiological minimum.

Be that as it may, the realist would have a further reply, though. Ferrajoli entrusts to constitutional scholarship a Herculean task. Furthermore, such a task, to be successfully carried out, requires the legal culture to be—not only technically sophisticated, but also—monolithic: namely, to be composed only of legal scholars that are cooperative, same-thinking, staunch guarentists *à la* Ferrajoli. Insofar as the legal culture is instead, like our present legal cultures, pluralist, insofar as different constitutional theories vie for hegemony, insofar as a conspicuous part of the legal profession adheres to the credo of principles constitutionalism, the Confinement Pattern Ferrajoli advocates is doomed to failure.

Of course, nothing prevents a revolutionary minority of jurists and judges from endorsing Ferrajoli's proposal and trying to carry it out within their own legal culture, realizing its requirements in individual cases, and advancing on adverse ground, step after step, towards the regulative ideal of complete cultural control.

So, to sum up: Ferrajoli's Confinement proposal contains at least one technically dubious ingredient (the equitable balancing of facts), and, as a whole, looks like a highly utopian "regulative ideal".

7 A Few Tentative Conclusions

Tentative analyses bring about tentative conclusions. As I have anticipated at the outset, the tentative conclusions that the preceding analysis of the four Patterns for coping with the realism-constitutional democracy puzzle suggests run apparently as follows.

[57] See, e.g., Comanducci (2005), pp. 105–117; Ruiz Manero (2014b).

One, the Neutralization Pattern—in the version considered by Barberis—is too good to be true.

Two, the Weakening Pattern—if grounded by appealing to the pretended virtues of legal (and constitutional) principles—is self-deluding wishful thinking.

Three, the Confinement Pattern—in the articulated version defended by Ferrajoli—requires, technical flaws apart, a veritable revolution in legal culture that looks like a highly utopian "regulative ideal".

Four, the Surrender Pattern combined with some dose of Confinement measures—as defended by Caracciolo—fares, apparently, as the only way-out that is so far immune from objections.

Five, by way of generalization, it seems reasonable to suppose that constitutional theory will never be able to meet the realistic challenge, except by a wise mixture of surrender (loosening) and confinement (strengthening).

Sometimes, a different conclusion is being drawn from the realistic challenge to constitutional democracy. Realism brings to the fore the failure of constitutional democracy as a viable form of government. Realism suggests, therefore, that such a form of government should be abandoned.[58] That conclusion, however, must be resisted. Realism—as a genuinely theoretical outlook—does not suggest throwing constitutional democracy away. Realism only urges constitutional theorists, and people at large, to entertain a realistic, not self-deluding, conception of constitutional democracy. It suggests that the institutional design of constitutional democracy be accommodated to the reality of adjudication, as depicted by realism. This may require, to begin with, moving to a more conscious balancing conception of the separation of powers (or to a mixed conception, combining relative specialization with checks and balances, as it frequently happens in existing constitutional states); it may also require, furthermore, the strengthening of social control—the control by a legally sophisticated "public opinion"—upon the judiciary. For instance, along lines like those pointed out by Caracciolo and Ferrajoli. And always with a clear perception of the fatally utopian, "regulative", flavour of the whole enterprise.

[58]This conclusion is drawn, e.g., in Martí (2002), p. 279 as I mentioned before. Martí proposes a way-out to the "radical" realism's challenge to liberal democracy so conceived. He points out to the (supposed) "axioms" ("empirically not demonstrable claims") of radical realism, and claims they should be turned down, because they are incompatible both with our "intuitions" about the law, and, above all, with the established "theories" of liberalism and democracy (pp. 279–281). A moderate realist, however, could reply to Martí's (ruinous) way-out by arguing that it is theoretically unsound and self-serving. To begin with, the pretended "axioms" of radical realism Martí considers are, his claim notwithstanding, *empirically demonstrable claims* (i.e., empirically grounded, truth-apt, claims): indeed, normative legal language *is* different from ordinary descriptive language, so far as the practice of its interpretation is concerned; this specificity *makes* interpretation of legal language *a matter of volition* (and not purely cognition, leaving aside the necessary cooperative or non cooperative attitude going along with ordinary conversations); legal norms *are not* (mysterious) objective entities out there, liable to be objectively known, but linguistic entities depending on acts of interpretation and normative integration. Furthermore, and consequently, if the supposed "axioms" of radical realism are in fact empirically demonstrable claims, their incompatibility with widespread "intuitions" and established theories of liberalism and democracy suggests that those intuitions and theories rest on false empirical presuppositions.

References

Barak A (1989) Judicial discretion. Yale University Press, New Haven
Barberis M (2004) Separazione dei poteri e teoría giusrealista dell'interpretazione. Analisi e Diritto:1–20
Barberis M (2016a) Filosofia del diritto. Una introduzione teorica. Giappichelli, Torino
Barberis M (2016b) Possono governare, le leggi? Il dilemma del rule of law. In: Pino G, Villa V (eds) Rule of law. Il Mulino, Bologna
Bobbio N (1985) Liberalismo e democrazia. Angeli, Milano
Bulygin E (1966) Judicial decisions and the creation of law. In: Bulygin E (ed) Essays in legal philosophy. Oxford University Press, Oxford, pp 75–87, 2015
Caracciolo R (2001) Discreción, respuesta correcta y función judicial. In: Caracciolo R (ed) El derecho desde la filosofía. Ensayos. Centro de Estudios Políticos y Constitucionales, Madrid, pp 251–260, 2009
Carrió R (1965) Notas sobre derecho y lenguaje. Abeledo Perrot, Buenos Aires
Celano B (2013) I diritti nello stato costituzionale. Il Mulino, Bologna
Celano B (2016a) Pre-conventions. A fragment of the background. Revus 30:9–32
Celano B (2016b) Rule of Law e particolarismo etico. In: Pino G, Villa V (eds) Rule of law. Il Mulino, Bologna
Chiassoni P (2014) Wiener realism. In: D'Almeida D, Gardner J, Green L (eds) Kelsen revisited: new essays on the pure theory of law. Hart, Oxford
Chiassoni P (2015) Some realism about legislation. Theory Practice Legis 3:173–186
Chiassoni P (2016a) Da Bentham a Kelsen. Sei capitoli per una storia della filosofia analitica del diritto. Giappichelli, Torino
Chiassoni P (2016b) Legal interpretation without truth. Revus 29:93–118
Chiassoni P (2019) Interpretation without truth. A realistic enquiry. Springer, Cham
Comanducci P (2005) Principios jurídicos e indeterminación del derecho. In: Comanducci P (ed) Hacia una teoría analítica del derecho. Ensayos escogidos. Centro de Estudios Políticos y Constitucionales, Madrid
Dworkin RM (1963) Judicial discretion. J Philos 60:624–638
Dworkin RM (1967) The model of rules. Univ Chicago Law Rev 35:14–46
Easterbrook FH (2004) Judicial discretion in statutory interpretation. Oklahoma Law Rev 57 (1):1–20
Endicott T (2014) Proportionality and incommensurability. In: Huscroft G, Miller BW, Webber G (eds) Proportionality and the rule of law. Rights, justification, reasoning. Cambridge University Press, Cambridge, pp 311–342
Ferrajoli L (1989) Diritto e ragione. Teoria del garantismo penale. Laterza, Roma-Bari
Ferrajoli L (2012) Constitucionalismo garantista y constitucionalismo principialista. In: Ferrajoli L, Ruiz Manero J (eds) Un debate sobre principios constitucionales. Palestra, Lima, 2014
Ferrajoli L (2013) La democrazia attraverso i diritti. Il costituzionalismo garantista come modello teorico e come progetto politico. Laterza, Roma-Bari
Ferrajoli L (2016a) La logica del diritto. Dieci aporie nell'opera di Hans Kelsen. Laterza, Roma-Bari
Ferrajoli L (2016b) La democrazia costituzionale. Il Mulino, Bologna
Ferrajoli L (2017) Costituzionalismo oltre lo stato. Mucchi, Modena
Guastini R (2011) Interpretare e argomentare. Giuffrè, Milano
Guastini R (2016) An exercise in legal realism. Paper presented at the at the International Conference "Interpreting Law – The Role of Judges in Contemporary Democracies", Faculty of Law, University of Belgrade, Belgrade, October 14, 2016
Hart HLA (1956) Discretion. Harv Law Rev 127:652. 2013
Hart HLA (1994) In: Raz J, Bulloch P 1961. The concept of law, Second Edition with a "Postscript", Oxford
Iglesias Vila M (2000) Judicial discretion and judicial positivism. www.ibrarian.net, pp 134–173

Kahneman D (2011) Thinking, fast and slow. Farrar, Strauss and Giroux, New York
Kelsen H (1960) Reine Rechtslehre, Zweite, vollständig neu bearbeitete und erweiterte Auflage. Verlag Österreich, Wien, 2000
Leiter B (2007) Naturalizing jurisprudence. Essays on American legal realism and naturalism in legal philosophy. Oxford University Press, Oxford
Lifante Vidal I (1989) Dos conceptos de discrecionalidad jurídica. Cuadernos de "Doxa" 25, Alicante: 2–62
Martí JL (2002) El realismo jurídico: ¿Una amenaza para el liberalismo y la democracia? Isonomía 17:259–282
Pino G, Villa V (eds) (2016) Rule of law. Il Mulino, Bologna
Raz J (1977) The rule of law and its virtues. In: Raz J (ed) The authority of law. Essays on law and morality. Clarendon Press, Oxford, 1979
Ruiz Manero J (2014a) In: Ferrajoli L, Ruiz Manero J (eds) Un debate sobre principios constitucionales. Palestra, Lima, 2014, pp 235–264
Ruiz Manero J (2014b) In: Ferrajoli L, Ruiz Manero J (eds) Un debate sobre principios constitucionales. Palestra, Lima, 2014, pp. 291–322
Ruiz Manero J (2014c) El legado del positivismo jurídico. Ocho ensayos sobre cinco autores positivistas: Hans Kelsen, Norberto Bobbio, Eugenio Bulygin, Luigi Ferrajoli, Riccardo Guastini. Palestra, Lima
Ruiz Manero J (2012) In: Ferrajoli L, Ruiz Manero J (eds) Dos modelos de constitucionalismo. Una conversación, Trotta, Madrid
Tarello G (1962) Il realismo giuridico americano. Giuffrè, Milano
Twining W (1973) Karl Llewellyn and the realist movement, 2nd edn. Cambridge University Press, Cambridge, 2012
von Wright GH (1984) Of human freedom, the Tanner lecture on human value. The University of Helsinki, Helsinki, May 16 and 17
Wroblewski J (1992) The judicial application of law. Kluwer, Dordrecht

Pierluigi Chiassoni is Professor of Jurisprudence at the University of Genova School of Law and a permanent fellow of Tarello Institute for Legal Philosophy. His jurisprudential interests span from economic analysis of law to legal interpretation and human rights. His main publications include Positivismo giuridico. Una investigazione analitica (Mucchi Editore, 2013), Tecnica dell'interpretazione giuridica (il Mulino, 2007), El discreto placer del positivismo jurídico (Externado de Colombia, 2016), La tradición analítica en la filosofia del derecho. De Bentham a Kelsen (Palestra, 2017), Ensayos de metajurisprudencia analítica (Olejnik, 2017), Interpretation without Truth (Springer, 2019).

On the (Un)Changing Judge Icons and Their Creators: On Deborah, Coke and Montesquieu, Posner and Barak, and Some Others

Jasminka Hasanbegović

Abstract This paper looks at the most important ideas and images of the judge throughout history. It is an attempt to provide an answer to the question whether the role of a judge in the society has remained the same since the dawn of time, or at least the birth of law and state, i.e. from the creation of courts and judges. Or does the role of judge perhaps differ from premodern to modern age? And if it does differ, are those differences negligible or important? In an attempt to provide a concise yet synthetic answer to these questions, this paper is divided into two parts. The first reviews the ancient origin of the modern idea of the judge as the mouth of the law, i.e. it scrutinises whether this idea originates in antiquity. In so doing, it elucidates the birth of the modern Coke-Montesquieu idea. Better still, depending on one's (modern) worldview (in particular one's understanding of modern law), the birth of two completely different modern ideas: Cokean and Montesquieuan. The question of whether it is one dialectically complex or two completely different ideas (perhaps even two completely different groups of ideas regarding the modern judge) is relevant for contemporary reflections on activism or restraint of judges, as well as for attempts to provide answers to which of the two is better. The second part of this paper thus considers the responses to these questions, specifically a critique of Posner's critique of Barak. The result demonstrates that the very attempt to make a clear distinction between activism and restraint of judges is not only theoretically impossible, but also practically unnecessary. For, as the second part of this paper will show, the essence and quality of a judge's attitude towards the constitution, laws, constitutionality and legality—whether that attitude is assessed as activist or restrained—is not reflected in a judge's stand regarding the letter, that is, literal text of the constitution and laws, nor on the nearly completely evasive and constantly changing spirit of the constitution, laws, constitutionality and legality; rather, they reside in the judge's attitude towards constitutionalism.

J. Hasanbegović
University of Belgrade Faculty of Law, Belgrade, Serbia

P. Chiassoni, B. Spaić (eds.), *Judges and Adjudication in Constitutional Democracies: A View from Legal Realism*, Law and Philosophy Library 135,
https://doi.org/10.1007/978-3-030-58186-2_4

The core of the identity of a judge, i.e. the judge's role in society, has remained more or less the same since biblical times (the second millennium BCE) or even longer. Its continuity can be traced back to the Book of Judges, i.e. the Seventh Book in the Old Testament, or according to the ideas of the Last Judgment in the eschatological worldviews of the Abrahamic religions (Judaism, Christianity and Islam) and Zoroastrianism, to the present day. This applies to both state court and tribunal/arbitration judges, and referees and judges in many other areas of social activity (such as those dealing with ethical issues relevant to different professions).

Let us review the basis for the opinion of constancy of the core identity of judges. The idea of the role of a judge was handed down a long time ago: if we read the Old Testament, especially the Book of Judges to the end (i.e. chapter 21, verse 25), we gain the insight and understand why judges are needed even when there are laws given by God. They are needed since people and nations do what is right in their own eyes, and not what is right according to laws. Judges, hence, have always been authorities to hear and decide contentious matters brought before them. Therefore, they need to be well versed in laws, as well as wise, just and fair, but also vested with the power to implement their decisions since the lack of implementation disrupts their authority and the authority of the laws.

This is probably why the role of judges in biblical times was given to tribal warlords who were neither elected nor had inherited their title, and who are sometimes imprecisely called kings.[1] It seems that in a tribal community—as described by the Old Testament—these kings/warlords/judges naturally imposed themselves through their authority. Even today judges are invited to measure our actions, words and thoughts during our earthly lives (prior to the Last Judgment) and declare them right or wrong, as well as establish consequences for these, because people and nations even today do what is right in their own eyes, and not what is right according to the laws.

It is also clear that the *authority* of divine laws, of earthly laws, and of judges themselves never suffices: justice requires *force*. Always. That insight as actual knowledge of lives of tribes and nations and their judges/warlords/kings described in *detailed* biblical *stories* from the second millennium BCE or much later eras (because the dating of almost all parts of the Old Testament is still in disarray),[2] would only come to be formulated in *abstract form* centuries later. Discussed by sophists—primarily, as far as we know, Hippias, Callicles and Trasymachus (fifth century BCE)[3]—it will become most *laconically and wisely* summarized by Blaise Pascal (1623–1662) again many centuries later: "Justice without force is powerless; force without justice is tyrannical" (Pascal 1969, p. 1160).

It should be noted that even in biblical times we encounter a female judge in the Book of Judges—Deborah (meaning *bee* in Hebrew). Indeed, not only a Judge, but

[1]On these *shoftim* (Hebrew—judges, *shofet* being the singular), see Coogan (2009), especially p. 426.

[2]On these extremely complex questions, comprehensively Barton (2014), *passim*.

[3]On these, thoroughly Đurić (2009).

the *Song of Deborah and Barak* (in the *Book of Judges*, chapters 4 and 5; Barak was a Judge after her, and his name means the lightening, enlightening) names her "mother of Israel" (*Book of Judges*, chapter 5, section 7). So, it was possible for a woman to be a judge in long gone biblical times, and what is perhaps more, a founding mother. Several millennia later, the decision of the Belgian Court of Cassation from November 11, 1889 states: "If the legislator did not exclude women from the Bar by some decree or any other official act, it was because this had been taken to be too obvious to be said *expressis verbis* as well, that the legal profession has been reserved for men only".[4] And this remained in force in Belgium until 1948. That *modern* history is silent about women—all women—as founding mothers when discussing founders of modern nation states does not even merit special mention, because it is a matter of undeniable historical fact. Only recently has history focused on founding mothers but solely as wives, daughters or helpers of founding fathers, providing them with "typically" female support, assistance and care (Roberts 2004).

A specific *legal* identity of the judge as holder of *judicial* power (as a form of state power) belongs to the *modern* era. And it is twinned with the idea, and in particular the practice, of separation of powers into legislative, executive and judicial. However, it is often wrongly thought that the notion of a judge as "only a mouth of law" has emerged in modern times. The metonymic phrase is spread as Montesquieu's (1995, p. 337), but the idea was tacitly accepted by many others, even if they did not use the same figure of speech, such as Bacon before Montesquieu, and Kant, Beccaria, or Bentham afterwards. Indeed there were those who saw the judge as a very sophisticated subsumptional, logical "automaton", special human objective "machine" for adjudication or in its contemporary version, a computer for adjudication. Or even (if one prefers Dworkinian language), the judge is considered the Hercules of adjudication, able to find (Dworkin's) single right solution for each case of decision-making, that is to say, that all these images of a judge are essentially similar.

It is Charles-Louis de Secondat, baron de La Brède et de Montesquieu (1689–1755) who is usually considered the creator and most prominent representative of this type of idea of the judge. However, this is incorrect. The idea of the judge as a speaking law, *lex loquens*, is not merely a Latinised original idea proposed by Montesquieu, but it is instead a considerably older, premodern idea, firmly rooted in antiquity.

The origin and meaning of the expression *iudex est lex loquens* is not unknown, but cannot be absolutely precisely determined.[5] We shall review this idea, its possible origin, its various linguistic expressions and their meanings in the first part of this paper by looking at, inter alia, Latin phrases or Latinised equivalents of phrases from different languages.

---

[4]Cited according to Perelman (1976a), pp. 129–131.

[5]On this, see Hanisch (2010), with extensive references to historical primary sources as well as their interpretation in other papers through history to the present (i.e. secondary sources and literature).

At first glance it might seem paradoxical to claim that the pre-origin of that expression could be found in Aristotle's (384–322) statement from *Nicomachean Ethics* that a judge is *dikaion empsychon*, i.e. *animated or breathing or living justness* (Aristotle 1934, bk. V, ch. IV, par. 7, or 1132a20-22). Aristotle's phrase—*dikaion empsychon*—is translated in different ways, as *the just in living form*, or *justice personified*, etc.[6] But, we deem the phrase *animated* or *living justness* better and more precise, and *animate justice* the best, among else, because it was already in antiquity translated into Latin as *iustitia animata*, i.e. animated justness (or animate justice).

This idea of Aristotle's (or even someone before him) will be expressed in Cicero's *On the Laws* in following words: the judge is a speaking law, while the law is a silent judge—*magistratum esse legem loquentem, legem autem mutum magistratum* (Cicero 1928, 3, 1, 2). It could be said that Cicero's ideas of judges and laws seem an echo of the aforementioned biblical idea of judges as necessary despite the existence of laws, but that remains to be proven. Yet, it could also be said that Aristotle's and Cicero's ideas of the judge are not exactly identical: Aristotle imagines a judge as a living, animate, breathing justice, and Cicero defines a judge as the law speaking, and the law as a silent judge. However, one should under no circumstances lose sight of the fact that Cicero implies that the law should be based on *recta ratio*, right reason, meaning that it should be just (cf. Cicero 1949, 1, 38). In that sense, both Aristotle's and Cicero's concepts of judges essentially state the same idea, which is only expressed through different figures of speech, that is, differently presented.

This idea will undergo considerable transformation already in antiquity, more precisely during the development of Roman law and society. Thus, Justinian's (482–565) *Corpus iuris* (sixth century) held that the Emperor is the animated law of the Earth: *Imperator est lex animata in terris* (*Corpus iuris civilis*, Novellae, 105. 2. 4). Accordingly, the Emperor takes the place of the judge as the living, breathing law. This, in turn, means the following: that the Emperor, being the animated law on earth, is not only the supreme judge, i.e. court on earth, but also that everything he likes (on earth) has the force of law (*quod principi placuit, legis habet vigorem*; *Digesta*, I, 4, 1 pr.).

It should be noted here that Cicero's idea of the judge as the speaking law (*magistratus est lex loquens*), most probably inspired by Aristotle's idea of the judge as animate, living justice (*dikaion empsychon* in Greek, and *iustitia animata* in Latin), did not undergo change out of thin air, being transformed into Justinian's (i.e. of *Corpus iuris*) idea on Emperor as the animated law on earth (*imperator est lex animata in terris*), hence, being concurrently the supreme judge and unlimited legislator on earth. Namely, the idea that everything a *princeps* likes has the force of law (*quod principi placuit, legis habet vigorem*) appeared already much earlier:

[6]Harris Rackham translated *dikaion empsychon* as *the just in living form*, or *justice personified*, e.g. Aristotle (1934), bk. V, ch. IV, par. 7, or 1132a20-22: "To go to a judge is to go to justice, for the ideal judge is so to speak justice personified."

this is Ulpian's (second century CE) view (*Digesta*, I, 4, 1 pr.), although he too borrows it from *Lex de imperio Vespasiani* from 69 BCE. And not only does it appear before and after the Principate, as well as in different places in *Corpus iuris* (e.g. in *Institutiones*, I. 1.2.6 too), it also reappears later, throughout Middle Ages and the Modern era. It even served in the formation of the idea of sovereignty, and indirectly (by opposing this political view and the practice based on it) the idea of modern constitution and constitutionalism as a political, i.e. state power limited by law.

In the history of influential Western ideas, one of the most prominent authors is certainly Thomas Aquinas (1225–1274), who famously embraced many of Aristotle's ideas, including the idea of animate justice. Aquinas provided this idea with a new dimension, claiming in his *Summa theologiae* (1265–1274) that animate justice is better than inanimate justice, so the justice of judges is better than justice only proclaimed from above (meaning, not necessarily applied in life), only contained in laws, existing only in them. Aquinas himself puts it thus:

> Praeterea, sicut dicit philosophus, in V Ethic., *ad iudicem confugiunt homines sicut ad iustum animatum*. Sed iustitia animata est melior quam inanimata, quae legibus continetur. Ergo melius fuisset ut executio iustitiae committeretur arbitrio iudicum, quam quod super hoc lex aliqua ederetur. (*Summa theologiae*, *De lege*, Ia-Iiae, Q. 95a1 arg. 2)

In the English translation:

> Further, as the Philosopher says (Ethic. v, 4), 'men have recourse to a judge as to animate justice.' But animate justice is better than inanimate justice, which is contained in laws. Therefore the execution of justice that is entrusted to the decision of judges is better than justice which is [only – J.H.] from above proclaimed by laws. (*Ibidem*)

Aquinas could have found inspiration for this new dimension—the view that justice proclaimed by judges is better than the one proclaimed by laws—in the Bible, in the aforementioned explanation of the need for judges even with the existence of laws given by God. So he could have applied that biblical insight to the earthly justice. Only one part of that terrestrial justice can be contained in (what we would call today) positive laws. These are the laws of the land as the laws in force within a country, and include only its statutes. The whole possible terrestrail justice, however, has to include also precedents and other judicial decisions of courts and tribunals, etc., when assessing the legal life on earth in a country. Then it can be viewed as the earthly justice in its entirety. But Aquinas could have also been inspired by Cicero's aforementioned opinion that a judge is speaking law, while law is (only) a silent judge. We are, however, unfamiliar with any studies focusing on this topic.

Parallel to this Aristotelian idea promoted by Thomas Aquinas, there was another one disseminated during the Middle Ages (and even later)—the Vespasianian-Ulpianian-Justinianian idea contained in *Corpus iuris civilis*. This was not only due to the fact that *Corpus iuris* was the most important legal source for the Bologna (and European) legal renaissance, but also because this idea was propagated by other important medieval authorities, such as William of Ockham (1285–1347) who reiterates in his *Dialogus* (1332–1347, 1476[1]) that the *emperor* is called the animated law: *imperator lex animata vocatur* (part. 3, tract. 2, lib. 1, cap. 1).

In subsequent periods, Aquinas' view that a judge's justice is better than a justice of laws will be interpreted and understood (as we shall soon demonstrate) as a belief that the ruler is above the law, inter alia, because the ruler—as animate justice or animate law—is and should be above other laws which—maybe slightly ironically—could be called inanimate laws (*leges inanimatae*). Such a view of the desirable relationship between the ruler, judges and laws will be both widespread and widely contested (perhaps successfully only for the first time with the *Magna Carta Libertatum* of 1215), and will later excite constitutional disputes, especially in seventeenth century England. These confrontations, disputes and conflicts regarding the desirable relationship between ruler, court and laws will mark the painful birth of modern constitutionalism, first in England, and then everywhere else, bringing with it the modern concept of the judiciary as one of the (at least) three technically separated state powers. This understanding of judicial power will become one of the necessary prerequisites, i.e. axioms of the state, societal and legal modernity, but shall remain disputed to this very day regarding almost every other aspect: defining the essence of judicial power, its content, exact ways of its constituting and functioning required to ensure the existence of that essence and the independence of judicial power.

Given that *Magna Carta Libertatum* is the historically most important *precursor* of modern declarations and acts constitutionalizing state power, identifying human rights, and introducing rule of law, we should note its famous provision 29, later renumbered and divided into two provisions (39 and 40), and which is still in force as a part of United Kingdom's positive law. It states:

> 39. Nullus liber homo capiatur, vel imprisonetur, aut disseisiatur, aut utlagetur, aut exuletur, aut aliquo modo destruatur, nec super eum ibimus, nec super eum mittemus, nisi per legale judicium parium suorum vel per legem terre.
>
> 40. Nulli vendemus, nulli negabimus aut differemus, rectum aut justiciam. (According to Holt 2010, pp. 460–461)

In English:

> 39. No free man shall be seized or imprisoned, or stripped of his rights or possessions, or outlawed or exiled, or deprived of his standing in any other way, nor will we proceed with force against him, or send others to do so, except by the lawful judgement of his equals or by the law of the land.
>
> 40. To no one will we sell, to no one will we refuse or delay, right or justice. (Again according to Holt 2010, *loc. cit.*)[7]

Or in the official translation:

> Section XXIX
>
> No Freeman shall be taken or imprisoned, or be disseized of his Freehold, or Liberties, or free Customs, or be outlawed, or exiled, or any other wise destroyed; nor will We pass upon him, nor condemn him, but by lawful judgment of his Peers, or by the Law of the Land. We will sell to no man, we will not deny or defer to any man either Justice or Right.

[7]Also available online, in different version dating from different years, in Latin and/or English, and in slightly differing English translations of the same Latin original.

This provision, thus, contains, *in nuce*, freedoms and rights of man (which will subsequently only be developed, more precisely determined and expanded). They can be denied solely *on the basis of a lawful judgement of (the defendant's) peers or the law of the land*. We should also highlight that the ruler *shall not sell, refuse or delay [anyone's] right or justice*, representing an important limitation to sovereign power.

Note that it was by the law adopted as early as 1354 that the provision 29 was revised by *freeman* becoming simply *man*, i.e. man of whatever estate or condition he may be, and the phrase "*due process of law*" (*for lawful judgement of his peers or the law of the land*) added. Revised, it reads:

> No Man shall be taken or imprisoned, or be disseized of his Freehold, or Liberties, or free Customs, or be outlawed, or exiled, or any other wise destroyed; nor will We pass upon him, nor condemn him, but in a due process of law by lawful judgment of his Peers, or by the Law of the Land. (According to Turner 2003, p. 157)

We can note that England is rightly considered the cradle and role model of constitutionalism, since the idea of existence of certain freedoms and rights of man (although, to be more precise, these were initially certain rights and freedoms of only certain men), which the ruler, i.e. government could deny him only on the basis of a lawful verdict delivered by peers and according to law of the land, was created and developed in this country as early as the thirteenth and fourteenth century.

In that sense, we should mention another precursor of constitutionalism: Henry de Bracton[8] (c. 1210—c. 1268), born during the reign of John Lackland (1166/1199–1216), but certainly prior to the issuing of *Magna Carta* (1215). He was an Oxford scholar and jurist of unusual cosmopolitan eclecticism and comprehensive knowledge of continental, received (Roman) law, member of clergy and advisor to king Henry III Plantagenet (1207/1216–1272).[9] Bracton is often called the thirteenth century Blackstone[10] for writing the famous *De Legibus et Consuetudinibus Angliae*

---

[8]Or Henry of Bracton, or Henricus Bracton, or Henry Bratton, or Henry Bretton.

[9]For more details on Bracton's life and work, see Maitland (1887[1]), especially vol. 1, pp. 1–33, also available online.

[10]This is unusual only at first glance, especially in professional circles, that somebody who appeared earlier (in the thirteenth century) is named after another who appeared a half millennium later (in the eighteenth century). However, from a didactic aspect, this is not the case. When Bracton was "unveiled" before the wider professional public in the nineteenth century, owing to new discoveries in the studies of his work (made by Paul Vinogradoff, Frederic William Maitland, etc.), as well as the first translations of his papers into English (by Sir Travers Twis), he was pronounced the thirteenth century Blackstone, given the enormous importance of Blackstone and his work from the previous (i.e. eighteenth) century. Thus, the unknown Bracton was described by means of the familiar and essentially similar Blackstone. In the same manner, the professional community calls Hippias of Elis (fifth century BCE) the ancient Hugo Grotius (seventeenth century) since it is assumed that the one closer to our era, namely Grotius as the father of modern natural law can explain the one who is less known and from a much older era, Hippias of Elis, representative of the Ionian Enlightenment (seventh century to fifth century BCE) and the first person to make the distinction between natural and (the later named) positive law. See Geffcken (1923), pp. 15–31, especially p. 23. In a similar manner, Bracton, as a less known figure from an earlier period, is called

(1235-1260), translated by Samuel E. Thorne as *On the Laws and Customs of England* (de Bracton 1968–1977, 1997^2), in which he paved the way for future case law, precedent law and *stare decisis* doctrines by collecting real and imaginary cases of role model adjudication. But Bracton was also a well-known opponent of despotic monarchy: he held the opinion that a ruler should be called a king only if he has assumed his power and exercised it pursuant to law.[11]

However, constitutionalization of state power, as limiting through law, has not gone without considerable political resistance, theoretical contestation and different formulations, even in the cradle of constitutionalism and modern democracy. Quite the contrary. For example, as was recorded by Samuel Rutherford (1600–1661) in *Lex Rex, or The Law and the Prince* in 1644 (Rutherford 1644, 1, 12, 208-255; *et passim*), Henry VIII Tudor (1491/1509–1547) considered that the king is given by God and the law is given by the king. Rutherford himself considered that while the king was indeed the law, this also necessarily implied the reverse: the law is king, so the king cannot do anything but what the law prescribes (at *loc. cit.*). Similar views on the relationship between king, law, God and judges and various interpretations thereof are encountered later as well, but opinions such as the one presented by Henry VIII remain prevalent in English history for a long time.

The position that *rex est lex* (the king is the law) was also promoted by James I Stuart (1566/1603–1625), and supported by Francis Bacon (1561–1626) and other (legal) authorities of the time. Francis Bacon (who was, incidentally, one of the fiercest opponents of Edward Coke) has special importance for this paper due to his 1612 essay, "Of Judicature", which starts with the following sentence:

---

thirteenth century Blackstone since Blackstone (with his *Comments*) remains one of the most important figures in the history of not only English law, but *common law* systems and legal orders in general. Sir William Blackstone (1723–1780) was an exceptional custom law expert, a lecturer at Oxford University, and the author of "Commentaries on the Laws of England" (1765–1769). The text is considered the best-known description of the English legal doctrines and used to this very day, while remaining the foundation for the education at English and North American faculties of law. According to Blackstone, the law declared by judges, law implemented by the courts, is at the heart of English law, because courts have to honour and protect the fundamental principles of state order. Although the legislator may even deviate therefrom, the courts must remain an obstacle to the unreasonable use of parliamentary authority. Expressed by modern vocabulary, courts not only have the last say on the content of legal provisions, but also represent the last legal defence and protection of the constitutionalism principles when these are breached by the legislator who passes unreasonable decisions. This is why Blackstone defines courts as "the living oracles, who must decide in all cases of doubt, and who are bound by an oath to decide according to the law of the Land". Blackstone also believes that judges—unlike members of Parliament—are able to be precisely that: living oracles identifying the law of the land in cases of doubt. Or, in modern terms, judges—unlike the members of Parliament—are able to be the last legal bulwark in the defense of constitutionalism. Still, for the sake of truthfulness, we must acknowledge that our concept of constitutionalism naturally differs (both historically and in view of Blackstone's political conservatism) from Blackstone's reconstructed opinions. For more details on Blackstone's aforementioned views on relationship between judicial and legislator's law in England, see Blackstone (1876), book I, part I, section III, p. 47; also available online as *Works by William Blackstone* at Project Gutenberg.

[11]For more details, see Pollock and Maitland (2010), vol. I, ch. VII, pp. 185–239, especially p.193.

> Judges ought to remember that their office is 'jus dicere,' and not 'jus dare,' to interpret law, and not to make law, or give law. (Bacon 1884, at the beginning)

This clearly indicates—although it is not explicit—that due to the relationship between the law and the king, judges hold no power, even though they perform—for the sake of law and justice—a very important office. We can clearly see this in Bacon's statement that "one foul sentence doth more hurt than many foul examples; for these do but corrupt the stream, the other corrupteth the fountain" (Bacon at *loc. cit.*). Bacon's metaphor, describing the law as a river flowing in a time long before and after our earthly lives, whose source has been renewing with every court sentence, demonstrates that the relationship between *jus dicere*, adjudication (always preceded by an interpretation of law), and *jus dare*, law giving (as creation of a law, or acknowledging of a right), could hardly be straightforward. This, in turn, made the relationship between the king as a sovereign holder of state power, and law extremely complex from the perspective of constitutionalism.

The successor to King James I, Charles I Stuart (1600/1625–1649) also promoted the same notion *rex est lex*, only in a milder form: *a Deo rex, a rege lex* (the king is from God, and the law is from the king). This view was primarily disputed by Edward Coke (1552–1634):[12] "The King himself should be under no man, but under God and the Law" (Coke 1738c, *The Reports*—Prohibitions del Roy, 12 Co. Rep. 63, *in fine*). Coke is referring directly to the authority of Henry de Bracton, i.e. to the same opinion stated in Bracton's *On the Laws and Customs of England*:

> PAREM autem non habet rex in regno suo, quia sic amitteret præceptum, cum par in parem non habeat imperium. Item nec multo fortius superiorem, neque potentiorem habere debet, quia sic esset inferior sibi subiectis, et inferiores pares esse non possunt potentioribus. Ipse autem rex non debet esse sub homine sed sub deo et sub lege, quia lex facit regem. (Bracton 1235–1260, vol. II, 33)

In English translation:

> The king has no equal within his realm, subjects cannot be the equals of the ruler, because he would thereby lose his rule, since equal can have no authority over equal, nor a fortiori has the king a superior, because he would then be subject to those subjected to him. The king must not be under man but under God and under the law, because law makes the king. Let him therefore bestow upon the law what the law bestows upon him, namely, rule and power. For there is no rex where will rules rather than lex. (Bracton at *loc. cit.*)

Thus, while searching for the answer to questions posed in the first part of our paper, we have chronologically arrived to the person who has become probably one of the most prominent iconographers of judges. According to everything we know regarding the history of legal thought and the history of ideas in general, Sir Edward Coke was the first to use the expression *the mouth of the Law* referring precisely to the phrase *Judex est lex loquens*.[13]

---

[12]For more on this, see Boyer (2003), pp. 242–244.

[13]Coke (1738b), p. 174, where he says: "[. . . ..] the mouth of the Law (for *Judex est lex loquens*)."

Certainly, we can say that Coke was the first only if we exclude Cicero's aforementioned words on judges, presented in his famous book *De legibus* (3,1,2): '*magistratus est lex loques*', i.e. the judge is the law speaking. Cicero's idea on the judge as the speaking law can be excluded for several reasons. First, the formal one, since the phrases used by both authors—*lex loquens*, i.e. *the law speaking*, and *the mouth of the law*—are not identical even in their mother tongues. Second, Cicero's term *lex loquens*, viewed from the aspect of language and rhetoric, is a metaphor or personification, while Coke's phrase *the mouth of the law*, form the same point of view, represents a metonymy. While observed as legal contents in their linguistic contexts, these expressions have or might have the same meaning; nevertheless, we can also exclude the aforementioned definition of judge provided by Cicero because it belongs to antiquity. For the time being, we can state with certainty that Coke was the first to use this expression in the *modern* era by describing the judge as "the mouth of the Law". He did so in his famous *Law Reports*, written from 1572 onwards, or, more precisely, in their Seventh Volume (or Part). It includes the *Report on Calvin's Case*, wherein Coke uses the phrase "the mouth of the Law" as an image stemming precisely from the view *Judex est lex loquens* (see fn 13 here). This expression was part of a larger comparison and presentation of arguments regarding the case of one Robert Calvin, and it certainly did not have the meaning it was later attributed by Montesquieu, and especially not the meaning attributed by later interpreters of Montesquieu.[14] Moreover, Coke's whole life and work demonstrate he understood differently the roles of king, judges and law. He also inclined stylistically towards metaphors,[15] so that Montesquieu's and subsequent considerably altered meanings of *the mouth of law* metonymy in the sense of *judge and his decisions* only confirm the full complexity of the reconstruction and comprehension of the history of ideas.

It might seem paradoxical, or (as Hegel would say) the cunning of reason in history, that the one who had coined and initially used the vivid term *mouth of the law* to depict a judge, his decisions and his role in the legal system, Sir Edward Coke, actually attested a completely different understanding of law, court and constitutionalism than the one proposed by Montesquieu, who is most deserving the credit for dissemination of that term. Coke is probably the best jurist of all time, what is attested by his entire life[16] with his exceptional, extremely comprehensive and varied legal body of work and accomplishments as a lawyer, prosecutor, judge, member of parliament, representative of the opposition, as well as his achievements in the field of nomotechnics, legal education, popularization of laws and many other. For the sake of illustration only, we shall mention but a few of these numerous exceptional and extremely varied Coke's legal achievements.

As a judge Coke was "from the first, excellent; ever perfectly upright and fearlessly independent, although he lived in days when the judges held their places

[14]For more details on this, see Hanisch (2010), especially pp. 141, 146–148, 160–161.

[15]On this, for more details, see Hostletter (1997).

[16]On this detailedly, see Johnson (1845^2) and Bowen (1957).

merely at the pleasure of the crown, and were, almost as a matter of course, expected to be high prerogative lawyers" (Johnson 1845^2, p. 222).

Coke's understanding of law, courts and constitutionalism might be best illustrated with the three following segments:

First, his statement that the "Magna Charta is such a fellow that he will have no sovereign".[17] Incredibly courageous words in a time when only a sovereign had no sovereign. Coke made this statement during a parliamentary debate when endeavouring to pressure the King to accept and sign the *Petition of Right*, in the drafting of which Coke played a central role, and which limited the King's power while explicitly referring to *Magna Carta.*

Second, Coke's 1610 decision in the Dr. Bonham's case, declaring that "[...] in many cases, the common law will controul Acts of Parliament, and sometimes adjudge them to be utterly void: for when an Act of Parliament is against common right and reason, or repugnant, or impossible to be performed, the common law will controul it, and adjudge such Act to be void."[18] This decision entailed judicial review and limiting of anyone's power exercised against the principles (spirit or values) of constitutionalism. It received support regarding one of its aspects, more precisely, that no one can concurrently be both a prosecutor and a judge in a single matter. Its other aspect, the judicial review of Parliament acts was rejected (even though it received initial approval), as opposed to the principle of Parliament sovereignty that was later supported also by Sir William Blackstone. In the North American colonies, however, this decision of Coke's had considerable impact, and was used as a rationale for annulment of several executive acts and the 1765 English Stamp Act (for opposing the natural equality of men, *Magna Carta* and natural laws). Yet, even there Blackstone's views were finally accepted in 1772. But then in 1803, a decision was delivered in the famous *Marbury v. Madison* case, which formed the basis for the exercise of judicial review in the United States, with referral to Article 3 of the Constitution and the use of words *void* and *repugnant*, most probably under the influence of Coke's decision, i.e. reasoning in the Dr. Bonham's case.[19]

And third, certain decisions, i.e. opinions of Coke's (like the opinion on the High Commission, and especially the one related to *Fuller's Case*, as well as the aforementioned *Prohibitions del Roy*, i.e. *Case of Prohibitions*) expressed in 1607–1608 at the beginning of his court career, have left a strong impact on the history of law and legal ideas. These are: delimiting of ecclesiastic and temporal court jurisdiction, accompanied by the limitation of the power of ecclesiastic courts, which strongly and directly influenced Roger Williams (1603–1683), one of the

[17]Coke (2003b). For more details on this, also see Gaunt (2015), pp. 1–13, especially p. 9.

[18]For entire text of the *Dr. Bonham's Case*, see Coke (2003b), vol. 1, especially pp. 264–283, or any of its online editions. For more details on the importance of the Dr. Bonam's case in the legal history and history of legal ideas, also see Williams (2006), pp. 111–128, especially p. 111.

[19]For more details on the literature and debate on this, see the references listed in the entry *Dr. Bonham's Case* at Wikipedia.

earliest proponents of the separation between church and state; proper argumentation which is not mere denying of the value of the opposing opinion; defence of the freedom of thought, right to silence, inviolability of home, and defence of other individual rights.[20] Perhaps above all was the effort to ensure the independence of judges[21] as a pillar of modern constitutionalism, as was clearly demonstrated by the wording of Coke's *Prohibitions del Roy* decision:

> The King in his own person cannot adjudge any case, either criminal or between party and party; but it ought to be determined and adjudged in some Court of Justice, according to the law and custom of England. The King may sit in the King's Bench, but the Court gives the judgment. No King after the conquest assumed to himself to give any judgment in any cause whatsoever which concerned the administration of justice, within the realm; but these causes were solely determined in the Courts of Justice. The King cannot arrest any man. (Coke 1607 at *loc. cit.*)

This three-part disposition was followed by Coke's exceptional and detailed reasoning containing other well-known statements, such as that the judges are not mere delegates of the King; that the opinions declared are not just Coke's but expressed in the presence and with the clear consent of all the judges of England, and Barons of the Exchequer. Special attention should be given to the famous argument presented by Coke to the King (who was in attendance) on why a King cannot adjudicate:

> [...] true it was, that God had endowed His Majesty with excellent science, and great endowments of nature; but His Majesty was not learned in the laws of his realm of England, and causes which concern the life, or inheritance, or goods, or fortunes of his subjects, are not to be decided by natural reason but by the artificial reason and judgment of law, which law is an act which requires long study and experience, before that a man can attain to the cognizance of it: that the law was the golden met-wand and measure to try the causes of the subjects; and which protected His Majesty in safety and peace: with which the King was greatly offended, and said, that then he should be under the law, which was treason to affirm, as he said; to which I said, that Bracton saith, quod Rex non debed {debet -?- J.H.} esse sub homine, sed sub Deo et lege [That the King ought not to be under any man but under God and the law.]. (Coke, 1738a, 2003a)

Montesquieu (1689–1755) had excellent knowledge of the English constitutional debate and saw the judges in a well ordered kingdom (which in his opinion cannot be despotic) only as mouths pronouncing the words of law:

> Des trois puissances dont nous avons parlé, celle de juger est en quelque façon nulle. [......
> ...] [L]es juges de la nation ne sont que la bouche qui prononce les paroles de la loi; des êtres inanimés qui n'en peuvent modérer ni la force ni la rigueur. (Montesquieu /1748[1]/ 1995, I, 337)

> Of the three powers above mentioned, the judiciary is in some measure next to nothing. [.........] The national judges are no more than the mouth that pronounces the words of the law, mere passive {= inanimate = lifeless – J.H.} beings, incapable of moderating either its force or rigour. (Montesquieu /1748[1]/ 1914, *ibidem*)

[20]For more details on these, see Bowen (1957), especially pp. 257, 260, 261.

[21]For more on this, see Campbell (1849), vol. 1, p. 237.

However, Montesquieu did not see judges as complete automatons, which was the view of many of his followers, including, in a certain way, Cesare Beccaria (1738–1794).[22] But, we should nevertheless acknowledge that Montesquieu himself contributed to this interpretation and idea of a judge as a human automaton who, when adjudicating, only declares the word of the law. He did so by referring to judges as merely the mouth of the law (*os legis*—in Latin) and inanimate beings, *être inanimé*, or in Latin: *ens inanimatum* or *entitas inanimata*.

Such a lifeless being whose mouth simply pronounces the words of law (*ens inanimatum per os eius solummodo verba legis locuta sunt*) irresistibly evokes a machine or automaton. Or else, if not entirely lifeless, inanimate, it irresistibly calls to mind a ventriloquist. Hence, the judge is the legislator's ventriloquist doll! And thus Montesquieuian judge can come in these two types: Like any machine, the judge has to be both designed and set in motion by a man, and may be either functioning or broken. Even as a state of the art machine for human voice generation and reading that only pronounces the words of laws, or as a less sophisticated someone who "swallowed" a record with laws, or a similar sound emitting device, either functioning or broken, or who "swallowed" even "only" the wrong *legal* records, which he then "plays", broadcasts from his belly like a good or bad, functioning or half broken "record player". But the judge as legislator's ventriloquist doll, by every *excellent* ventriloquist, who is *in constant dialogue* with *another* person *inside* him (i.e. his *doll*), in the case of judge-ventriloquist doll, who is seemingly in legislator's "belly", but in fact in his head and soul, would imply a constant dialogue of the legislator-ventriloquist with his doll-judge. Since this is impossible mission, the revers happens: The excellent judge-ventriloquist is in constant dialogue with his doll-legislator. So, the verdict that he delivers—regardless of whether one assesses it positively or negatively—*clearly* stems from this dialogue and thanks to this dialogue, which is nothing else but the confronting of arguments, reasoning for such a verdict.

In any case, Montesquieu's judges as lifeless (or inanimate) entities (or creatures) pronouncing the words of the law (*entia inanimata ora eorum solummodo verba legum locuta sunt*) differ greatly from the entire previous tradition:

First, they are very different from the Aristotelian idea *iudex est iustitia animata* (i.e. *dikaion empsychon*)—living justness, animate justice.

They are also different from the Ciceronian idea that judge is the speaking law, and law is the silent judge (*magistratus est lex loquens, lex autem mutus magistratus*). To be more precise, Cicero's notion should be divided into two parts, i.e. viewed from two aspects. As we already mentioned, the first part, the idea of the judge as the speaking law—*lex loquens*, could be understood as *identical* with the concept of judge as the one speaking the words of law (*qui verba legis loquit*), even though these are completely different from the aspect of language, style and rhetoric; but it can also be understood as a *completely different*, even *opposite* idea, precisely because, besides everything previously mentioned, a judge,

[22]For more on this, see Hanisch (2010), especially pp. 131, 150, 152, 154, 157.

magistratus is a man, and Montesquieu's judge is some kind of inanimate being—*ens inanimatum* or *entitas inanimata*. However, the second part of Cicero's idea, according to which the law is a silent (or even mute) judge, and where the judge is in the background, makes it quite clear that—unlike the law, i.e. legislator—a judge cannot and should not be silent. Indeed, whether he can, may and should only inanimately pronounce the words of law, is a completely different, Montesquieuian rather than Ciceronian question.

As far as the Vespasianian-Ulpianian-Justinianian idea in which the *imperator est lex animata in terris*, it should be noted that it was prevalent even outside of England, not only in Jean Bodin's time (1530–1596), but even later. Seen through the lens of this Vespasianian-Ulpianian-Justinianian idea, Montesquieu's judges can be seen as inanimate beings who only pronounce the words of the emperor, i.e. whose mouths are only the channel for the words of the emperor (regardless of who the emperor is, which exact title he holds, or what principles he embodies), as the highest law and court in the country (*entia inanimata per ora eorum solummodo verba imperatoris qua suprema lex Curiaque in terris locuta sunt*).

Finally, Montesquieu is essentially different even to the Thomistic school of thought, according to which, as we have seen, judicial justice is better than the justice of earthly laws (alone), as the judicial inanimate beings only speak the words of law that refer to a concrete case. Their justice cannot be better than the justice of laws, but at best, only equal to it or inferior. The problem becomes even more complicated when compared to Thomistic tradition. Namely, Montesquieu's position, even if it (accidentally) achieves a justice of laws, can in no case achieve *equity*. And it is *equity* (as established since Aristotle), which as *justice in a concrete case* is both better and superior to justice, i.e. justness, including the justice of laws.

Recall that in *Les Six livres de la Républiqu*e (1576) Bodin says: "[*L*]*e Prince* [...] *est la loi vive* [...]" (Bodin 1576, p. 378). And the king is not only the animate law (i.e. *lex animata*), but he should also exert judicial power. Which is where Bodin and Montesquieu differ. Montesquieu failed to express the essence of judicial power in the best possible manner, given that he saw judges as mouths of the law, i.e. inanimate beings only pronouncing the word of the law (*ora legum, i.e. entia inanimata qua solummodo verba legum loquuntur*). Nevertheless, his insistence on technical separation of judicial from the other two powers, i.e. on deconcentrated state power, and thus, independence of courts, should be seen as his biggest contribution to modern conceptualization and constitutionalisation of courts.

When discussing Montesquieu's understanding of judges, we should under no circumstances disregard the fact that he (as Beccaria after him) was referring to criminal law implementation, that is criminal court judges (as we would call them today). And in this area of paradigmatically strict and precise laws, it is not difficult to imagine the logical, i.e. syllogistic automatism of law implementation. Judicial power is limited by laws, thus almost no power whatsoever, which is a guarantee of freedom and legal safety for Montesquieu, Beccaria and their followers.[23]

---

[23]For more details, see Hanisch (2010), pp. 133, 135–137, 140, 144, 148, 155.

Ultimately, it should be noted that Montesquieu never thought that judges in England had no freedom in legal interpretation, nor that the freedom they had made them not subject to the law. And he especially did not think that owing to that freedom (which included the interpretation of not only the letter but also the spirit of law, i.e. implementation of law in accordance with the equity principle) they possessed a specific legislative function. No. Judges in England are free to interpret the law, but that freedom is considerably reduced by precedents and the letter of the law.[24]

In summary, it could be said that, although there is no proof that Montesquieu was directly influenced by the premodern history of the idea *iudex—lex loquens* (*qua iustitia animata*), we should acknowledge certain indirect influences caused by social needs and the spirit of the time. Regarding the pre-Montesquieu modern era, we should highlight Coke's concept of judge and judiciary, not only (nor even primarily) because Coke was the first one to use the expression *mouth of the law*, basing it precisely on the phrase *iudex est lex loquens*, but because he understood much better than Montesquieu the *essence* of the speaking law. And although Coke understood the need for that speaking law to be independent and knowledgeable in law (in a word, highly professional, as we would put it nowadays), being himself also limited by the circumstances and spirit of his time, he did not manage to reach the postulate of deconcentration of state power through its technical separation into three parts. Coke is, thus, significant primarily for his comprehensive and functional definition of the independence of skilled judges, i.e. judiciary, where he explicitly states that the king cannot adjudicate in any legal disputes; that judges are not king's delegates; that the king, after taking the throne, i.e. power, cannot decide on any matters related to administration of the judiciary within his kingdom, but must leave all such matters, including trials, exclusively to the courts; and that a king cannot arrest anyone.

When it comes to the professionalism of judges, which can also be seen as one of the requirements for their independence, Coke defines it precisely by explaining why the king cannot adjudicate: wide breadth of knowledge and exceptional natural talent do not suffice for adjudication, it also requires *legal* knowledge about the law in one's country, in order to adjudicate in matters pertaining to lives of others, or inheritance, or goods, or property *not* on the basis of natural, good sense, but the artificial, legal reasoning on the laws. This demands *considerable study and experience* before one gains insights into law that provides the golden met-wand, i.e. the perfect measure and criteria for adjudication in legal disputes.

Montesquieu's lesson on the necessity for deconcentration, i.e. separation of state powers, is another postulate of the modern era that retains great importance to this day, since we are constantly facing widespread examples of concentration of power and authority. We see this in totalitarian, authoritarian and (neo)bonapartist regimes, military juntas and dictatorships, as well as other more or less disguised examples of similar systems in illiberal and populist democracies. Maybe the reason for such

[24]For more of historically relevant details on this, see Hanisch (2010).

widespread concentration of state power and authority should be found in the fact that constitutionalism—as one of the most important modern political and legal ideas—requires considerable effort, toil and time to spread and take root, but deteriorates quite easily and quickly if not nurtured.

Ultimately, we can conclude that the *origin* of the image of judge as a mouth pronouncing the words of the law belongs to premodern times; but the *image itself* is, however, an important characteristic of the modern era. Its creator (as far as we know) is Coke, but Montesquieu must be given credit for its propagation and popularity. Still, the image itself of the judge as a mouth that (only) pronounces the words of the law operates like the Rorschach inkblot, or dual image, since it both theoretically and practically depicts two quite different types of judges, which we shall, provisionally, call the Cokeian and Montesquieuian image of the judge. This image of the judge (as the mouth pronouncing the words of the law), or these two completely different images of the judge (Cokeian and Montesquieuian), or even many of these different images of the judge (since both of them have many variants), have marked the modern era, especially the modern judiciary, both in legal theory and practice of judicature, that is, all of legal reality. It seems that they, probably unconsciously, also mark the basic ideas behind the recent contemporary debate on judicial activism and restraint, although, as far as we know, no one has explicitly referred to them in the context of said debate. This shall be discussed in detail later.

This would be a pertinent moment to clarify why we consider that the ideal image of the judge in a modern (and especially contemporary) democracy should be identified rather within Coke's image of a judge (or versions thereof), than in Montesquieu's. This is the lesson that history of modern law has already taught us.

Let us recall how the French Revolution gave rise to the concept of law as a set of positive laws, i.e. statutes, which are the expression of national sovereignty. This conception of national sovereignty, on the one hand, and the principle of separation of powers, on the other, are the reasons why the role of the judge in the then modern revolutionary France was reduced—in a truly Montesquieuian manner—to the very minimum. The power of adjudication was understood solely as the application of the text of the law to an individual case through simple deduction, and without venturing into the area of legal interpretation, which would pose the risk of deforming the will of the legislator.

For the rare cases where the text of the law was unclear or insufficient, *The Law on Organization of Courts of August 16–24, 1790* (that is to say in the very beginning of the Revolution) established a new legal remedy in the interest of all courts: *the request for a temporary decision of general character*, i.e. a request for interpretation or amendment of specific regulations. Article 12 of this law states that "they [i.e. courts] shall not make regulations, but they shall have recourse to the legislative body, whenever they think necessary either to interpret a law or to amand it". (According to Perelman 1976b, p. 17).

Apart from this, the law obliged the judges to provide a rationale behind their decisions, and established the Court of Cassation with competences to ensure that judges are not breaking the law when believing that they are interpreting it. The Court of Cassation was thus considered a police officer created by the legislative power in order to supervise the work of the judiciary, and which had to occasionally report on the success of that mission to the legislator.

In practice, however, this institute of request for a temporary decision of general character turned out to be a very bad legal solution, since the judges tended to overuse it out of fear of interpretation of laws. It, thus, not only obstructed the sound functioning of the judiciary and buried the legislator under an avalanche of requests of that kind, but it also breached the principle of separation of powers in the most direct manner, since the legislator actually resolved the dispute in favour of one of the parties by interpreting the law in a particular way, thus itself also becoming a judge. *Ergo, summa separatio—summa confusio!* Or, *summa separatio potestatis (in trias potestates)—summa confusio earum (i.e. potestatarum).* In other words, maximal separation of power (in three "totally" separated state powers) leads to maximal confusion of those powers.

This is why, during the drafting of the *Code Civil* (adopted in 1804), the institute of request for a temporary decision of general character was replaced by the famous Article 4 stating: "Le juge qui refusera de juger sous prétexte du silence, de l'obscurité ou de l'insuffisance de la loi, pourra être poursuivi comme coupable de déni de justice". Or in English: "The judge who refuses to judge under the pretext of the silence, the obscurity or the insufficiency of the law, can be prosecuted as guilty of denial of justice (*déni de justice*)".[25]

After this historical experience, the need for judicial interpretation of laws, and sometimes even their amendment, becomes glaringly obvious. The differentiation of creation and implementation of law remains important, although somewhat relativized, especially due to hierarchies of sources of law, as well as of acts of law implementation, and particularly by the hierarchy in control of constitutionality and legality of acts in a legal order. But, the *creative* element in application of law can no longer be denied.[26] This is precisely why it is necessary to seek the ideal image of the judge in modern (and *a fortiori* contemporary) democracies within the Cokeian variants. However, since modern democracy is also a modern constitutional democracy,[27] the question of the role of the judge in the contemporary constitutional democracy presents itself.

In searching for the ideal image of the judge within contemporary constitutional democracy, the second part of this paper focuses only on Barak's (1936-) image of the judge in a contemporary democracy as it appears in his entire legal legacy (having in mind that his theoretical legacy remains open, while the judicial ended with his retirement). It directs our attention primarily at the image given in his book *The Judge in a Democracy* (Barak 2006). Has Barak presented something in his judicial practice and writing that has not been previously known?[28] And is Barak's

[25]For more details, see Huberlan (1968), pp. 47–54; Košutić (1973), pp. 9–37, especially p. 32 (and fn 96) and pp. 153–154; Perelman (1976b), pp. 16–18; Hasanbegović (1988), pp. 165–168.

[26]For more on this, see Košutić (1973).

[27]For more on this, see Hasanbegović et al. (2016), pp. 47–59.

[28]On this and other relevant Barak's stands more detailedly, see also Košutić et al. (2016).

image of the judge in modem democracy different from the image depicted by his contemporary Richard Posner (1939-), also judge and legal scholar, in his book *How Judges Think* (Posner 2008)?

The impetus and core of the revaluation, reassessment and reappraisal of Barak's image of the judge in a contemporary democracy were provided and determined by Posner's criticism of Barak contained principally in his article *Enlightened Despot* (Posner 2007, p. 53),[29] later also published in his book *How Judges Think.* So, carefully studied through a double critical lens, this search for the image of a model judge in contemporary democracy strives to answer the question of who Barak or Posner—or maybe both, or neither, even though both fall within Cokeian ideal judge versions—has delivered something of value, something enlightening. Who has provided important new critical insights (or at least enabled them), and whose theoretical approach to the judiciary is more appropriate for the contemporary democracy?

We think that this critical review of Barak's image of the judge in contemporary democracy, based on Posner's criticism of said image, will clarify why the differentiation between active, or even hyperactive, and restrained judiciary is not inherently valuable. Neither (hyper)activism nor restraint of judges *by itself* results in disloyalty and loyalty, respectively, to a given constitution. This is because, as we hope to demonstrate, a judge's loyalty or disloyalty to the constitution *by itself* and *for itself* is not crucial. What is crucial is a judge's loyalty or disloyalty to *constitutionalism*, which this double criticism strives to prove.

One could immediately pose the question why Posner's criticism of Barak's book *The Judge in a Democracy*, published under the title *Enlightened Despot*, is important. Why is it worthy of legal or general attention, or, indeed, relevant to every contemporary political and legal community? Succinctly put, because it relates to the most important legal issues of the world we inhabit, and because it reflects and refracts them. Let us take a closer look.

As far as the basic aforementioned texts—Posner's *Enlightened Despot* and Barak's *The Judge in a Democracy*—are concerned, the following should be noted:

Although Posner is known for his extreme sharpness and harshness of legal views even in his judgements[30]—let alone anywhere else—to such an extent that is phenomenally close to what psychologists call *acting out*,[31] it should be noted that

[29]Posner's *Enlightened Despot* was first published in 2007 in the US magazine *New Republic* on the p. 53, and since the *New Republic* has printed as well as online edition, and Posner's text in both editions covers a single page, in order to facilitate the orientation in the text, we refer to its specific paragraphs (as § or §§), which are, of course, not marked with numbers (1, 2, 3, 4, etc.) in the original.

[30]To provide just one example: Posner has stated in his decision from 1997 in the case of *State Oil Co. v. Khan* that the US Supreme Court decision from 1968 establishing the anti-monopole precedent (and which, *nota bene*, he himself has invoked and relied on in his decision!) is "*moth-eaten*", "*wobbly*", and "*unsound*". On this, see Parloff (2000).

[31]Only for the sake of illustrations, we can refer to what Robert Boynton wrote in his review of Posner's book *Public Intellectuals: A Study of Decline*, in *The Washington Post*, where he states his

Posner did not write *Enlightened Despot* overnight. Nor did he publish the text in the influential US magazine *New Republic* in 2007 spurred by rage against Barak's views on the judiciary presented specifically in *The Judge in a Democracy* (2006) or elsewhere. Unlike judicial decisions, which judges cannot change after pronouncing them, authors of scientific papers can change their texts, and those changes, additions, abridgments, etc. are usually introduced during preparations for new editions. However, Posner republished unchanged *Enlightened Despot* in 2008 and 2010 in his book *How Judges Think*,[32] thus demonstrating that he has maintained his views and arguments supporting them as presented in 2007.

Barak's book *The Judge in a Democracy* examines the role of judges in contemporary democracies, the tools for implementation of that role, the relationship between the judiciary and other branches of state power, and finally the evaluation of the role of the judge. Even though it focuses on the courts of legal systems belonging to the *common law* family and some other mixed systems, Barak, quite rightfully, considers his book also relevant for Romano-Germanic, Scandinavian and post-socialist systems (Barak 2006, p. XVII). His opinions on almost all of the issues raised in this book were already elaborated in previous papers, especially in his 2005 book dedicated to interpretation of the law—*Purposive Interpretation in Law*. So, Barak's *The Judge in a Democracy* does not represent a theoretical shift but further theoretical development and finalization of the author's views on judicature in practice.

When Robert Alexy was asked which teachings or theory of legal interpretation within the framework of common law or anglophone world he would recommend, he chose Barak's with no second thoughts.[33] Barak has also briefly presented his basic concepts of legal interpretation theory (for new purposes) in the book *The Judge in a Democracy* (Barak 2006, especially 122–154) and continued developing them in his book *Proportionality: Constitutional Rights and their Limitations* (Barak 2012).

belief that Posner will never sit on the U.S. Supreme Court because, in spite of his "obvious brilliance" Posner would be criticised for his occasional "outrageous conclusion", such as his assertion that "the rule of law is an accidental and readily dispensable element of our legal ideology", or his argument in favour of buying and selling babies on the free market in lieu of government-regulated adoption, or his support for the legalization of marijuana and LSD (Boynton 2002). Or, even recently, in 2015 and 2016, Posner was criticised by the right-wing media for the column he wrote for *Slate* and for what he said about the Constitution: "I see absolutely no value to a judge of spending decades, years, months, weeks, day, hours, minutes, or seconds studying the Constitution, the history of its enactment, its amendments, and its implementation" (Posner 2016; *** /Critique on Posner/ at MEDIAite.com).

[32]To put it more precisely, Posner republished *Enlightened Despot* in 2008 and 2010 in his *How Judges Think* within its Chapter 12: *Judicial Cosmopolitanism* (pp. 347–368), specifically at pp. 362–368 with a few minor changes.

[33]This took place at a *Fundamental Rights: Justification & Interpretation* conference, organized at the Belgarde University Faculty of Law by the Serbian Association for Legal and Social Philosophy on October 24–25, 2014.

Hence, when two judges belonging to the very pinnacle of the profession—and who are also highly esteemed legal theorists—discuss the role of the judge in contemporary constitutional democracy, deliberate on when the judge is characterized by reserve, activity or hyperactivity in his/her performance of the judge's role, as well as whether s/he should be characterised by reserve, activity or hyperactivity, and especially when they express incompatible views on that issue, then that surely deserves attention and thorough analysis.

In order to be precise, we should add three more remarks to our critique of Posner's critique of Barak's judicial practice and his book *The Judge in a Democracy*. For reasons of space, we shall refrain from reviewing *other critiques of Barak*'s book (for example, that of Jabareen 2005) as well as *other critiques of Posner*'s critique of Barak (for example, that of Barak Medina from 2007). Although some arguments by Barak Medina are considered (Medina 2007), delving into Medina's critique of Posner's critique of Barak would necessarily require a critical review of Medina's own views which falls outside of the scope of this paper. And finally, we shall refrain from reviewing *all* of Posner's critical opinions of Barak, especially those focusing on Barak's personality and psychological profile, as well as some historical comparisons, since these belong (according to traditional logic) to arguments *ad hominem* or *ad personam*. (We admit, however, that the results of such an analysis, professionally conducted, might be very interesting for both.) We shall, instead, review only those critical opinions relevant to the identification and evaluation of the role of the judge in contemporary constitutional democracy.

The critique of Posner's critique of Barak, focusing on core issues and succinctly presented, needs to be carried out in at least four basic steps.

First. Posner grounds his criticism of Barak's views on the role of judge in democracy and his judicial practice in the Supreme Court of Israel by criticizing Barak's interpretation of Israeli Basic Laws as the constitution of Israel. He states: "But, only in Israel (as far as I know) do judges confer the power of abstract review on themselves, without benefit of a constitutional or legislative provision" (Posner 2007, §4; repeated completely in Posner 2008, p. 364). And Israeli judges cannot refer to a constitutional provision since, according to Posner, Israel lacks a constitution.

Posner is explicit: "Israel does not have a constitution" (Posner 2007, §2). He expresses this view first indirectly, by comparing Israel's Chief Justice Barak with the US Chief Justice John Marshall, and then quite directly by saying: "Barak is John Marshall without a constitution to expound [...]. Israel does not have a constitution." (*ibidem*). This has been slightly altered in *How Judges Think*: "Barak is John Marshall without a constitution to expound. Israel does not have a constitution in the usual sense" (Posner 2008, p. 363).

Hence, however strange this statement might seem, it has been explicitly and clearly expressed, and repeated. It is quite strange since it is the equivalent of a renowned legal scholar saying that the United Kingdom (or New Zealand) does not have a constitution. But why does Posner think so about Israel? Because in his eyes, Israeli Basic Laws, passed by the Knesset, could also be repealed by the Knesset. It should be noted that eleven such laws were passed in the period 1958–1992.[34] But, first let us see what precisely Posner says:

> Israel does not have a constitution. It has 'Basic Laws' passed by the Knesset, Israel's parliament, which Barak has equated to a constitution by holding that the Knesset cannot repeal them. (Posner 2007, §2)

The same view is presented in *How Judges Think*, this time expressed slightly more comprehensively and precisely:

> "Israel does not have a constitution in the usual sense. The Knesset (the Israeli parliament) has passed several 'basic laws,' one of which – Basic Law: Human Dignity and Freedom – provides that 'the life, body or dignity of any person shall not be violated' and that 'every person is entitled to protection of his life, body and dignity.' (Barak 2006, at 85 n. 154) But while the Knesset can call some of its laws 'basic' if it wants to, there is grave doubt that it is authorized to promulgate constitutional as well as ordinary statutory provisions. (Segev 2007)" (Posner 2008, p. 363)

Now it is quite clear that Posner does not differentiate between the constitution and constitutionalism.

The first question that arises is the importance of the fact that Posner does not differentiate between constitutions (be it written or unwritten bodies of legal and other rules regulating the foundations of political and social life in a society, i.e. state)[35] and constitutionalism (as practice or body of ideas, attitudes, and rules as patterns of behaviour, *limiting* political powers and all other authorities in a society by means of so-called basic laws).[36] This lack of differentiation is important because it prevents (Posner, or anyone else who fails to make that difference) from noticing that should the Knesset repeal the Basic Laws, Israel would become an undemocratic state with an undemocratic constitution. It also keeps him from noticing that Israel would be an undemocratic state if the Basic Laws were implemented contrary to the principles of constitutionalism.

Posner considers—as we have seen above—that abstract judicial review has to be conferred to judges exclusively by an (explicit, written) constitutional or legislative provision. This is also very strange. At least if we take into account that in the United States (and similarly in Australia) the federal and state courts (at all levels, both

---

[34]For more on this, see "older" papers such as Bin-Nun (1990), especially pp. 8–88 *et passim*, and regarding more recent literature, see Jacobsohn (1994), Cohen and Susser (2000) and Mazie (2006).

[35]Constitutions are defined in many other similar ways, but they always relate primarily to the sets of legal rules regulating said matter. According to type, they encompass both premodern and modern, autocratic and democratic constitutions.

[36]There is also a lot of reference material on the difference between constitutionalism and constitutions. Just for the sake of illustration, see Fellman (1973/1974), Fehrenbacher (1989), Gordon (1999) and Waluchow (2014), and also the cited reference papers there. Constitutionalism as a limitation of power through fundamental superior laws is predominantly a modern phenomenon. We encounter this difference under different names, e.g. material, substantial, a certain value system oriented, or modern constitution. In Serbian, the most information on the differentiation between constitutions and constitutionalism can be found in the papers of Lidija R. Basta, who is consistent in theoretically differentiating between the two.

appellate and trial) are empowered to review and declare the (un)constitutionality of legislative acts in any case within their jurisdiction, or, in other words, that all courts are empowered to review concrete statute and declare unconstitutionality (Corwin 2014; Patrick et al. 2001).

In the US, this capacity of all courts is commonly held to have been established in the case of *Marbury v. Madison* (5 U.S. 137, 1803), argued before the Supreme Court in 1803, and in Australia in the case of *Australian Communist Party v. Commonwealth* (1951, 83 CLR 1 AustLII) in 1951. With that in mind, according to Posner, a concrete judicial review in the USA (or Australia) could have been established by the Supreme Court, which therefor did not need an explicit, written constitutional or legislative provision, nor would Posner therefore describe the Supreme (or any other) Court in the United States as usurpative when reviewing constitutionality. But the same does not go for abstract judicial review in Israel. Posner has declared the Supreme Court of Israel as usurpative when it performs an abstract review of constitutionality, because it lacks an explicit, written constitutional or legislative provision therefor. Posner states: "He [Barak] takes for granted that judges have inherent authority to override statutes. Such an approach can accurately be described as usurpative" (Posner 2007, §5 *in fine*). However, in *How Judges Think* Posner himself has redacted this entire paragraph (Posner 2008, p. 364).

We must wonder why Posner does not consider the establishment of specific review of constitutionality of laws by the US or Australian Supreme Courts as usurpation, and does consider the establishment of the abstract review of constitutionality of laws by the Supreme Court of Israel as usurpation. Maybe he believes that *quod licet Iovi non licet bovi*. But, the problem with this in principle justifiable double standard is not only related to determining who is Jove in this case, and who an ox, nor why, but the issue is actually much larger. This is the most important issue of any constitutional democracy: which power is entitled to the constitutionalisation of the legal system in a given state. In the case of Israel, if not the Knesset and the Supreme Court of Israel, than what authority is entitled to the constitutionalisation of Israel? But, this problem does not exist for Posner, since he fails to differentiate between the constitution and constitutionalism.

Second. Posner argues that Barak's idea of the courts' enforcing a set of rights that they find to be a component of "substantive" democracy actually involves a curtailing of democracy and results in a "hyperactive judiciary" because courts do not limit themselves to protect just democratic political rights as only human rights. To be completely clear, here is Posner:

> For Barak, however, democracy has a 'substantive' component, namely a set of rights ('human rights' not limited to political rights, such as the right to criticize public officials, that support democracy), enforced by the judiciary, that clips the wings of the elected officials. That is not a justification for a hyperactive judiciary, it is merely a redefinition of it. (Posner 2007, §6 *in fine*; identically phrased in Posner 2008, p. 364)

Here we also encounter Posner's explicitly defined concept of modern democracy:

> Political democracy in the modern sense means a system of government in which the key officials stand for election at relatively short intervals and thus are accountable to the citizenry. (Posner 2007, §6; identically phrased in Posner 2008, p. 364)

This is, however, the reduction of the concept of modem democracy to the (formal) concept of majority rule, and more precisely, to rule of representatives determined by any of applied majoritarian principles. Consequently, though representative and not direct, it remains premodern democracy, because majority rule (either representative or direct) may be (substantively) tyrannical as well. But modern democracy should be able to hinder the tyranny of majority. So, modern democracy has to be defined as something more than majority rule.

Put simply, modem democracy consists of majority rule (as its formal or procedural component) and the effective protection of the minority (as its substantive and substantial component). In the beginning of modem history that minority was political, protected by *both civil and political rights*, guaranteed to *all*. This is to say: Posner is wrong. Human rights (previously, rights of man, or rights of man and citizen) must not be limited to political ones, and they have never been, not even in their most important forerunner—the *Magna Carta Libertatum*.[37]

And if effective protection of human rights makes tyranny of majority impossible, then in order to be effective that protection has to encompass: (a) not only political but also civil rights, as it did in the beginning of modern history, and then afterwards also amended contingently by some economic, social and cultural rights, whether as individual or collective, minority rights; (b) the effective protection of human rights by means of an independent judiciary, which in legal terms may also be expressed as a (human) right to an independent (or even natural) judge; and c) the legal possibility to override any statute which diminishes or even denies any established human right (Hasanbegović, *ibidem*).

What Posner does not understand is that modern democracy is, in the aforementioned sense, a substantive democracy, and that it actually *per se* involves a curtailing of democracy reduced to majority rule, and further has to be legally able to "clip the wings of the elected officials" whenever they transgress their constitutional, legislative or any otherwise legally determined limits. Let us quote Posner once again in order to demonstrate his obvious lack of understanding regarding modern constitutional democracy:

> Political democracy in the modern sense means a system of government in which the key officials stand for election at relatively short intervals and thus are accountable to the citizenry. A judiciary that is free to override the decisions of those officials curtails democracy. For Barak, however, democracy has a 'substantive' component, namely a set of rights ('human rights' not limited to political rights, such as the right to criticize public officials, that support democracy), enforced by the judiciary, that clips the wings of the elected officials. That is not a justification for a hyperactive judiciary, it is merely a redefinition of it. (Posner 2007, §6; identically phrased in Posner 2008, p. 364)

[37] On this in more detail, see Hasanbegović (2016), pp. 47–59.

Now we have to wonder whether Posner's aforementioned view that the "hyper-activity of courts" by definition exists whenever the judges strive to effectively protect human rights from the legislator who has flown so high that he has endangered not the political, but "merely" certain among the other human rights of the individuals in the legal order. In order to answer this question, one should take into account that in both theory and practice (regardless of the growing number of relevant papers[38]) judicial activism, judicial restraint as well as judicial hyperactivism are still nothing more than individual, highly personal labels for an estimation of judicial practices which by themselves (and this seems essential to us) can be neither good nor bad. And if it is true that "most people use the term *judicial activism* to explain decisions that they don't like" (Wallace and Olson 2010)[39] then Posner's "judicial hyperactivism" would be nothing but his label for judicial practice he *hyper*-dislikes, because he prefers formal to substantive democracy, and also greatly prefers only formal constitutionality and legality to constitutionalism. Posner openly exhibits his hyper-dislike by saying:

> It is thus the court that makes Israel's statutory law, using the statutes themselves as first drafts that the court is free to rewrite. (Posner 2007, §8 *in fine*)

And in *How Judges Think* as well, only slightly rephrased:

> The court treated the statute as a first draft that the judges were free to rewrite. (Posner 2008, p. 365)

Still, Posner is certainly familiar with the history of Anglo-American legal theory—where Bishop Benjamin Hoadly, William Blackstone, Oliver Wendell Holmes Jr., Roscoe Pound, John Chipman Gray, Jerome Frank, Karl Llewellyn and many others have stated that enforcement of law by judges uses the same laws in order to find in them—through interpretation—the meanings they consider as most appropriate for specific cases, and which, thus, through that interpretation by judges (and especially the judges of supreme courts) become the true meanings of laws. Of course, and not only in Israel.

Third. Posner claims that Barak's approach to the interpretation of laws involves, in practice, interpretation in the context of the judge's own personal ideal system,

---

[38]For a beginning it is enough to see Canon (1983), pp. 236–247; Lewis (1999); Kmiec (2004), pp. 1441–1477—who notes here that the term *judicial activism* had been discussed in over five thousand articles since 1990; Bonventre (2005), pp. 557–576; Roosevelt (2006); Cross and Lindquist (2007), pp. 1752–1784; Green (2009), pp. 1195–1263; Tamanaha (2010) as well as the references provided in these texts.

[39]This view was first (as far as we know) presented by Supreme Court Justice Anthony Kennedy: "An activist court is a court that makes a decision you don't like."—Kennedy (2010).

For details on the lack of sound criteria for both the differentiation between judicial activism and restraint, and the assessing of these practices as goood or bad, as well as on uncritical adoption of the very division to judicial activism and restraint, and accordingly, the senselessness of such a division, especially in Europe, with references to new papers describing this (for example: Prochazka 2002; Sadurski 2003), see criticism in Smilov (2004); Marinković (2016), pp. 96–115, especially pp. 102–105.

and "opens up a vast realm for discretionary judgment", rather than providing for an objective interpretation of the law (Posner 2007, especially §§ 8 & 13; the same in Posner 2008, pp. 365 & 367). The scope of this paper does not allow us to analyse and assess Barak's legal interpretation theory which has been, as previously stated, presented in detail in two of Barak's books: *Purposive Interpretation in Law*, and *Proportionality: Constitutional Rights and their Limitations*. It will suffice to refer to the aforementioned Alexy's assessment of Barak's interpretation theory. However, it should be highlighted that Posner is incorrect when equating judicial discretion in interpreting a statute by aspiring to achieve justice with judicial subjectivism (Posner 2007, especially §§ 10 & 15; in Posner 2008, §10 is repeated at 366, while §15 has been left out).[40] This is erroneous because the modern concept of justice (unlike all premodern ones, starting with Aristotle's fifth book of *Nicomachean Ethics*) is not empty;[41] quite the opposite, it is filled with human rights which can be enjoyed or effectively protected by laws and courts in a specific legal order, and which, thus, make the very substance of rather precisely identified content of the concept of justice in the said legal order.[42]

And, finally, fourth. Posner is also highly critical of Barak's view of the separation of powers (Posner 2007, especially §§ 9 & 10; nearly identical phrasing in Posner 2008, pp. 365–366, but the first two sentences from §10 have been omitted: "In Barak's conception of the separation of powers, the judicial power is unlimited and the legislature cannot remove judges. (And in Israel, judges participate in the selection of judges.)") Here it becomes evident that Posner lacks some insights into political philosophy and theory, and the modern history of different democratic practices, as well as comparative knowledge of different contemporary democratic systems.[43] The separation of powers in the technical sense, as organizing of (at least) three powers (legislative, executive and judicial), becomes unavoidable in modern history, with the emergence of nation states, due to their size (in territory and number of inhabitants).

The technical separation of powers thus exists in all systems of organization of powers: in presidential (such as the US), parliamentary (such as the UK), and presidential-parliamentary (such as France), but also in assembly-governed (such as Switzerland). This separation of powers persists, hence, in both democratic and non-democratic systems (e.g. in South Africa until 1990, in socialist, i.e. communist, several South American and post-communist systems, etc.). Technical separation of powers, hence, should not under any circumstances be equated with a checks-and-balances system, which, for example, does not exist in (democratic) Switzerland. Nor should technical separation of powers be equated with the independent

[40]For a criticism (of not only Posner, but in general) of the viewpoint that everything that is a matter of will, i.e. decision, i.e. choice is *per se* tyranny, see Spaić (2016), pp. 121–147.

[41]For a critique of contemporary analytic philosophy and its empty ideas, see Unger (2014).

[42]For more on this, see Hasanbegović (2016).

[43]On this confusion, both phenomenal and conceptual, in detail, see Posner (2007), especially §9; Posner (2008), pp. 365–366.

judiciary, since technically separated authorities, including courts (separated from legislative and executive branches) do not necessarily imply an independent judiciary. Accordingly, a checks-and-balances system is not a prerequisite for a modern constitutional democracy, but an independent judiciary is, which is clearly demonstrated by the example of Switzerland. Thus, Posner is prejudiced and also wrong when equating unlimited judicial power with incompetency of the legislator to remove judges.[44]

Finally, we can conclude that both Barak and Posner definitely belong to the circle of the best judges, not only in their countries, but also in the entire contemporary world and that we can learn a lot from their jurisprudences in the sense of court practices. But when we observe jurisprudence as legal theory, especially as constitutional theory and theory of the interpretation of law, Barak can serve as a model constitutional theoretician and legal interpretation theorist.

Posner, unlike Barak, does not even intend to create a *comprehensive* theory or doctrine on law, or interpretation of law, or judiciary, or even their cultural, civilizational and spiritual environment, although as a prolific legal writer he has touched upon many different social spheres. And as a highly educated and knowledgeable person, he has left us many lucid and sharp observations, insights and descriptions even in areas beyond the judiciary and law. He has also left us several intellectual *actings out*, one of which is his review of Barak's *Judge in a Democracy*; nevertheless, the critical analysis of this review has resulted in further insights, so we owe him gratitude for those *actings out* as well.

The unity and harmony of Barak's achievements in legal theory and practice, in which his practical results still exceed the theoretical ones, on the one side, and our critique of Posner's critique of Barak, on the other, have provided us with an important new insight that Barak himself failed to make. We have gained it precisely by critically reviewing Posner's criticism of Barak, and the insight can be expressed in somewhat contemporized Iheringian way: The struggle for law in our time should not under any circumstances be reduced to the struggle for a constitution—either in an activist or restrained manner—since a struggle for law should be the struggle for *constitutionalism* by means of constitution, laws, and especially practice of knowledgeable, independent and honorable judiciary, among other means. And both activists and those who are restrained can provide considerable assistance in that struggle, but they can also considerably hinder it. This is precisely why neither activism nor restraint are important *per se*. What is important is the societal and especially judges' attitude towards constitutionalism.

[44]More detailed explication and explanation on this in Hasanbegović (2016, 2018).

References

*** (Critique on Posner), *Federal Judge: 'US Constitution Is Outdated, Judges Should Stop Studying It'*, June 2016. http://www.mediaite.com/online/federal-judge-u-s-constitution-is-outdated-judges-should-stop-studying-it/; or elsewhere under federal-judge-u-s-constitution-is-outdated-judges-should-stop-studying-it

Aquinas T, Summa theologiae, De lege, Available online http://www.corpusthomisticum.org/sth2095.html; or other English translations available online: http://www.summatheologica.info/summa/questions/?q=214&a=1086

Aristotle (1934) Nicomachean ethics. In: Rackham H (ed) Loeb classical library. Harvard University Press, Cambridge

Australian Communist Party v. Commonwealth (1951) 83 CLR 1 AustLII, http://www.austlii.edu.au/au/cases/cth/HCA/1951/5.html

Bacon F (1884) The works of Francis Bacon, Volume I: essays, LVI essay: of judicature, ed. Also available online at https://en.wikisource.org/wiki/The_Works_of_Francis_Bacon,_Volume_1/Essays/Of_Judicature

Barak A (2005) Purposive interpretation in law (trans: Hebrew by Sari Bashi). Princeton University Press, Princeton

Barak A (2006) The judge in a democracy. Princeton University Press, Princeton

Barak A (2012) Proportionality: constitutional rights and their limitations (trans: Hebrew by Doron Kalir). Cambridge University Press, Cambridge

Barton J (2014) Ethics in ancient Israel. Oxford University Press, Oxford

Bin-Nun A (1990) In: Furman DC (ed) The law of the state of Israel: an introduction [Einfuerung in das Recht des Staats Israel] (1983[1]) (trans: Menachem Eichelberg). Rubin Mass Ltd, Jerusalem. updated and approved by the author

Blackstone W (1876) Commentaries on the laws of England. John Murray, (1765[1]), London

Bodin J (1576) Les Six livres de la République, un abrégé du texte de l'édition de Paris de 1583, par Gérard Mairet. LGF, Paris

Bonventre VM (2005) [Issues facing the judiciary –] Judicial activism, Judges' speech, and merit selection: conventional wisdom and nonsense. Albany Law Rev 68(1/6):557–576

Bowen CD (1957) The Lion and the throne: the life and times of Sir Edward Coke (1552-1634). Little, Brown, and Company, Boston

Boyer AD (2003) Sir Edward Coke and the Elizabethan Age. Stanford University Press, Stanford

Boynton RS (20 January 2002) "Sounding Off", a review of Richard Posner's public intellectuals: a study of decline. In: The Washington Post Book World, http://www.robertboynton.com/articleDisplay.php?article_id=75

Campbell J (1849) The lives of the Chief Justices of England, vol 1. John Murray, London, also available online at https://archive.org/stream/liveschiefjusti06campgoog#page/n261/mode/2up

Canon BC (1983) Defining the dimensions of judicial activism. Judicature 66(6):236–247

Cicero MT (1928) De legibus (trans: Keyes CW). Loeb Classical Library/Harvard University Press, Cambridge

Cicero MT (1949) De inventione (trans: Harry Mortimer Hubbell). Loeb Classical Library/William Heinemann Ltd/Harvard University Press, London/Cambridge

Cohen A, Susser B (2000) Israel and the politics of Jewish identity: the secular-religious impasse. Johns Hopkins University Press, Baltimore

Coke E (November 1607) Prohibitions del Roy. Also available online at http://www.bailii.org/ew/cases/EWHC/KB/1607/J23.html

Coke E (1738a) The reports of Sir Edward Coke, Kt. in English, in Thirteen Parts Compleat (with References to All the Ancient and Modern Books of the Law), London, In the Savoy: Printed by E. and R. Nutt, and R. Gosling, for R. Gosling, the George Wythe Collection – also available online at http://lawlibrary.wm.edu/wythepedia/index.php/Reports_of_Sir_Edward_Coke

Coke E (1738b) The Reports of Sir Edward Coke, Part VII, 4a, Calvin's Case, also available online at http://files.libertyfund.org/files/911/0462-01_LFeBk.pdf

Coke E (1738c) The Reports of Sir Edward Coke, Prohibitions del Roy, 12 Co. Rep. 63, also available online at http://www.uniset.ca/other/cs4/77ER1342.html
Coke E (2003a) In: Sheppard S (ed) The selected writings and speeches of Sir Edward Coke, 3 volumes. Liberty Fund, Indianapolis, also available online at http://oll.libertyfund.org/titles/911
Coke E (2003b) The speech on the 15th of May 1628 in the house of commons. In: Sir Edward Coke (ed) The selected writings and speeches of Sir Edward Coke, vol 1, Also available online at http://oll.libertyfund.org/titles/911
Coogan MD (2009) A brief introduction to the old testament: the Hebrew Bible in its context. Oxford University Press, Oxford
Corpus iuris civilis, (Latin edition), Hrsg. von Mommsen und Hildesheim, 1889[1], or Paul Krüger, Theodor Mommsen, Rudolf Schöll, Wilhelm Kroll, Cambridge UK, Cambridge University Press, 2014; available online https://archive.org/details/corpusjuriscivil00krueuoft
Corwin ES (2014) The doctrine of judicial review: its legal and historical basis and other essays. Transaction Publishers, Piscataway
Cross FB, Lindquist SA (2007) The scientific study of judicial activism. Minnesota Law Rev 6 (15):1752–1784
de Bracton H (1968–1977) De Legibus et Consuetudinibus Angliae (On the Laws and Customs of England), 1235–1260. In: Woodbine GE (ed) 4 volumes (trans: Thorne SE). Publications of the Selden Society, London. reprint. Buffalo, W.S. Hein, 1997
de Bracton H, De Legibus et Consuetudinibus Angliae (On the Laws and Customs of England), 1235–1260, Available online in Latin, with English translation at http://bracton.law.harvard.edu/Framed/mframe.htm
Dr. Bonham's Case, the entry at Wikipedia, https://en.wikipedia.org/wiki/Dr._Bonham%27s_Case#cite_ref-11
Đurić M (2009) Ideja prirodnog prava kod grčkih sofista [The idea of natural law by Greek Sophists], (1956[1]). In: Sabrani spisi Mihaila Đurića [Collected Writings of Mihailo Đurić], knjiga I. Službeni glasnik & Pravni fakultet u Beogradu, Beograd
Fehrenbacher DE (1989) Constitutions and constitutionalism in the slaveholding South. University of Georgia Press, Athens
Fellman D (1973/1974) Constitutionalism. In: Wiener PP (ed) Dictionary of the History of Ideas: studies of selected pivotal ideas, vol 1. Scribner, New York, pp 485–492
Gaunt J (May 2015) "Magna Charta is such a fellow that he will have no sovereign.": Five Knights for Freedom: The Story of the Petition of Right 1628, pp. 1–13, available only online at the *Falcon Chambers* website http://www.falcon-chambers.com/images/uploads/articles/JG_-_Magna-Carta.pdf
Geffcken J (1923) Die griechische Aufklärung. Neue Jahrbücher für das klassische Altertum (51–52):15–31
Gordon S (1999) Controlling the State: constitutionalism from ancient athens to today. Harvard University Press, Cambridge
Green C (2009) An intellectual history of judicial activism. Emory Law J 58(5):1195–1263
Hanisch T (2010) La puissance de juger chez Montesquieu face à la tradition juridique anglaise. Annuaire de l'Institut Michel Villey 2:131–165
Hasanbegović J (1988) Perelmanova pravna logika kao nova retorika [Perelman's Legal Logic as New Rhetoric]. IICSSO, Beograd, (1986[1])
Hasanbegović J (2018) "O tri principa – legitimitetu, *checks and balances* i vladavini prava tj. pravnoj državi – i njihovoj (i)relevantnosti za valjano pravosuđe [On Three Principles – Legitimacy, Checks and Balances, and Rule of Law – and Their (Ir)Relevance for a Good Judiciary]" & "Constituional Amendments Draft on the Judiciary and Prosecutor Office: Towards an Independent Judiciary in Serbia or in the Opposite Direction". In: Testimony – Preparation for the Changes to the 2006 Constitution and the Legal Profession. Judges' Association of Serbia, Belgrade, pp 310–317. (in Serbian part of the book) & pp 263–274 (in English part of the book)

Hasanbegović J (2016) Why do we need fundamental rights, not only in practice, but also in theory? In: Himma KE, Spaić B (eds) Fundamental rights: justification and implementation. Eleven International Publishing, The Hague, pp 47–59

Holt JC (2010) Magna Carta, 2nd edn. Cambridge University Press, Cambridge

Hostletter J (1997) Sir Edward Coke: a force for freedom. Barry Rose Law Publishers, Chichester

Huberlan C (1968) Les mécanismes institués pour combler les lacunes de la loi. In: Perelman C (ed) Le problème des lacunes en droit. Bruylant, Bruxelles, pp 47–54

Jabareen H (June 2005) "Ignoring the 'Other': book review of 'Shofet Behevra Demokratit' ('A Judge in a Democratic Society') by Aharon Barak, Nevo Publishing, 551 pages, NIS 128 (Hebrew)", Review was first published in *Ha'aretz* newspaper on 06/17/2005, and then in *Adalah's Newsletter*, vol. 14, Also available online https://www.adalah.org/uploads/oldfiles/newsletter/eng/jun05/rev.pdf

Jacobsohn GJ (1994) Apple of Gold: constitutionalism in Israel and the United States. Princeton, Princeton University Press

Johnson CW (1845) The life of Sir Edward Coke, Lord Chief Justice of England in the Reign of James I: with memoirs of his contemporaries. Henry Colburn, London, in 2 volumes, also available online at https://archive.org/details/lifeofsiredwardc01john, https://archive.org/details/lifeofsiredwardc02john

Kennedy H (14 May 2010) Anthony, Address at Forum Club of the Palm Beaches, Florida. Available at http://www.c-span.org/video/?293521-1/justice-kennedy-remarks-supreme-court

Kmiec KD (2004) The origin and current meanings of 'Judicial Activism'. California Law Rev 92 (5):1441–1477

Košutić B (1973) Sudska presuda kao izvor prava [Judicial decision as source of law]. Savremena administracija, Beograd

Košutić BP, Hasanbegović J, Mirić MK, Marinković T, Spaić B, Kršljanin N, Vukotić M, Eror V (2016) Aron Barak: Sudija i teoretičar prava [Aharon Barak: judge and legal theorist]. Srpsko udruženje za pravnu i socijalnu filozofiju & Dosije Studio, Beograd

Lewis FP (1999) The context of judicial activism: the endurance of the warren court legacy in a conservative age. Rowman & Littlefield, Lanham

Magna Carta Libertatum (1215*) Also available online http://www.orbilat.com/Languages/Latin/Texts/06_Medieval_period/Legal_Documents/Magna_Carta.html; official translation of Sec. 29 also available online http://www.legislation.gov.uk/aep/Edw1cc1929/25/9/section/XXIX

Maitland FW (1887) In: Maitland FW (ed) Introduction to Bracton's note-book: a collection of cases decided in the King's courts during the reign of Henry the Third, Annotated by a lawyer of that time, seemingly Henry of Bracton. C.J. Clay & Sons, London. in 3 volumes, reissued by Cambridge University Press, 2010, also available online at: https://archive.org/stream/bractonsnoteboo00maitgoog#page/n64/mode/2up

Marbury v. Madison, 5 U.S. 137 (1803), https://supreme.justia.com/cases/federal/us/5/137/.

Marinković T (2016) Barakova doktrina ciljnog tumačenja u pravu kao mogući obrazac interpretativne odanosti konstitucionalizmu [Barak's doctrine of purposive interpretation in law as a posible model of interpretative fidelity to constitutionalism]. In: Košutić BP, Hasanbegović J, Mirić MK, Marinković T, Spaić B, Kršljanin N, Vukotić M, Eror V (eds) Aron Barak: Sudija i teoretičar prava [Aharon Barak: Judge and Legal Theorist]. Srpsko udruženje za pravnu i socijalnu filozofiju & Dosije Studio, Beograd, pp 96–115

Mazie SV (2006) Israel's higher law: religion and liberal democracy in the Jewish State. Lexington Books, Lanham

Medina B (June 2007) "Four Myths of Judicial Review: A Response to Richard Posner's Criticism of Aharon Barak's Judicial Activism", also published in *Harvard International Law Journal*, vol. 49 – August 16, 2007, see http://law.huji.ac.il/upload/Medina_response_to_Posner1.pdf

Montesquieu C (1914) The spirit of laws (trans: Thomas Nugent), revised by J. V. Prichard, based on a public domain edition published in 1914. G. Bell & Sons, Ltd, London, rendered into HTML and text by Jon Roland of the Constitution Society; also available online at http://www.constitution.org/cm/sol.htm

Montesquieu C (1995) De l'Esprit des lois, (1748[1]). Gallimard, Paris
Ockham, William of, *Dialogus*, (1332-1347*, 1476[1]), available online at http://www.britac.ac.uk/pubs/dialogus/w32d1atx.html
Parloff R (10 January 2000) "The Negotiator: No one doubts that Richard Posner is a brilliant judge and...", *Fortune Magazine*, http://archive.fortune.com/magazines/fortune/fortune_archive/2000/01/10/271747/index.htm
Pascal B (1969) Pensées, (1660[1]). In: Pascal B (ed) Œuvres complètes. Pléiade, Paris
Patrick JJ, Pious RM, Ritchie DA (2001) Judicial review. In: The Oxford Guide to the United States Government. Oxford University Press, New York, pp 348–351
Perelman C (1976a) Le problème des lacunes en droit. In: Perelman C (ed) Droit, morale et philosophie. L.G.D.J, Paris, pp 129–131
Perelman C (1976b) Logique juridique: Nouvelle rhétorique. Dalloz, Paris
Pollock F, Maitland FW (eds) (2010) The History of English Law before the Time of Edward I, 1895[1], reprint of 2nd edition, with a selected bibliography and notes by Professor S.F. Milsom. Liberty Fund, Indianapolis, in 2 volumes, also available online at http://oll.libertyfund.org/titles/pollock-the-history-of-english-law-before-the-time-of-edward-i-2-vols
Posner RA (23 April 2007) "Enlightened Despot". In: The New Republic, https://newrepublic.com/article/60919/enlightened-despot
Posner RA (2008) How judges think. Harvard University Press, Cambridge
Posner RA (2010) How judges think. Harvard University Press, first paperback edition, Cambridge
Posner RA Law school professors need more practical experience & US constitution is outdated, judges should stop studying it, at *Slate* blog in June 2016. http://www.slate.com/articles/news_and_politics/the_breakfast_table/features/2016/supreme_court_breakfast_table_for_june_2016/law_school_professors_need_more_practical_experience.html?wpsrc=sh_all_mob_tw_top
Prochazka R (2002) Mission accomplished: on founding constitutional adjudication in central Europe. Central European University Press, Budapest
Roberts C (2004) Founding mothers: the women who raised Our Nation. William Morrow/HarperCollins Publishers, New York
Roosevelt K (2006) The Myth of judicial activism: making sense of Supreme Court decisions. Yale University Press, New Haven
Rutherford S (1644) Lex Rex, or the law and the prince, London, also available online at http://www.portagepub.com/dl/caa/sr-lexrex17.pdf
Sadurski W (ed) (2003) Constitutional justice, East and West: democratic legitimacy and constitutional courts in post-comunist Europe in a comparative perspective. Kluwer, The Hague
Segev J (2007) Who needs a constitution? In defense of the non-decision constitution-making tactic in Israel. Albany Law Rev 70:409–489
Smilov D (2004) The character and legitimacy of constitutional review: Eastern European perspectives. Int J Constit Law 2(1):177–194
Spaić B (2016) Institucionalno rješavanje problema semantičke neodređenosti u pravnom tumačenju [Institutional Solution for Semantically Undetermined Problems in Legal Interpretation]. In: Spaić B, Banović D (eds) Savremeni problemi pravne i političke filozofije [Contemporary Problems of Legal and Political Philosophy]. Šahinpašić, Sarajevo, pp 121–147
Tamanaha BZ (2010) Beyond the formalist-realist divide: the role of politics in judging. Princeton University Press, Princeton
The Bible, Old Testament, also available online, e.g. at https://www.kingjamesbibleonline.org/
Turner RV (2003) Magna Carta. Longman, London
Unger P (2014) Empty ideas: a critique of analytic philosophy. Oxford University Press, Oxford
Wallace C (interviewer), Olson T (interviewee) (8 August 2010) "Ted Olson on Debate Over Judicial Activism and Same-Sex Marriage", http://www.foxnews.com/on-air/fox-news-sunday/transcript/ted-olson-debate-over-judicial-activism-and-same-sex-marriage#p//v/924499914001

Waluchow W (Spring 2014 Edition) "Constitutionalism". In: Zalta EN (ed) The Stanford encyclopedia of philosophy, http://plato.stanford.edu/archives/spr2014/entries/constitutionalism/
Williams I (2006) Dr. Bonham's Case and 'void' statutes. J Legal History 27(2):111–128

Jasminka Hasanbegović (University of Belgrade) is professor of Jurisprudence at the University of Belgrade Faculty of Law. Her publications focus the traditions of rhetoric and topic, with a special emphasis on the work of Chaim Perelman.

An Exercise in Legal Realism

Riccardo Guastini

Abstract This paper is an exercise in legal realism. I shall argue in favour of seven purely realistic theses, concerning namely: (1) the relationship between legal realism and legal positivism; (2) the concept of validity; (3) the theory of interpretation; (4) the ontology of law; (5) the epistemology of legal cognition; (6) the nature of the so-called rule of recognition; (7) the concept of obligation.

1 Introduction

This paper is an exercise in legal realism. However, I will not even try to present a comprehensive picture of legal realism. I shall confine myself to arguing, in a straightforward way, in favour of seven purely realistic theses.

2 Legal Positivism

I shall begin by discussing a mostly "domestic" issue,[1] related to Italian literature. Beyond its domestic character, it gives me the opportunity to clarify some basic features of legal realism (and legal positivism too).

In Italian legal-philosophical literature, legal realism is often distinguished from and contrasted to legal positivism.[2] This view can be explained only by an odd and narrow concept of legal positivism, identified more or less with the doctrines of

[1]Not only domestic, however: see Leiter (2007), esp. 59 ff.

[2]See e.g. Bobbio (1961a), p. 141 ff:, Pattaro (1971); Jori (1987). See also Barrère Unzueta (1990), ch. 3.

R. Guastini (✉)
University of Genova, Tarello Institute for Legal Philosophy, Genova, Italy
e-mail: guastini@unige.it

P. Chiassoni, B. Spaić (eds.), *Judges and Adjudication in Constitutional Democracies: A View from Legal Realism*, Law and Philosophy Library 135,
https://doi.org/10.1007/978-3-030-58186-2_5

nineteenth century continental legal scholars—who were used to identify the law in force with the set of normative sentences (especially: codes) enacted by the law-giving authorities, assumed such set of sentences to be complete (gapless) and consistent, and moreover conceived legal interpretation as a merely cognitive enterprise (Bobbio 1961a, b, pt. 2).

Nowadays, however, this is widely considered as a misleading account of legal positivism (Ross 1963; Bulygin 2007). Rather, legal positivism is generally regarded as a methodological attitude toward the law. Its main theses are the following.

1. First, legal positivism, properly understood, amounts to deny the existence of so-called natural law (however conceived), since according to legal positivism law is a human artefact. This is true for whatever form of legal positivism. There are no norms in the very nature of "things" or human relationships—no norm exists without a human act of normative creation. As Kelsen (echoing W. Dubislav) rightly says: "Kein Imperativ ohne Imperator", that is, no command without anyone commanding (Kelsen 1965, p. 237).[3]

In other words, as stated by Hume, no norms can (logically) flow from facts or knowledge of facts, no normative sentence may be logically derived from a set of purely cognitive premises, such as propositions describing the nature (or any other kind of facts whatsoever). Norms can only stem from those human acts that enact—"posit"—them by uttering normative sentences.

This does not imply—contrary to Kelsen (1965)—that a norm cannot be logically entailed by other norms. This is simply meant to underline that deducing is not deciding; thus, an entailed norm comes to "legal existence", that is, acquires membership in a legal system, only when it is actually "posited" by a law-creating agency (see Alchourrón and Bulygin 1989).

By the way, this formulation of the no-natural-law thesis is *not* equivalent to the so-called "social sources thesis". From the standpoint of legal positivism, that law is (or stems from) some kind of social fact is a matter of course. But the "social sources thesis" is a quite unhappy way to state this point. This is so for at least two reasons. On the one hand, such a thesis suggests (or seems to suggest) law to be a set of "social rules" (in Hart's parlance), that is, customary rules – on the contrary, with the exception of international law, modern (state) law is essentially a set of "posited" rules, issued by some sort of "sovereign" authority. On the other hand, the "social sources" thesis looks compatible with a form of the natural law doctrine, namely, the doctrine of the so-called "variable natural law", according to which law does not stems (only) from voluntary human acts, but (also) flows spontaneously from "society", "social relationships", "social conscience", "Volksgeist", or the like, and changes accordingly over time.

2. Second, the core of legal positivism, since Bentham and Austin, is the distinction between expository and censorial jurisprudence—that is, between the law as it

[3]According to legal positivism, the so-called "natural law", is not law properly understood, but a critical moraity.

actually is and the law as it ought to be (according to some standard of evaluation).[4] Describing the existing law and evaluating it are two different and independent intellectual enterprises.[5]

3. Third, as a consequence, no "objective" obligation to obey the law can exist—the knowledge of legal norms does not involve any obligation to obey them. Sure, obedience is what lawmakers demand, but (contrary to Kelsen's view) no binding force, no obligation to obey, is conceptually entailed by the very existence or legal validity of a norm. Obedience presupposes not only cognition, or "recognition", but also axiological acceptance by the addressees.[6]

All such three features of legal positivism (properly understood) are shared by legal realism. Legal realism is an openly positivistic view about the law. Not all positivist legal scholars are realist, but all realists are positivists.

3 Validity

The third feature of legal positivism introduced in the preceding section deserves some development.

A widely accepted unrealistic view—that can be traced back to Kelsen (1934, 1960)—is that any valid norm is *thereby* binding, obligatory for its addressees. Since validity is nothing but binding force. If a rule R states, for example,

(R) Income taxes ought to be paid,

the validity judgment about this rule will be

(VJ1) The rule R is valid.

But, since validity is conceptually equivalent to bindingness, (VJ1) is equivalent, in turn, to a sentence stating that the same rule is obligatory:

(VJ2) The rule R ought to be obeyed.

This view—sharply criticized by Ross (1961)—is somehow astonishing. The content of the obligation imposed by (VJ2) is clearly nothing but obedience to (R), that is, the very same behaviour commanded by (R.) Hence, the difference between (R) and (VJ2), if any, does not lie in the behaviour requested—it can only lie in the nature of the obligation at hand. If the *legal* obligation stated by (R) is paying income taxes, this further obligation stated by (VJ2) cannot be anything other than a *non-legal* obligation, hence a moral or political one.

---

[4]Bentham (1780), p. 293 f.; Austin (1879), p. I, 220. See Chiassoni (2016), ch.s 1 and 2.

[5]By the way, it is precisely this feature of legal positivism that is currently refused by non-positivist legal scholars. See e.g. Atienza and Ruiz Manero (2009).

[6]"According to the non-cognitive view, acceptance is constitutive" of binding force (Ross 1968, p. 61).

A different argument to state the same point is the following. If every legal norm is obligatory, binding, then the law as a whole is binding—there is an obligation to obey the law in general, *the law as such*. Now, the sentence "The law ought to be obeyed" is a meta-linguistic sentence, whose object-language is the law. Hence, the obligation to obey the law cannot be—for purely logical reasons—a *legal* obligation: it is necessarily a *meta-legal* obligation, an obligation with respect to the law. In other words, it must be some sort of moral or political obligation (Guastini 2016).

The thesis according to which there is a moral obligation to obey the law, however, is distinctive of the so-called "ideological" or "ethical" legal positivism—a moral (or political) doctrine very close to natural law—that has nothing to do with legal positivism properly understood, especially in its realistic version (Bobbio 1961a, ch. 7; Ross 1961).

Moreover, the sentence (VJ2) does not seem to allow for any descriptive interpretation—it is a manifestly prescriptive sentence, since it imposes an obligation. Hence, it has no truth-value. Being prescriptive—neither true nor false—it has no place within "expository jurisprudence", that is, a scientific (descriptive) discourse about the law. Admitting prescriptive sentences in legal-scientific discourse is incompatible with the scientific program of legal positivism, especially in its realistic version.

4 Interpretation

Nowadays—after Hart's *Concept of Law*—the predominant view as to legal interpretation runs more or less like this.[7]

Legal texts are framed in natural languages. In natural languages meaning is determined by actual linguistic conventions. Therefore each legal text has an objective meaning so determined.[8] However, legal texts are formulated by means of "general classifying terms" (that is, predicates in the logical sense: terms that denote classes), and such terms are fatally vague or open textured. As a consequence, given any rule whatsoever, there are cases that surely fall under its scope, as well as cases that do not. But, side by side with such "easy" cases, there are also "hard", marginal, cases to which the application of the rule is dubious and disputable. In easy cases judges have no interpretive discretion. Hence in such cases one can distinguish between legally correct and incorrect interpretations. In hard cases, on the contrary, the chosen interpretation is the result of a discretionary decision about the extension

[7]See e.g. Hart (1961), ch, 7; Carrió (1994), p. 49 ff.; Bulygin (1995). Some criticism in Guastini (2011).

[8]This view has a tacit prescriptive implication: legal texts ought to be interpreted according to the dictionary and syntax of the natural language in which they are formulated. But why should not one interpret, for example, according to the (supposed) intention of the lawgiving authorities? And, moreover, what should not one use the whole panoply of interpretive arguments, such as *a contrariis*, *a simili*, systemic coherence, and so on?

or reference of the concepts expressed by general terms, in such a way that there is no room for correctness or incorrectness judgments.

To fully appreciate this theory one must pay attention most of all to what it *does not* say.

First, this theory has no definite view as to juristic (legal scholars') interpretation—it is focused only on judicial interpretation. This is a serious shortcoming, for two main reasons. On the one hand, juristic and judicial interpretations deserve separate accounts since they are not necessarily identical from the point of view of logical analysis: for example, legal scholars' interpretation does not involve the solution of any particular case, while judicial interpretation necessarily does; judges must solve the ambiguity and vagueness of legal texts, they cannot confine themselves to detecting them impartially, while academic jurists can; etc. On the other hand, it is legal scholars who equip judges with concepts, doctrines, interpretive tools, forms of reasoning—as a matter of fact, the interpretive and dogmatic practice of legal scholarship conditions the very *forma mentis* of judges. Judicial interpretation is biased by legal dogmatics and cannot be understood without reference to it.[9]

Second, and more important, the theory at hand is focused on the issue whether a (previously identified) rule applies to a particular situation or not. This way, the theory completely overlooks the previous identification of the rule as such, hence the central features of judicial and, most of all, juristic job, that is (a) text-oriented interpretation ("in abstracto", that is, with no reference to particular cases) and (b) the construction of unexpressed, unformulated, rules in order to fill gaps, concretize principles, and so on (Guastini 2013).

1. *Text-oriented interpretation*. Before asking whether a given rule is, or is not, applicable to a particular case, one has to identify the rule at stake. The identification of the rule (or rules) expressed by a legal text is no matter of subsumption of a specified case under the extension of a concept—it is a matter of deciding the meaning of a complete normative sentence. In most cases, one and the same normative sentence is liable to different and competing meaning-ascriptions—depending on the interpretive technique to which it is submitted, on the competing juristic doctrines on the matter, on the different moral feelings of interpreters—in such a way that different rules can be derived from it. From a logical (not psychological) point of view, subsumption presupposes a decision "in abstracto" about the meaning-content of legal texts.

Just an example. Article 13.1 of the French Constitution (1958) states: "The President of the Republic shall sign the ordinances and decrees deliberated upon in the Council of Ministers". Does it mean that the President has the power to sign those ordinances and decrees, or that he/she has the obligation to sign? There is no problem of open texture, no problem of subsumption, here: in such circumstances interpreters are faced with a completely different issue—not the application of a rule

[9]Tarello (1968).

to a definite case, but the very identification of the rule itself (Troper 1994, p. 275 ff.).

But even the silly example usually put forward by the followers of the mentioned theory can be used to depict the difference between interpreting a text "in abstracto" and subsuming a case under a (previously identified) rule. "No vehicle in the park", said the law-giver. All right: cars and trucks are certainly included in the scope of the rule. But what about ambulances? If the sentence is understood literally, then the rule prohibits the entering of "vehicles" with no further specification—ambulances are not admitted. But the same sentence may be interpreted (with the aid of a counter-factual sentence pointing at the supposed intention of the lawgiver) as expressing a different rule, referring to "vehicles except ambulances"—in such a way that ambulances are admitted in the park. The problem is not subsuming or not ambulances under the concept of "vehicle", since, no doubt, they are vehicles. The problem is identifying the very content of the rule to be applied.

2. *Construction of unexpressed rules*. By the way, the most (and primary) part of juristic and judicial job consists in a great deal of inferential operations by means of which new rules, that the lawgivers never formulated, are added to the legal system. Such unexpressed rules are usually labelled as "implicit", but they are not implicit in the strict (that is, logical) sense since they are derived from explicit rules by means of non-deductive arguments.

Just one simple example, in view of clarifying what I mean by "unexpressed rule". According to Justice Marshall (*Marbury,* 1803):[10] "a legislative act contrary to the constitution is not law [. . .]. Certainly all those who have framed written constitutions contemplate them as forming the fundamental and paramount law of the nation, and, consequently, the theory of such government must be that an act of the legislature, repugnant to the constitution, is void". Justice Marshall assumes that, according to the intention of the framers, the Constitution is superior to (more valued than) legislative acts, and derives from such a "theoretical" assumption two outstanding normative consequences—first, any legislative act contrary to the constitution is void; second, the Court is entitled to declare such an act void. Both consequences are but unexpressed rules, that have no counterpart in the constitutional text and that the Supreme Court is adding to the Constitution.[11]

Thus, the dominant view as to legal interpretation is completely blind about the very core of legal interpretation (and reasoning). It assumes interpreting, ascribing meaning to legal texts, to be a cognitive (or mainly cognitive) activity, that depends on accepted linguistic conventions—the only room for interpretive discretion stems from the vagueness (the open texture) of predicates. This is a quite unrealistic view. And as matter of fact it is unsound.

[10] *Marbury v. Madison*, 5 U.S. (1 Cranch) 137, 2 L.Ed. 60.

[11] See Troper (2011), p. 139 ff.

The realistic view about legal interpretation is that the law, understood as a set of rules, is the result of juristic and judicial interpretation and construction of legal texts.

5 Ontology

According to an unrealistic view, widespread especially among legal philosophers, law is a set of abstract entities such as rules (or norms) or even a set of enigmatic deontic (or Hohfeldian) entities such as obligations and rights.

Thus, accounting for the law in force would consist precisely in describing the content of rules, and the proper way to do this would be by means of deontic sentences, that is, sentences iterating like an echo the rules they refer to and/or describing the deontic properties of actions: "It is obligatory that *p*", "It is prohibited that *q*", etc.[12]

From a realistic—empiricist—point of view, on the contrary, law is but a set of (quite peculiar) facts, namely linguistic utterances and interpretive practices: the linguistic utterances of the law-giving authorities and the interpretive practices of legal scholars and judges.

Accordingly, accounting for the law in force may consist either in cognitive interpretation or in descriptive meta-jurisprudence.

(a) Cognitive interpretation is the uncommitted analysis of the normative sentences enacted by the lawgivers, with a view to detecting their plausible meanings in the light of existing linguistic conventions, interpretive methods, juristic theories, and past judicial decisions (if any).
(b) Descriptive meta-jurisprudence, in turn, consists in analysing and accounting for past judicial decisions.

Both cognitive interpretation and descriptive meta-jurisprudence are meant to predicting (or, better, attempting to predict) future judicial decisions.

From this standpoint, the so-called "normative propositions"—the propositions by which jurists describe[13] the law in force—are not (they cannot be) deontic sentences about the normative qualification of behaviour ("It is obligatory that *p*" or the like). They are true or false *propositions* (in the logical sense): "normative" because of their object, not because of their normative inferential capacity—they do not admit any normative or practical inference (Bulygin 1981, 1982).

Normative propositions—according to their (either manifest or concealed) logical form—are existential propositions about rules or norms, in the sense that they state

[12]Once more: Kelsen (1934, 1960). I will get back later to this point, when discussing the so-called "internal point of view".

[13]Sometimes they do, although this is not the core of legal scholarship—in most cases jurists do not describe the law, but contribute to frame it.

the existence of rules *within* a given legal system, their membership in the system. For example: "The rule 'It is obligatory that *p*' exists (is in force) in the legal system S". In such a proposition, the rule is not stated or iterated, but mentioned in inverted commas. From such a proposition alone no one can validly infer that *p* ought to be done.

The truth condition of such propositions is the prevailing interpretive practice of jurists and applying practice of judges (Ross 1958). In other words, normative propositions are but pieces of descriptive meta-jurisprudence.

6 Legal Cognition

According to a quite unrealistic view, no significant cognition of law is possible from the so-called "external" point of view, that is from the standpoint of those uncommitted people (either jurists or laymen) who do not "participate" to the legal game and limit themselves to observing the actual behaviour (the linguistic behaviour included) of "participants". No genuine cognition, no sound description, of law is possible unless one assumes the "internal" point of view. Such a point of view, however, presupposes acceptance of the law itself: at least, acceptance of the ultimate "rule of recognition" by which the valid rules of the legal system at stake are identified. Acceptance is conceived as a necessary requisite for taking cognizance of the law (Hart 1961; Scarpelli 1965).

No need to say that "validity" in this context—as in Kelsen's pure theory of law—entails (or amounts to) binding force: a valid rule is a rule that ought to be obeyed. Hence it is not surprising at all that the supporters of the internal point view maintain that so-called "internal statements" are committed sentences by which people approve and/or criticize behaviours by reference to the rules of the system, make claims justified by such rules, and so forth. This amounts to say that the internal point of view is the standpoint not of "expository jurisprudence" (in Bentham's parlance), but of lawyers and judges.

So, it is quite evident that internal statements do not "bear upon" rules, do not describe them—they *apply* rules. They are normative in character and, therefore, have no truth-values (Bulygin 1981, 1982). Hence, they have no place in a "scientific", axiologically neutral, description of the law in force. Apparently the supporters of the internal-point-of-view thesis are unable to distinguish between genuine expository jurisprudence—"legal science" in Continental parlance—and legal dogmatics, the latter being a practice "internal" to the law, quite different from its detached description.

By the way, the view at stake has a troubling natural-law shade, since it tacitly assumes the intrinsic bindingness of law as such—the so-called "normativity of law". As I already said, such an assumption is the core of "ethical" or "ideological" positivism. But, at the same time, this assumption is shared by natural law doctrine: *lex iniusta non est lex*—positive law incompatible with natural law is no law at all, which means that it does not deserve obedience, while "genuine" law is, by definition, just, and that means that it demands obedience.

The realistic view on the matter is that the only genuine uncommitted cognition of the law is purely "external". Cognitive or "expository" jurisprudence can only be a set of detached statements of facts (Ross 1962). Once more: legal science is a set of normative propositions, whose truth-conditions are the prevailing interpretive practice of jurists and applying practice of judges.

It seems that the supporters of the internal-point-of-view thesis do not even conceive the very possibility of an uncommitted account of the law in force. This is proven, among other things, by their treatment of the concept of obligation, too, as we shall see in a moment.

7 Rule of Recognition

Legal cognition, the topic discussed in the preceding section, suggests a look at Hart's rule of recognition. Well, what kind of rule is this? It is no surprise that two competing views exist in legal-theoretical literature on the issue—a realistic view and an unrealistic one.

The unrealistic thesis—another feature of the internal-point-of-view theory—is that such a rule is a genuine rule, that is, a rule of behaviour, namely, a (void, incomplete) meta-rule that does not states directly what is to be done, but commands people to obey the (further) rules that will be issued by the "sovereign".[14]

As a consequence, the acceptance of such a (meta-)rule is definitely axiological and involves the disposition to comply with the sovereign's commands. This is why the point of view "internal" to the rule of recognition is normatively committed—the commands issued by the sovereign are valid law and they ought to be obeyed as the rule of recognition commands.

The realistic view, on the contrary, is that the rule of recognition is but a criterion of identification of the valid rules of the system—a conceptual rule, not a rule of behaviour (Bulygin 1976, 1991).[15]

Accordingly, the "acceptance" of the rule of recognition is a cognitive, epistemic, not axiological, move (Guastini 1998). It has no normative import. Its only purpose, as its name suggests, is "recognizing", that is, identifying valid law with the aim of describing it.

Once more: the knowledge of the existing law does not involve any obligation to obey.

---

[14]Raz (1971), p. 93; Hacker (1977), p. 23; MacCormick (1981); Ruiz Manero (1990), p. 135 ss.

[15]By the way, contrary to a suggestion of Cristina Redondo (in a private conversation), one cannot maintain that the rule of recognition accomplishes both tasks—provides an identification criterion of the law and, at the same time, commands obedience to the law so identified. This is so for a very simple reason: the criterion and the command are two *logically different* rules—a conceptual rule and a rule of behaviour respectively.

8 Obligation

The unrealistic trend about the concept of legal obligation appears in the form of refusal and criticism of Bentham's "strongly positivist conception" (Hart 1966, p. 143) on the topic.

According to Bentham, obligation is a "fictitious entity", in the sense that the word "obligation" (as well as other related words: "right", for example) is devoid of any semantic reference. So the only way to clarify its meaning is what is (nowadays) usually called a "definition in use", which amounts to translate a complete sentence where the word (the *definiendum*) does appear into a different complete sentence, provided with the same meaning, where the word does not appear. A deontic sentence such as "The subject S has the obligation to do the action A"—according to its (concealed) logical, not linguistic form—can be translated without loss of meaning into a sentence predicting that the subject S will probably be punished if he/she will not do A (Bentham 1780, ch. 3).

The supporters of the unrealistic view (namely Hart 1961, p. 79 ff.; Hart 1966) object that, in the common usage of lawyers and judges (as well as laymen), this is not at all the actual *normative* meaning of deontic sentences. According to the ordinary usage of such sentences, it is not contradictory to say that a subject has an obligation although he/she probably will not be punished in case of disobedience; moreover, it is not redundant to say that a subject has an obligation and moreover he/she is likely to incur in a sanction for disobedience. Most of all, when a judge states that someone has an obligation, it is a matter of course that he/she is not predicting his/her own decision—judicial deontic sentences are meant not to predict, but to *justify* decisions. Punishment is not the actual consequence of disobedience—rather, disobedience is the *reason* for punishment.

Accordingly, stating the existence of an obligation presupposes reference to some previously accepted rule or norm and amounts to either accounting for its content or "iterating" it like an echo (Hart 1963; Scarpelli 1967).

Prima facie, the unrealistic view looks right: it is a matter of course that the "normal" use of deontic language is normative, prescriptive. And it is surely the case when judicial (as well as legislative) language is at stake. Nonetheless, the unrealistic view is wrong.

Sure, from the *internal* point of view one can assert that, if a rule (an accepted rule) exists, then—for that reason alone—an obligation exists, since such an obligation is but the "content" of that rule. From the *external* point of view, however, can one seriously assert the same?

The conceptual issue ("What does 'obligation' mean?") hides an epistemic problem related to legal cognition: what are the truth conditions of a sentence asserting the existence of an obligation, that is the existence in the legal system of a rule imposing an obligation? Can expository jurisprudence seriously assert the existence of an obligation if non-compliance is devoid of any practical consequence?[16]

Unrealistic scholars clearly misunderstand the object and point of Bentham's "predictive theory". Bentham did not refer in any way to judicial language—when analysing the concept of obligation, he was interested in *expository* jurisprudence: in legal cognition, not in legal practice and the application of law.[17] The deontic sentences he had in mind are not sentences uttered by some legal authority—they are sentences by which an uncommitted legal scholar purports to describe the law in force.

Moreover, unrealistic scholars seem to think that judicial deontic sentences are descriptive, hence true or false, sentences. "Internal" statements, although—admittedly—normative, are supposed to *describe* the content of (previously accepted) rules. Is it the case? It seems that such statements do not describe at all, but *iterate* or *apply* the rules they presuppose (and tacitly refer to). So, the unrealistic tenet is contradictory: no sentence can be at the same time both normative and descriptive (Bulygin 1982). Moreover, a descriptive sentence about norms (a "normative *proposition*") cannot justify any prescriptive conclusion, such as a judicial decision. A prescriptive conclusion can be drawn only from normative premises.

Once more, unrealistic people seem unable to even conceive the very possibility of a neutral account of the law in force, which is the scientific program of legal realism.

References

Alchourrón CE, Bulygin E (1989) Von Wright on deontic logic and the philosophy of law. In: Bulygin E, Paulson S et al (eds) Essays in legal philosophy. Oxford University Press, Oxford, 2015

Atienza M, Ruiz Manero J (2009) Para una teoría postpositivsta del Derecho. Palestra-Temis, Lima-Bogotá

Austin J (1879) In: Campbell R (ed) Lectures on jurisprudence or the philosophy of positive law, 4th edn. John Murray, London

Barrère Unzueta MA (1990) La Escuela de Bobbio. Reglas y normas en la filosofía jurídica italiana de insipiración analítica. Tecnos, Madrid

Bentham J (1780) In: Burns JH, Hart HLA (eds) An introduction to the principles of morals and legislation. Clarendon Press, Oxford, 1996

Bobbio N (1961a) Il positivismo giuridico, 2nd edn. Giappichelli, Torino, 1996

Bobbio N (1961b) Comandi e consigli. In: Bobbio N, Greco T (eds) Studi per una teoria ganerale del diritto, 2nd edn. Giappichelli, Torino, Introduction by R. Guastini, 2012

[16]By the way, without any reference to sanction in case of disobedience, it becomes impossible to distinguish law from morality (Schauer 2015), commands from advices (Bobbio 1961b).

[17]By the way, the same holds for Holmes' view about the law as a prophecy of what courts will probably do. It is a matter of course that Holmes did not refer (literally) to "the law", in the sense of law-givers' and judges' language, but to "legal doctrine", understood as uncommitted description of the law in force.

Bulygin E (1976) On the rule of recognition. In: Bulygin E, Paulson SL et al (eds) Essays in legal philosophy. Oxford University Press, Oxford
Bulygin E (1981) Legal statements and positivism: a reply to Joseph Raz. In: Bulygin E, Paulson SL et al (eds) Essays in legal philosophy. Oxford University Press, Oxford
Bulygin E (1982) Norms, normative propositions, and legal statements. In: Bulygin E, Paulson SL et al (eds) Essays in legal philosophy. Oxford University Press, Oxford
Bulygin E (1991) Algunas consideraciones sobre los sistemas juridicos. Doxa 9:257–279
Bulygin E (1995) Cognition and interpretation of law. In: Gianformaggio L, Paulson SL (eds) Cognition and interpretation of law. Giappichelli, Torino
Bulygin E (2007) In: Chiassoni P, Guastini R, Ratti GB (eds) Il positivismo giuridico (trans: Chiassoni P, Guastini R, Ratti GB). Giuffré, Milano
Carrió GR (1994) Notas sobre derecho y lenguaje, 4th edn. Abeledo-Perrot, Buenos Aires
Chiassoni P (2016) Da Bentham a Kelsen. Sei capitoli per una storia della filosofia analitica del diritto. Giappichelli, Torino
Guastini R (1998) Conoscenza senza accettazione. In: Gianformaggio L, Jori M (eds) Scritti per Uberto Scarpelli. Giuffré, Milano
Guastini R (2011) Rule-scepticism restated. In: Green L, Leiter B (eds) Oxford studies in philosophy of law, vol 1. Oxford University Press, Oxford
Guastini R (2013) Juristenrecht. Inventing rights, obligations, and powers. In: Ferrer Beltrán J, Moreso JJ, Papayannis DM (eds) Neutrality and theory of law. Springer, Dordrecht
Guastini R (2016) "Kelsen on Validity (once more)", to be published in Ratio Juris
Hacker PMS (1977) Hart's philosophy of law. In: Hacker PMS, Raz J (eds) Law, morality, and society. Essays in honour of H.L.A. Hart. Clarendon Press, Oxford
Hart HLA (1961) In: Bulloch PA, Raz J (eds) The concept of law, 2nd edn. Clarendon Press, Oxford. with a Postscript, 1994
Hart HLA (1963) Kelsen visited. In: Hart HLA (ed) Essays in jurisprudence and philosophy. Clarendon Press, Oxford, 1983
Hart HLA (1966) Legal duty and obligation. In: Hart HLA (ed) Essays on Bentham. Jurisprudence and political theory. Clarendon Press, Oxford, 1982
Jori M (1987) Il positivismo analitico italiano prima e dopo la crisi. Giuffré, Milano
Kelsen H (1934) Introduction to the problems of legal theory (trans: Litschewski Paulson B, Paulson SL). Clarendon Press, Oxford, 1992
Kelsen H (1960) Pure theory of law (trans: Max Knight). University of California Press, Berkeley, 1967
Kelsen H (1965) Law and logic. In: Kelsen H, Weinberger O (eds) Essays in legal and moral philosophy (trans: Heath P). Reidel, Dordrecht, 1973
Leiter B (2007) Naturalizing jurisprudence. Essays on American legal realism and naturalism in legal philosophy. Oxford University Press, Oxford
MacCormick N (1981) H.L.A. Hart. Edward Arnold, London
Pattaro E (1971) Il realismo giuridico come alternativa al positivismo giuridico. Rivista internazionale di filosofia del diritto XLVIII:61–126
Raz J (1971) The identity of legal systems. In: Raz J (ed) The authority of law. Essays on law and morality. Clarendon Press, Oxford, 1979
Ross A (1958) On law and justice. Stevens & Sons, London
Ross A (1961) Validity and the conflict between legal positivism and natural law. In: Paulson SL, Litschewski Paulson B (eds) Normativity and norms. Critical perspectives on Kelsenian themes. Clarendon Press, Oxford, 1998
Ross A (1962) "Review" of H.L.A. Hart's the concept of law. Yale Law J LXXI
Ross A (1963) Giusnaturalismo contro positivismo giuridico. In: Castignone S, Guastini R (eds) Realismo giuridico e analisi del linguaggio. Testi di Karl Olivecrona e Alf Ross, 2nd edn. ECIG, Genova. (Italian trans: Siciliano S), 1990
Ross A (1968) Directives and norms. Routledge, London

Ruiz Manero J (1990) Jurisdicción y normas. Dos estudios sobre función jurisdiccional y teoría del derecho. Centro de estudios constitucionales, Madrid
Scarpelli U (1965) Cos'è il positivismo giuridico. Comunità, Milano
Scarpelli U (1967) Le proposizioni giuridiche come precetti reiterati. Rivista internazionale di filosofia del diritto XLIV:465–482
Schauer F (2015) The force of the law. Harvard University Press, Cambridge
Tarello G (1968) La semantica del neustico. Osservazioni sulla parte descrittiva degli enunciati precettivi. In: Tarello G (ed) Diritto, enunciati, usi. Studi di teoria e metateoria del diritto. Il mulino, Bologna, 1974
Troper M (1994) La signature des ordonnaces: fonctions d'une controverse. In: Troper M (ed) Pour une théorie juridique de l'État. P.U.F, Paris
Troper M (2011) Marshall, Kelsen, Barak et le sophisme constitutionnaliste. In: Troper M (ed) Le droit et la nécessité. PUF, Paris

Riccardo Guastini is emeritus professor of Jurisprudence in the University of Genoa and a permanent fellow of the Tarello Institute for Legal Philosophy. His current research interests include general jurisprudence, constitutional theory, and the theory of legal interpretation. He is co-editor of the journals *Analisi e diritto*, *Materiali per una storia della cultura giuridica*, and *Ragion pratica*. His last books include *Le fonti del diritto* (2010), *Leçons de théorie constitutionnelle* (2010), *Interpretare e argomentare* (2011), *La sintassi del diritto* (2nd ed., 2014), *Discutendo* (2017), *Filosofía del Derecho positivo* (2018).

A Causal View of Judicial Interpretation

Michel Troper

Abstract The skeptical version of the realist theory holds that judicial interpretation, performed by an authentic interpreter, is an act of the will, that interpretation cannot be true or false and is necessarily valid, whatever its content, that it is the interpreter who is the real producer of the norm and not the author of the text subject to interpretation. Such a theory faces some serious objections. According to one of the most difficult, if this were true, judges would not be bound to follow any rule; they would be free to decide according to their preferences or even their whims; their decisions would be without coherence or continuity. Yet, we see that law, even judge made law, possesses the characteristics of a system and follows certain patterns. Using the classic distinction between having an obligation and being obliged, I will show that, while judges have no obligation to issue certain decisions, they are obliged or constrained by the system. Such an answer presupposes a causal theory of law and I will then argue in favor of such a theory.

1 Introduction

Legal Realists, like other positivists seek to describe not what ought to happen according to the law, but what really happens. Regarding adjudication, they share the idea that legal reasons that judges invoke in their opinions are justifications "providing post-hoc rationales for decisions reached on other grounds" (Leiter 2011). One common argument in favor of this view is that these legal reasons refer to preexisting rules that judges pretend to apply to a case, while in fact they have produced them themselves by way of legal interpretation.

Being descriptive as opposed to prescriptive or normative a realist theory of interpretation does not recommend any particular method of interpretation. However, it does not aim at describing the meaning of some legal document, such as the

M. Troper (✉)
University Paris Nanterre, Nanterre, France

P. Chiassoni, B. Spaić (eds.), *Judges and Adjudication in Constitutional Democracies: A View from Legal Realism*, Law and Philosophy Library 135,
https://doi.org/10.1007/978-3-030-58186-2_6

constitution, a statute, an international treaty or a contract. What it describes is not a meaning but the nature of the process of interpretation, i.e. the process that legal authorities follow when they interpret legal documents.

According to realists, legal interpretation is a function not of knowledge but of the will. Some authorities like for example judges, but not exclusively judges, have been empowered to give interpretations that are legally valid not because of some correspondence with the preexisting meaning of the text but only because of its author, who is the *authentic interpreter.* Thus, a legal interpreter does not discover the meaning, but rather decides it. Realists share this view with some other positivists, such as Kelsen or Hart, who also believe that, in some cases at least, interpreters make a decision.

Nevertheless, this view comes in different versions.[1] According to the most radical, before an act of interpretation the text has no meaning at all and the legal interpreter is the true author of the norm. Some realists like to quote Hoadley *"whoever hath an absolute authority to interpret any written or spoken laws, it is he who is truly the Law-giver to all intents and purposes, and not the person who first wrote or spoke them"*. One could say the same thing in quasi Kelsenian terms: If, as Kelsen claims, a norm is the meaning of an action or of a text, deciding on the meaning amounts to deciding on the norm. Naturally, all realists do not subscribe to this radical form of rule-skepticism.

Whatever the variety, the realist view faces a number of serious objections. According to one of them, the realists tell us that courts do not make a decision by applying a preexistent rule, but without resorting to a psychological or sociological explanation, they cannot tell us how judges do decide. One should remark that Kelsen, although strongly opposed to realist theories, could very well subscribe to the realist explanation of the behavior of judges. In the same way that he would say that, although the law maker applies the constitution, the substance of the law reflects their political or moral preferences, he would agree that whenever a judge has a margin of discretion he too decides according to his moral or political preferences, which in turn can be attributed to social or psychological factors. It is thus not inconsistent with Kelsen's anti-sociological legal theory to assume that, even though actors are legally unbound, they are at the same time psychologically or socially determined. However, it is not for the legal scholar but for the political scientist or the sociologist to say what these factors are. In other words, just as other legal theorists, realists, even as they view norms as facts, are forced either to remain silent about what causes those facts or to resort to other disciplines.

Another, not altogether unrelated objection, is that realists are incapable of explaining the coherence or continuity of the jurisprudence of the courts. If it were true that legal interpreters are unbound and that they enjoy complete discretion, then they would be free to act as legislators and create law that fits their own political or moral preferences or even to act on whims or toss a coin and abandon all pretenses at following precedents. Yet, when we look at the body of case law, we find that,

[1]Guastini, *ibid.*

although there are occasional changes, it is relatively stable and coherent. In spite of dramatic political and ideological changes in France in the last 100 years, the courts have kept using the same fundamental principles in tort law or administrative law. One might certainly argue that coherence is due to the fact that legal interpreters, especially judges, form a homogeneous social group, that they have received the same education, have the same interests and share the same ideology of the rule of law.

But that is not enough because we observe similar stability and coherence in international courts where interpreters are more heterogeneous, or in countries where some judges are cynical and do not believe in the morality of the law. A realist theory would not explain why a change in the composition of courts does not bring about a rapid change in the substance of case law in the same way a change of majority in parliament leads to fundamental change. And it would not explain why courts apply or seem to apply rules or why they interpret them consistently when they could easily change their interpretation.

We thus seem to be in need of an explanation and since legal theorists cannot find it in the logic of legal reasoning they must look for a causal explanation. But they seem to be facing a dilemma: either they look for this explanation in disciplines other than legal theory and leave the job to sociologists, psychologists or political scientists; or they stick to legal theory and must confront the dominant view that a legal decision is not in a causal relation with other legal decisions, in other words that relations between norms cannot be causal.

In order to escape the dilemma, we must therefore challenge the dominant view and imagine some form of analysis that would be at the same time legal and causal. I will thus proceed in three steps: first examine Kelsen's theory on the relation between law and causality, then propose an alternative view and finally I will show that this alternative view is capable of reconciling legal and causal analysis.

2 The Dominant View: Legal Science and Causality

Most legal philosophers do not normally consider that law functions according to the principle of causality and that law could be a causal science. It is Hans Kelsen who most explicitly defended the thesis that legal science is not and cannot be a causal science. He makes a fundamental distinction between on one hand natural science, which is a causal science, and on the other hand normative science. Nature, he writes, is "a certain order of things or a system of elements that are linked by cause-effect relationships, i.e. according to a principle that is called causality". Human behavior also can be viewed as "an element of nature, i.e. as governed by the principle of causality". Therefore, when a science describes and explains human behavior in that way, as social science does, this science is not fundamentally different from the natural sciences".

However, men also make statements relating facts according to another principle, entirely different from the principle of causality. He calls that principle "imputation".

Both principles establish a link between two facts but in different ways. The principle of causality states that "If A then B", the principle of imputation that "if A then B *ought to be*".

Both principles are *a priori*. Every science constructs its object and analyzes it in the light of its own principle. But this is precisely the reason why they are so different: if we want normative science to be different from the natural sciences, we must construct its object in the light of a different principle and comprehend society as an object different from nature.

Yet, in Kelsen's theory, there is an important difference between causality and imputation, although he does not seem to be fully aware of it. The causal relation between facts is not part of nature but imposed by the human mind, but for Kelsen imputation is not a construction of legal science; it is already directly present and visible in the object itself, because it is what makes the very structure of the norm. Norm propositions, because they describe norms, have exactly the same structure "if A then B ought to be", but unlike norms, even if they are formulated with the copula "ought" they are not prescriptions, but mere descriptions of norms so that attempting to understand the meaning of this "ought", Kelsen has to come up with the strange expression of a "descriptive ought", which does not explain much.

Thus, imputation is not only the principle in the light of which legal science analyzes its object; it is present in the object of legal science, in the law itself. It is an objective reality. And since legal science describes a reality that is non causal by means of norm propositions that have the same structure and contain an ought, that science cannot be a causal science.

As already mentioned, Kelsen does not deny that there are causal relations between social or psychological facts and the will of the men who create norms. The will of men is indeed an effect of certain causes and so is the content of the norm that has been created, but these causes are entirely external to the law and legal science cannot analyze them. They are an object for sociology or psychology. Understanding these causes does not allow us to understand why a norm is valid, in other words why a norm is a norm. The will may have a cause, but the will is not the cause for the validity of the norm, which is based only on a superior norm. Similarly, the superior norm (the constitution e.g.) does not *cause* the validity of the inferior norm (the act of parliament). It is only the basis for this validity.

However, this reasoning fails if we accept as realists that norms are facts, because, if this is the case, it is conceivable to have causal relations in the law.

3 An Alternative Conception

Let us start with a metaphor. In a game of chess, there are situations when a player may choose between different moves, all of which are permitted by the rules. However, a competent player may recognize that all of those moves, save one, would inevitably bring defeat. He is under no obligation to make that one move that can save him. If he makes another move, he does not break any rule. Nevertheless, if he does make the move that will save him, he can say that he was constrained, and a competent observer can say that this was objectively the case. This type of constraint is not external to the game. An expert, analyzing the game, would not look for an explanation in the psychology, or the religious and political beliefs of the player and any other competent player would have made the same move.

The constraint therefore only comes from the situation of the game itself, and this situation is the result of all the moves that have been made so far, each being made anticipating the probable reaction from the other player, etc. One can therefore say that the constraint has been caused by the system of chess and the situation of the game at one given moment.

In the legal system as in the game of chess, we can encounter behaviors that can be viewed as consequences of a situation at a specific moment. Some constitutions are precisely based on such assumptions and seek to bring about behaviors not by way of commands, but rather by creating situations where authorities would be constrained to act in a certain manner. Take Montesquieu's model of the balance of powers, which is also that of Madison or of some of the leaders of the beginning of the French Revolution. The division of powers between the House of Commons, the House of Lords and the King is not only meant to protect civil liberty against possible attempts at despotism. By requiring the consent of three authorities, whose interests are different, for the enactment of a new law, the system guarantees that none will prevail and that laws will be made by a series of compromise, to the effect that legislation will necessarily be moderate. By preventing the King from making laws alone, the system guarantees that he will only act on the basis of a previous law, which is the very definition of political liberty, the right of everyone to be subject not to men, but to laws only. Men will behave according to the law not because they have been so ordered or because of their virtue, but because they will have no other choice. It is indeed the constitutional system that is expected to produce such results, because it is made of relations between political authorities, i.e. between empowering norms. Naturally, the system did not produce the results that Montesquieu or Madison expected, but the very construction of such models suffices to show that law makers do reason in causal terms. As Montesquieu wrote at the end of his famous chapter "on the constitution of England", "*It is not my business to examine whether the English actually enjoy this liberty, or nor: Sufficient it is for my purpose to observe, that it is established by their laws; and I inquire no further*" (Montesquieu 1750 Bk XI, chap. 6).

However, we can not only discover that the makers of a new constitution occasionally reason in causal terms, but also use causality from an external point of view as an instrument of analysis and attempt explaining actual behaviors as produced by constraints.

We could analyze in this manner all sorts of behaviors by all sorts of authority. Indeed, we find an example of such analysis in any book on the parliamentary system. It is well known that it was born out the practice of ministers in eighteenth century England resigning after a threat of impeachment or in France in the nineteenth century after a threat by the lower house of refusing to vote the budget. We have here a situation, where given the power of the lower house in England to impeach and the power of the house of Lords to punish a crime that is not or very vaguely defined the only sensible thing to do for ministers. Only later was this constraint perceived as an obligation. Similarly, in France, resignation of the cabinet is the only sensible thing when there is a serious possibility that the proposed budget be rejected (Troper 2001, pp. 147s).

It is not only political authorities that are subject to such constraints. It is also true of courts and we can explain in that manner both general patterns of behavior, but also some specific decisions.

As far as general patterns are concerned, we can observe that lower courts by and large follow the jurisprudence of higher courts. In some system this cannot be explained by saying that the lower courts are under an obligation to defer to the jurisprudence of the higher courts, because all legal systems do not have a formal rule to that effect. In France, since the Revolution, the only official source of law is statutory law, that is presumed to express the general will. Any attempt by courts, to openly create law would therefore be considered a usurpation of the legislative power and a crime. Courts used to claim to be bound by statutes only, now by the constitution, never by precedents. Thus, with few exceptions, precedents do not bind the courts and can only be used as authoritative arguments (Grzegorczyk and Troper 1997, p. 103).

Following a precedent therefore must be disguised as an application of a statute. Obviously, no statute can be applied without being interpreted, but the French Revolution assumed that interpretation amounts to law creation and established a general prohibition of judicial interpretation, which remained prevalent in the civil code, that does not contain one single article dealing with statutory interpretation. Courts then must pretend that they apply a statute without interpreting it.

If in practice, civil and criminal courts in France do follow the jurisprudence of the court of Cassation, administrative courts follow that of the Council of State, this can only be explained in factual terms. Using an oxymoron, French scholars speak of a *de facto bindingness* due to several factors. The most important is obviously the hierarchy of courts. Lower courts follow higher courts, for fear of being overruled. The influence of the hierarchy is greatest when judges are civil servants, conscious of their careers, when these careers depend in part on judgment by their superiors, and when this judgment is often based on the rate of reversal by the higher courts. As for the chess player constrained to make a certain move, it is in the best interest of lower courts to follow higher courts.

The highest courts pose a different problem. They are no more bound by their own precedents than the lower courts but being at the top of the hierarchy, they do not fear being reversed, except perhaps by the legislative power. Then why do they follow some patterns and try to be coherent rather than deciding on whims or according to their political or moral preferences, or at least to try to reconcile them with the general principles of their former doctrines?

One possible answer, for those courts that cannot select cases and must make thousands of decisions a year, is that following routine saves time and energy. Moreover, an individual member of the court cannot push in favor of a particular decision and hope to convince his colleagues just by openly saying that it corresponds to his political or moral preferences. He must use the language accepted in this context, i.e. arguments drawn from the jurisprudence of the court. And the court as a whole is also constrained by the informal rules of the game. It is in its best interest to be as coherent and predictable as possible. We may assume that the best interest of any authority is to maximize its power and that power is the capacity to influence the behavior of others. Obviously, one can influence the behavior of a larger number of people with general rules rather than with an incoherent series of particular decisions. Particular decisions only affect the parties to the case, but if third parties can be persuaded that a decision is based on a general principle that will probably remain stable, they will be able to use this principle to predict the consequences of their actions and adapt their behavior. From a normative point of view, one could say, as does Montesquieu, that being subject to general principles is the guarantee of political liberty. What he had in mind was legislation, not because the will of the lawmaker corresponds in any way to the will of the subjects, but only because laws are general and stable. But from the point of view of the court, we can see that the generality of the rules it produces, and the coherence of its jurisprudence is thus the best way for the court to influence that behavior.

On the other hand, even a supreme court is not alone in the legal environment. In a given legal system, as in several continental countries, there may be several supreme courts competing—or in the politically correct vocabulary "In dialogue"—to produce general concepts. National courts are also in "dialogue" with international or supranational courts. This constitutes a further incentive for a court to use the concepts and doctrine in a consistent manner to resist the influence of other courts. For example, the French Constitutional Council has long resisted the European Court of Justice, by using its own earlier doctrine that international treaties prevail only on statutory law but not on constitutional law.

This shows that it is possible to explain not only a general behavior of the courts, following their own precedents in easy cases, but also at least some specific decisions in hard cases. We can distinguish two types of constraints.

Firstly, constraints that result from the interaction between a specific court and other institutions, other courts or political institutions. In 2008, a constitutional amendment in France authorized the priority question of constitutionality, allowing parties to a case before a lower court, when the issue depends on the constitutionality of an applicable statute, to refer the question to the Constitutional Council, but only indirectly, through the court of Cassation or the Council of State, who act as filters and verify that the question is serious. The court of Cassation, obviously lacking enthusiasm for this new procedure that diminished its power, made in 2010 the best possible move to try and avoid it: a preliminary reference to the European Court of Justice, in the hope that the European Court would decide that the new procedure would jeopardize the supremacy of European law over domestic law, since the Constitutional Council at the time considered that the French constitution is the highest norm and abstained from making preliminary reference to the ECJ (Molfessis 2011/2).

But constraints can also arise from the context of argumentation. Here, we can even observe patterns of behavior and explain the similarity of some court decisions in different countries at different times by the similarity of argumentative situations. One good example is that of decisions manipulating the hierarchy of norms. In order to maximize their power courts must be able to invalidate norms, for example legislative norms and find a conflict with a higher norm. However there are cases when such a higher norm is not readily available and the only way then is to create it by interpreting some document and argue not only that it contains such a higher norm but also that this supremacy implies the power of the court to invalidate a lower norm. This is precisely the reasoning in Marbury arguing that (a) any constitution is higher than acts of Congress since ordinary legislation cannot amend the constitution; (b) therefore ordinary legislation in conflict with the constitution is void and it is the business of courts to invalidate it. The reasoning is flawed because while it is true that all constitutions contain some special amending procedures, not all constitutions allow courts to invalidate statutes. The former does not imply the latter. Every constitution is above legislation in a procedural sense, not in a substantive sense.

True the American constitution is above legislation in both senses, but only after Marbury has decided that courts have the power to invalidate acts of Congress. In other words, the hierarchy of norms did not exist before Marbury, but only after the court created it.

But this is not specific to the US. Already under the French monarchy, the courts called "*parlements*", decided that they had the power to review the king's legislation. In order to confront the laws with higher norms, they invoked a range of unwritten—and extremely vague—principles that, they argued, stood above the king's laws and that even the sovereign could not change.

The same happened in France in 1971. The 1958 constitution had given the Constitutional Council the power to review the conformity of statutes with the constitution. At first, statutes were only confronted with the numbered articles of the constitution, but in 1971 the Council decided that the preamble was part of the constitution. Until that date the preamble, mentioning that the French people proclaims its attachment to the declaration of the rights of man, the preamble of the 1946 constitution, was considered to be a philosophical or political statement without any binding force. By the 1971 decision, not only did it become a binding norm, but it was also promoted at the constitution level.

Similarly, a court may be constrained to build even higher levels in the hierarchy of norms. In a series of decision, the supreme court of India, in order to invalidate a constitutional amendment, decided that there were some principles forming the basic structure of the Indian constitution, that could not be subject to amendments. Several other constitutional or supreme courts later used the same reasoning.

Sometimes a court can be constrained to create a new concept because it is the only possible means that could permit to justify the decision that the court wanted to reach. In 1962, the French president de Gaulle decided to amend the constitution in order to have the president elected by universal suffrage. The normal amending procedure requires two steps. First the two houses of Parliament must both approve with a simple majority a bill proposed by the President; then in a second stage the President submits the bill to the Congress, composed of both houses sitting together. The Congress must approve the bill with a 3/5 majority. Alternatively, the President, instead of submitting the bill to the Congress, may submits it to popular referendum. In 1962, the Senate was strongly opposed to de Gaulle's proposal and would never have approved the bill. De Gaulle then decided unilaterally to bypass Parliament and submit the bill directly to a popular referendum, which he won. However, the new amendment was referred to the Constitutional Council, who declined to review it on the merits, i.e. not because the amending procedure had not been followed, but because "laws adopted by the People by referendum are the direct expression of national sovereignty", thus making a new distinction between laws adopted by the people through representatives and laws adopted by the people by referendum. Only the former can be reviewed by the council. The constitution does not make that distinction. Obviously, the Council had powerful reasons to make it. In 1962, the Council was a very young and weak institution and there is no doubt that, had they invalidated the amendment, de Gaulle would have crushed it or its members, but the best possible legal argument was that the new constitutional law was the direct expression of national sovereignty.

However, by using that argument, the Council introduced unknowingly another distinction, which the constitution does not make, between two peoples. Article 3 reads: "National sovereignty shall vest in the people, who shall exercise it through their representatives and by means of referendum". Thus, according to article 3 it is the very same people that exercises sovereignty by two different means. When the people are being represented, it is composed not only of voters, but of all citizens, included all those who cannot vote for different reasons. This is the reason why in the French legal tradition members of Parliament are not representatives of their constituencies or the electorate but of the people as a whole, why they are never subject to the control of voters, why there is an absolute presumption that they express the general will. In this tradition representation is not a relation between two entities, the representative and the represented, the represented has no will that could serve as a standard to measure the will expressed by the representative. However, when the Council decides that laws adopted by referendum are the direct expression of national sovereignty, they unwillingly refer to a different people reduced to the voters. It may very well be that this new concept of the people is more coherent with the modern views of representative democracies, but it is undoubtedly a new concept.

4 An Explanation Both Legal and Causal

We must distinguish between three different questions:

- Does the analysis of these actions or justifications amount to an explanation?
- Is the explanation causal?
- Is the explanation legal?

The first question is whether this analysis amount to an explanation? We have seen that at least some actions and some justifications provided by the actors result from situations when these actors have no other choice or when there is one or a limited number of good choices. Obviously, this analysis is only partial. What we explain is sometimes the action itself (de Gaulle's use of the referendum in 1962), sometimes only the type of arguments that actors must use. We do not explain why the American Supreme Court, or the French Constitutional Council wanted to maximize their power at a specific moment and review the constitutionality of statutes but only why they used the specific technique of playing with the hierarchy of norms.

It must be also be stressed that the question whether we have produced an explanation is different from the question of the truth of the explanation. The only question, as Davidson rightly pointed out is whether we have produced an explanation in the logical sense and this depends on what we mean by "explanation" and by "causal explanation" (Davidson 1967, pp. 691–703).

We can distinguish between two kinds of causal explanations. In a strong sense, to explain is to subsume under a general Law, like subsuming the fall of this particular apple on this particular day under the Law of gravity. The great French historian Paul Veyne therefore rightly claims that History can never be a causal science in this sense, since there are no covering laws of this type. And this is also true of legal science, because we can never come up with a covering Law similar to the Law of gravity (Veyne 1996).

However, there is another model, that of a weak causal analysis. According to Ricœur, following William Dray, a causal analysis is possible without any reference to covering Laws. It simply aims at verifying the titles of the candidates to be a cause, i.e. "its title to support its claim to occupy the place of the 'because' as an answer to the question 'why?'".[2] The test is that the factor in question must have been necessary: "without it the event to be explained, would not have happened and we must have a good reason to select this factor among all the conditions that taken together constitute the sufficient reason for the event" (Ricœur 2006, p. 225).

Dray also describes an explanation by means of reasons consisting in a reconstruction of the calculation by an agent of the means he should use in order to achieve the end he has chosen in the light of the situation where he was placed (Ricœur 2006, p. 232). Thus, explaining is showing that the agent's action was appropriate given the circumstances.

What we have provided is thus a causal explanation in that sense, because it enables us to understand why some event happened or some justification was provided. Again, the explanation may not be true, but it is an explanation.

In the world of legal constraints, we are dealing with a weak causality because we can never be certain that in a particular situation one particular move will necessarily be made. In the real world, chess players are more or less competent; sometimes they may not wish to win. Suffice it to say that if a rational player will make such move, the cause of his behavior lies in the situation of the game. On the other hand, the causal link is only indirect. The situation can cause the player to make the move only

[2]Summarized by par Ricœur (2006), pp. 225s.

because he has analyzed the situation. The move is only the consequence of his perception of the situation, the analysis and the strategic calculation he has made. Nevertheless, to the extent that we assume a totally rational player, like a computer, with no preference other than winning, we can safely eliminate from the explanation factors that are external to the system.

While we have provided an explanation without using a covering law, the explanation is nevertheless general in a sense, because we can argue that "if y is a good reason for A to do x, y would be a good reason for anyone resembling A to do x in a similar situation".

At this point, someone might object that the explanation may be causal, but not really a legal explanation, because in order to fully understand some action, we must take into account all the factors, some of which are psychological—Marbury can be partly explained by the animosity between Marshall and Jefferson- and some political. For example, the Minerva Mills decision was an episode in the political battle about an agrarian law, that Indira Gandhi wanted to promote and that the group of large landowners and members of the court strongly opposed.

However, we are not trying to give a total historical explanation, but only to show that it is possible to give an explanation pointing to a cause identified as a legal situation.

The remaining difficulty, then, is to decide what counts as "legal", but we can use at least two different tools. In some cases, the difficulty is not so great, because both the explanandum, i.e. Marbury v. Madison, and the explanans, i.e. the argument from the supremacy of the constitution as the only possible argument, present themselves as legal. In other cases, what is to be explained is an action; a specific move made by one of the actors, resigning from office, proposing a constitutional amendment for referendum, etc., we understand that he used an explicit or implicit empowering norm, taking into account the possible counteractions by other actors, on the basis of other empowering norms. We have therefore remained in a legal universe and it the situation of that universe at a given moment that we may consider to be the cause of some legal actions.

References

Davidson D (1967) Causal relations. J Philos 64:691–703

Grzegorczyk C, Troper M (1997) Precedent in France. In: MacCormick N, Summers R (eds) Interpreting precedents. A comparative study. Dartmouth, Aldershot

Leiter B (2011) Rule-skepticism restated. In: Green L, Leiter B (eds) Oxford studies in philosophy of law. Oxford University Press, Oxford

Molfessis N (2011/2) The immediate resistance of the court of cassation to the priority preliminary ruling on the issue of constitutionality. In: Pouvoirs N°137, https://www.cairn-int.info/article-E_POUV_137_0083%2D%2Dthe-immediate-resistance-of-the-court-of.htm

Montesquieu (1750) The Spirit of Laws, 1st English translation by Thomas Nugent, Bk XI, chap. 6

Ricœur P (2006) L'intrigue et le récit historique. Temps et récit, t 1. Éd. du Seuil, Paris

Troper M (2001) Le droit, la théorie du droit, l'Etat. PUF, Paris

Veyne P (1996) Comment on écrit l'histoire: texte intégral. Nouv. éd. Ed. du Seuil, Paris

Michel Troper is emeritus professor at the Université de Paris-Nanterre, where he taught Jurisprudence and Constitutional Law. His main jurisprudential interests are in epistemology of legal science, legal interpretation and theory of the State. Among his publications are *Pour une théorie juridique de l'État* (Presses universitaires de France, 1994), La *philosophie du droit* (Presses Universitaires de France, 2011).

Rule(s) of Recognition and Canons of Interpretation

Luka Burazin and Giovanni Battista Ratti

Abstract It is sometimes claimed (in Anglo-American jurisprudential literature) that the rule of recognition sets the criteria for identifying legal norms and that this, therefore, means that canons of interpretation are also part of these criteria. Such a view then faces the problem of theoretical disagreements that call into question the rule of recognition itself and legal positivistic accounts of law. The paper argues that the rule of recognition sets the criteria only for sources of law and not legal norms themselves and that a theory of interpretation that distinguishes between normative texts (sources of law) and legal norms (as meanings of legal texts) can help explain why the rule of recognition might still be conceived as a conventional rule based on the convergent practice of officials and the fact that officials sometimes disagree about the correct interpretation of legal texts.

1 Introduction

It is sometimes argued, more or less explicitly, that canons of interpretation (interpretive methods, techniques or standards) are a conceptually necessary part of the criteria of validity set by the rule of recognition. Roughly, the reasoning behind this might be the following: (a) the rule of recognition sets the criteria for identifying valid legal norms (i.e., the criteria of validity); (b) the "what is the law" question cannot be answered only on the basis of the formal criteria of validity (i.e., whether a norm was enacted by a competent authority in a duly prescribed procedure); (c) in order to determine what is the norm in force, one needs to determine its content; (d) in order to determine the content of the norm, one needs to interpret its linguistic

L. Burazin (✉)
University of Zagreb, Zagreb, Croatia
e-mail: lburazin@pravo.hr

G. B. Ratti (✉)
University of Genoa, Genoa, Italy
e-mail: gbratti@unige.it

P. Chiassoni, B. Spaić (eds.), *Judges and Adjudication in Constitutional Democracies: A View from Legal Realism*, Law and Philosophy Library 135,
https://doi.org/10.1007/978-3-030-58186-2_7

formulation (i.e., the sentence expressing it or the norm-formulation); (e) hence, the rule of recognition necessarily includes among its criteria of validity canons of interpretation.

This leads to the theoretical disagreements objection. Roughly, the objection might go as follows: (a) the rule of recognition is constituted by the convergent social practice of judges with respect to the criteria for identifying the legally valid norms of their system, which include or presuppose canons of interpretation; (b) judges often disagree on how to interpret a norm-formulation they are supposed to apply and thus disagree about its content, i.e., they disagree about what the legally valid law is (about what is prescribed by a legal order); hence, (c) the rule of recognition, as conceived by legal conventionalists, does not really exist and/or (d) it cannot be a conceptual tool for explaining theoretical disagreements.

The paper argues that the rule of recognition sets the criteria only for sources of law and not legal norms themselves and that a theory of interpretation that distinguishes between normative texts (sources of law) and legal norms (as meanings of legal texts) can help explain why the rule of recognition might still be conceived as a conventional rule based on the convergent practice of officials and the fact that officials sometimes disagree about the correct interpretation of legal texts.

To this purpose, the paper first sets out the view that there are conceptual connections between the rule of recognition and canons of interpretation, based on the analysis of Hart's conception of the rule of recognition and his (implicit) doctrine of interpretation (Sect. 2). Section 3 introduces Dworkin's theoretical disagreements argument against Hart and conventional legal positivism, seeking to show that both Hart's and Dworkin's views stem from the lack of a full-fledged theory of interpretation, required to address the issue of interpretive disagreements and the relations between canons and the rule of recognition. Section 4 gives a brief account of the basic elements of one such theory of interpretation, making conceptual space for distinguishing between different levels of the rule of recognition and determining their relations with canons of interpretation. Finally, Sect. 5 presents a kind of legal positivism (which we propose to call "critical positivism") which could more easily account for the twofold fact that there is often among lawyers general agreement on "legitimate" sources and at the same time wide disagreement on their interpretation.

2 Hart's Conception of the Rule of Recognition and Canons of Interpretation

Hart's rule of recognition includes the criteria for identifying legal norms (rules) as norms belonging to a particular legal system (or norms of the relevant community). These criteria are often labelled as the criteria of validity or the criteria of legality. According to Hart (1994, p. 94), the rule of recognition specifies "some feature or features possession of which by a suggested rule is taken as a conclusive affirmative indication that it is a rule of the group to be supported by the social pressure it exerts". The rule has the following conditional structure: "If x meets criteria c, then x is a legally valid norm of a legal system LS". Thus, all xs that meet criteria c count as the law in a given LS. One can argue that, as such, the rule of recognition is in fact a definitional (and a constitutive) rule, i.e., a rule defining what a legally valid norm in a given legal system is.[1]

The rule of recognition can take on various forms, i.e., it can set different criteria of identification by listing different features that a rule must have in order for it to be a rule of the relevant community. The simplest criterion of identification is a reference to some authoritative text of rules (Hart 1994, p. 94). All the rules that have the feature of being written down in a text are the rules of the legal system having this particular rule of recognition. More complex criteria of identification consist in listing some more general features. These can be "the fact of their [rules] having been enacted by a specific body, or their long customary practice, or their relation to judicial decisions" (Hart 1994, p. 95).

It is evident from the above examples of identification criteria that these criteria in fact represent type-sources of law in a given legal system.[2] There is even a sentence in *The Concept of Law* in which Hart (1994, p. 106) expressly equates the criteria of legal validity with sources of law: "We may say that a criterion of legal validity or source of law [...]". Further textual support can be found on p. 134: "The acknowledgement of precedent as a criterion of legal validity [...]" or p. 266: "a rule of recognition specifying the sources of law and the relationships of superiority and subordination holding between them" or "[...] something very like a rule of recognition identifying the authoritative sources of law as described in this book is necessary" or "[...] I ascribe the general agreement found among judges as to the criteria for the identification of the sources of law to their shared acceptance of [...]". Thus, the feature "enacted by a legislative body" listed in the rule of recognition identifies in fact statutes as a source of law, the feature "long customary practice" identifies customs as a source of law, and the feature "relation to a judicial decision" identifies precedents as a source of law. As put by Hart (1994, p. 101; emphasis ours):

> In a modern legal system where there are a variety of 'sources' of law, the rule of recognition is correspondingly more complex: the criteria for identifying the law are multiple and commonly include a *written constitution*, *enactment by a legislature*, and *judicial precedents*.

This conclusion also draws on Hart's claim that a rule of recognition setting more than one such general feature as criteria of identification can provide a solution to a possible conflict among the criteria. A solution might consist in their "arrangement in an order of superiority, as by the common subordination of custom or precedent to statute, the latter being a 'superior source' of law" (Hart 1994, p. 95).

---

[1]For an account of Hart's rule of recognition as a definition of 'valid law' and thus a conceptual rule see Bulygin (2015).

[2]Cf. also Ross (1962, p. 1186).

Thus, one can argue that Hart's rule of recognition in fact determines or specifies type-sources of law in a particular legal system, and that it takes membership in the thus determined type-sources of law as the criterion for identifying a particular rule as a rule of a legal system, as a rule belonging to a particular legal system, i.e., as a criterion of legal validity.

According to this view, we can reformulate Hart's version of the rule of recognition by using the following conditional: "If x belongs to the accepted type-source (s) of law SL, then x is a legally valid norm of a given legal system LS". As such, the rule of recognition is a double definitional (and constitutive rule). It defines not only what a legally valid norm in a given legal system is, but also what its legal sources are. Or, perhaps more precisely, one could claim that there are in fact (at least) two rules of recognition: one defining type-sources of law in a given community (the rule of recognition of type-sources) and the other defining legally valid norms (in the sense yet to be explained) in a given community (the rule of recognition of 'norms'). The view that Hart's rule of recognition determines type-sources of law in a particular legal system, and that it takes membership in the thus determined sources of law as the criterion for identifying a particular rule as a rule of a legal system, is reflected in Hart's claim that, e.g., British judges "identify a particular statute as law in their courts, on the footing that what the Queen in Parliament enacts is law" (Hart 1994, p. 115).

Concerning the content determining which feature is to serve as an identification criterion, it seems that, according to Hart, general reference suffices. Thus, for example, if a rule of recognition refers to legislation as an identification criterion,

> it need not refer to all the details of procedure involved in legislation. Usually some official certificate or official copy will, under the rules of recognition, be taken as a sufficient proof of due enactment. Of course, if there is a social structure so simple that the only 'source of law' is legislation, the rule of recognition will simply specify enactment as the unique identifying mark or criterion of validity of the rules (Hart 1994, p. 96).

From this it follows that, according to Hart, a rule can be identified as a legal rule belonging to a particular legal system already on the basis of the fact that, e.g., its linguistic formulation is found in a document enacted by the legislature, sufficient proof of which could be some official certificate or official copy of the enacted document. Hence, one could claim that Hart's rule of recognition sets the criteria of legal validity in such a way that the object of the identification performed by officials on the basis of the rule of recognition is in fact only the *linguistic formulation of a legal norm*, which is sufficient to at least *prima facie* identify a particular legal norm as belonging to a legal system. Since it is from linguistic formulations of legal norms (i.e., normative texts) that legal norms can be derived, such linguistic formulations are not norms themselves but their sources. Therefore, Hart's rule of recognition could be interpreted as in fact setting the criteria of identification of legally valid 'norms' in the sense of token-sources of law.[3]

---

[3]One might dub this rule of recognition 'the rule of recognition of token-sources of law'. This would be very interesting from the systematic point of view since the rule of recognition of type-sources

Hence, when Hart (1994, p. 115; emphasis ours), in his already quoted text, says that British judges "identify *a particular statute* as law in their courts, on the footing that what the Queen in Parliament enacts is law", it means that judges identify this particular statute as a token-source of law (and in this sense "*as law* in their courts") since it belongs to legislation as a type-source of law (defined by the RoR of type-sources) in their legal system. The same interpretation applies to Hart's exemplification of the process of identification of 'legally valid rules', where legally valid 'rules' seem to be understood by Hart (1994, p. 107; emphasis ours) as (legally valid) token-sources of law:

> If the question is raised whether some suggested *rule* is *legally valid*, we must, in order to answer the question, use a criterion of validity provided by some other rule. Is *this purported by-law* of the Oxfordshire County Council valid? [...] At this first stage the *statutory order* [made by the Minister of Health] provides the criteria in terms of which the validity of the by-law is assessed. [...] We may query the validity of the statutory order and assess its validity in terms of the *statute* empowering the minister to make such orders. Finally, when the validity of the statute has been queried and assessed by reference to the rule that what the Queen in Parliament enacts is law, we are brought to a stop in inquiries concerning validity [...].

Since the object of identification by judges is in fact a norm-formulation, on the basis of which we infer that a norm, the formulation of which has been identified, belongs to a particular legal system, it is sufficient for the purpose of identification to determine whether the norm-formulation in question was enacted by a body (at least *prima facie*) competent to create it. Namely, it is sufficient to determine whether a norm meets (at least some of) the formal criteria of validity (in the sense of criteria of conformity with the norms on the production of law).[4] This also ensues from the answer Hart (1994, p. 107; emphasis ours) gives to the above quoted question ("Is this purported by-law of the Oxfordshire County Council valid?"): "Yes: because it was made *in exercise of the powers conferred*, and *in accordance with the procedure specified*, by a statutory order made by the Minister of Health".

It is surely enough to at least *prima facie* identify the existence of a particular (written) legal norm within a legal system (and in this sense to identify it as legally valid) by identifying its linguistic formulation (in the above demonstrated way). But what about the identification of the content of legal norms? At one point Hart (1994, p. 269; emphasis ours) actually says that, according to his theory, both "the existence and *content* of the law can be identified by reference to the social sources of the law

---

would have as its members classes (viz. the classes of the possible instantiations of the source "legislation", say) whereas the rule of recognition of token-sources would have as its elements particular pieces of legislation or custom. However, one must be careful when adopting this stance because the rule of recognition of token-sources would be merely extensional (something similar to what happens to the "supreme norm" in Alchourrón's and Bulygin's definition of valid law in Alchourrón and Bulygin (1979)) and, so, in this sense would lack the intensional aspect one tends to ascribe to rules of recognition.

[4]See Guastini (2014, p. 248). Note, however, that the formal criteria of validity are a sufficient, but not a necessary condition of legal existence (namely, there are some norms the existence of which is based, e.g., on the principle of effectiveness). See ibid.

(e.g. legislation, judicial decisions, social customs)". Unfortunately, Hart does not say much about how the content of law is identified. The only thing he says is that the content (just like the existence) of a norm is identified *by reference to the social sources of the law*. For example, in the case of a statutory norm, by pointing to the fact that the text of the norm in question was promulgated by the legislator. Thus, it seems that, for Hart, there is no real difference between identifying the existence and the content of (written) legal norms, or more specifically, norm-formulations and their meaning (i.e. the norms themselves). This is in line with Hart's belief that

> the life of the law consists to a very large extent in the guidance both of officials and private individuals by *determinate* [emphasis ours] rules which, unlike the applications of variable standards, do *not* require from them a fresh judgment from case to case. This salient fact of social life remains true, even though uncertainties may break out as to the applicability of any rule (whether written or communicated by precedent) to a concrete case (Hart 1994, p. 135).

Of course, the norm-formulation and the norm are not one and the same thing. The (expressed) norm is the meaning of its linguistic formulation, acquired through the process of interpretation (Guastini 2011, pp. 63–74). So, the fact that Hart pretty much equated legal rules with their linguistic formulations seems to presuppose the view that normative texts should be interpreted according to their plain, settled meaning, i.e., by using the literal or plain-meaning interpretation. Hence, one could claim that Hart's prescriptive doctrine of interpretation (i.e., the view that normative texts *should* be interpreted according to their plain meaning) and his consequential failure to distinguish between norm-formulations and norms forced Hart to at least implicitly endorse the view that canons of interpretation (namely, the literal interpretation canon) are necessarily a part of the rule of recognition. Of course, one might argue that there is still no general conceptual implication between the rule of recognition and the canons, since the norms to be recognized may well all be customary norms.[5] So, in Hart's theory, the interpretive implication would be contingent on there being norms to be identified by means of interpreting legal texts. That said, in so far as texts are recognized as sources under the rule of recognition, the connection between the rule of recognition and at least one canon is unavoidable and, in this weaker sense, "necessary".

Of course, if a rule of recognition of a legal system incorporated in its criteria of validity principles of justice or substantive moral values that do not have a "pedigree", which Hart (1994, p. 247) admits is possible, then obviously judges would have to identify legally valid norms not only on the basis of some formal criteria, but also by using substantive ones. That is to say, they would have to determine whether a particular norm (of course, only if these principles and values are taken to be the

[5]It should be noted, however, that even the practice forming the basis of customary norms must be "read" in the light of some criterion. Still, interpreting customary law and interpreting statutory law are two quite different activities, the first being a classification of facts and the second the attribution of meaning to texts. On this point, see Guastini (2011, pp. 8–12).

criteria of identification and not of creation of the law)[6] conforms to the content of the said principles and values in order that it be identified as a legally valid norm of their legal system. It could thus be argued that incorporating canons of interpretation into the rule of recognition would in that case be necessary in order that a judge be able to identify a legally valid norm of a system. However, as has been shown, Hart's rule of recognition defines the sources of law of a given legal system and identifies legally valid norms as norms belonging to these sources. Where the rule of recognition incorporates non-pedigreed principles of justice or substantive moral values, these principles and values are determined by the convergent practice of officials as type-sources of law in their legal system. Officials agree that these principles and values are the sources of law of their legal system and that they are therefore part of the criteria of validity despite their sometimes disagreeing about the results of identifying, on the basis of these criteria, norms as legal norms (Hart 1994, pp. 258–259). Whether or not officials (i.e., judges) also agree on which canons of interpretation they should use in order to get the same result more often (or always) is an empirical matter. Canons of interpretation may well be set by the rule of recognition itself, but they may also be set by other legal rules of the system (Ratti 2012, p. 84) or not even be set at all. Of course, if such principles were formulated in, e.g., a constitutional or a statutory provision, they would be identifiable by the same criteria as other expressly formulated legal norms (Hart 1994, pp. 265–266).

Finally, despite the fact that Hart seems to implicitly endorse the view that there is a necessary connection between canons and the rule of recognition (at least in the case of written law), it should be noted that nothing in Hart's theory of the rule of recognition itself, at least in so far as the rule of recognition is conceived as setting the criteria for identifying legally valid 'norms' in the sense of token-sources of law, warrants the claim that canons are necessarily part of it. As shown, no canon of interpretation is required to identify legally valid norms in the sense of token-sources of law. Also, nothing in the positivist conventionality thesis warrants such a claim. The rule of recognition is, according to Hart (1994, pp. 256, 266–267), a conventional social rule, "a form of judicial customary rule existing only if it is accepted and practised in the law-identifying and law-applying operations of the courts", i.e., "a conventional form of judicial consensus". It is constituted by the social practice of judges. Hence, the judges' social practice determines its content. Therefore, as long as the rule of recognition fulfils its conceptual function of identifying type- and

[6]In replying to Dworkin's criticisms, Hart resorts to Raz's view that in cases where judges are required to apply moral standards, they do not identify pre-existing law, but rather create new law. See Hart (1994, p. 254) and Raz (1986, pp. 1115–1116). According to this view, it seems that if moral standards were included among the rule of recognition's criteria of validity, their status would be different from that of the other criteria. While the other criteria would be the criteria for identifying preexisting norms as legal norms, moral standards would be the criteria for exercising discretion and creating new law. Of course, if taken as such, their being part of the rule of recognition would not imply that canons of interpretation are also included in the rule of recognition. One can interpret only something that exists and that can be subject to interpretation and that is surely not the case with law yet to be created by judges applying moral standards.

token-sources of law in a given legal system, whether or not it also includes canons of interpretation among its criteria is only a contingent fact. Thus, for example, if Hart had endorsed the sceptical theory of interpretation, rather than the cognitivist one, his rule of recognition would be read as setting the criteria of legal validity only of texts expressing valid legal norms, and not of legal norms in the sense of meanings of those texts.

3 The Argument from Theoretical Disagreements

However, although nothing in Hart's theory of the rule of recognition itself and the positivist conventionality thesis warrants the claim that there is a necessary connection between canons and the rule of recognition, Hart's implicit view that canons of interpretation are necessarily included in the rule of recognition and are thus covered by a consensus or convention among officials gave rise to Dworkin's powerful theoretical disagreements objection. Indeed, Dworkin refers to examples of disagreements on the interpretation of legal sources in order to maintain that the rule of recognition cannot be reconstructed in conventional terms. Shapiro (2011, p. 283) sums up Dworkin's attack in the following words:

> Debates about proper interpretive method pose an even greater difficulty for legal positivism. As Ronald Dworkin has argued, the mere fact that such disputes take place indicates that law cannot rest on the kind of facts that positivists believe form the foundation of legal systems. For positivists have maintained that the criteria of legal validity are determined by convention and consensus. But debates over interpretive methodology demonstrate that no such convention or consensus exists. In other words, disagreements about interpretive method are impossible on the legal positivist position. Nevertheless, they seem not only possible, but pervasive.

This leads Dworkin to hold that the rule of recognition is not a theoretical tool that one can fruitfully employ to reconstruct legal practices in contemporary societies. When Dworkin discusses the issue of disagreements as a challenge to legal positivism, he refers to well-known cases such as *Riggs v. Palmer* and *TVA v. Hill*, in which—at least from the perspective adopted by the "second" Dworkin—the interpretation of certain legal provisions is discussed. However, by doing so, Dworkin—and with him a huge part of common-law legal theory—seems to confuse different problems, deriving from disagreements about the interpretation of sources the presence of the disagreement about the identification of the ultimate criteria of recognition of a legal system (Dolcetti and Ratti 2013, pp. 305–308). This inference (quite mistaken in our view) seems to be founded on an affirmative reply to the question of whether interpretive canons are part of the criteria contained in the rule of recognition. As we have seen, this is probably due to the fact that Hart did not give much thought to this issue, for in his view the relation between sources and norms is not problematic (Guastini 2011, pp. 427–431), so the rule of recognition identifies, at the same time, sources and norms.

According to our view, Dworkin's attack on conventionalism hits an easy target by means of the argument on disagreements, since common law legal positivism seemingly does not have a full-fledged theory of legal interpretation, which is necessary to explain interpretive disagreements and the relations between canons and the rule of recognition. The basic elements of a full-fledged theory of legal interpretation, some of which (e.g. norm-formulation vs norm distinction) we have already used in reconstructing Hart's view, will be therefore briefly set out and explained in the following section.

Indeed, attempts at solving the (supposed) puzzle raised by Dworkin have gone in two main directions: (a) a sociological-empirical thesis that aims at denying the pervasive character of disagreements within contemporary legal systems; (b) a conception of law that contains a theoretical explanation of interpretive disagreements. The first approach was elaborated by Brian Leiter, while the second was put forward by Scott Shapiro. In our view, both approaches are saddled by some theoretical difficulties.

The first approach seems to be undermined by the fallacy of improper generalization, in so far as it derives from the (supposed) absence of interpretive disagreements in the lower levels of the US judiciary system a general thesis according to which legal systems in general are not characterized by the presence of widespread interpretive disagreements (Leiter 2009, pp. 1226–1227). The second approach is a peculiar mixture of descriptive and prescriptive tenets (Beltrán and Ratti 2013, pp. 181–185), since it presupposes that, in the absence of a shared interpretive methodology, conventionalism must inevitably admit that there is no "right" way of identifying legal norms (Shapiro 2011, p. 382): which *presupposes*, in a problematic way, a necessary connection between the rule of recognition and legally admissible interpretive methods.

At any rate, both proposals fail to clarify whether it is possible to make a case for a conceptual connection between the rule of recognition and the canons of interpretation: which is what really interests us here. The argument commonly framed or presupposed in the relevant literature is as follows: since the rule of recognition identifies norms (and not simply texts), it is necessary to include canons, which allow one to pass from relevant sources to norms (Marmor 2005, p. 95).[7] A possible strategy for denying a conceptual connection between canons and the rule of recognition consists in negating one of the premises and maintaining that the rule of recognition identifies texts, and not norms. As we have seen, there are some passages in *The Concept of Law* that suggest this was indeed Hart's idea.

In any case, going beyond Hartian philology, it is logically necessary that one can count on some criteria that identify the type-sources from which one (supposedly) can derive certain norms, before such norms can be identified. In other words, in order to know what the system of norms, which are in force in a given community, is, we must be able to determine the type-sources of law in that community, from which such norms can be derived. For this operation to be carried out, no canon of

[7]On this argument see Bayón (2002, pp. 60–64).

interpretation is needed. We only have to know the *master book* (in Alchourrón's terminology) (Alchourrón 2012, pp. 44–50)[8] that is generally used by lawyers to solve the questions they normally deal with. If this is correct, the concept of the rule of recognition—as mentioned before—should be divided into two more specific concepts: one bearing on the identification of type-sources of law (the rule of recognition of type-sources) and the other bearing on the identification of norms (the rule of recognition of norms). It is easy to see that the second concept is parasitic on the first, for one cannot construe any norm which is not derived, more or less directly, from a source. However, in order to explain interpretive disagreements and the relations between canons and the rule of recognition in this way it is—as we already pointed out—necessary to provide at least some basic elements of a theory of legal interpretation.

4 Basic Elements of a Theory of Legal Interpretation

So far we have spoken in terms of norm-formulations, sources and norms. Let us be more accurate. We use the term "norm-formulation" to designate any text issued by a competent authority within a certain legal system. In this sense, norm-formulations are particular instances of legal sources (or token-sources of law): they are the sources put into existence by an act of voluntary promulgation carried out by a certain organ at least *prima facie* vested with the power to do so. We call a "norm" any meaning possibly attributable to a norm-formulation.

In juristic language norms and norm-formulations are seldom kept separate. Jurists commonly use the word "norm" (or "rule") to refer both to norms and norm-formulations. And this due to a received (neo-)formalistic view, according to which words have a "proper" and "easily graspable" meaning (or at least a core of proper meaning), and norm-formulations express, in the majority of cases, only one (more or less vague) norm (Guastini 1991).

From the theoretical perspective, however, the two concepts have to be neatly distinguished. Norm-formulations are segments of prescriptive discourse, i.e., the discourse whose principal function is to direct human behaviour. Norms are the meaning-contents of norm-formulations. Norms can be regarded as the prescriptive analogue of propositions in descriptive language (Alchourrón and Bulygin 1981, p. 96). They are meanings just like propositions, but unlike propositions they are prescriptive in character, hence neither true nor false (Kelsen 1960, pp. 269–276). Norms depend on interpretation and constitute its product. As a consequence, when jurists affirm they are carrying out "an interpretation of norms," this should be understood as "an interpretation of norm-formulations," since norms are the product,

[8]The "master book" is defined by Alchourrón as the "totality of all legal texts".

and not the object, of the interpreting activity.[9] Interpretation is what relates norms to norm-formulations. More precisely, legal interpretation can be conceived of as the process of associating a meaning (a norm) to one or more norm-formulations.

There is no such thing as a necessary bi-univocal relationship or a one-to-one correspondence between the norm and the norm-formulation. A norm-formulation can, in fact, at the same time express more than one norm, both disjunctively and conjunctively, as well as less than one norm (a fragment of a norm, as is usually said) or no norm at all. Analogously, a norm is not necessarily the expression of just one norm-formulation: frequently, it is necessary to put together several norm-formulations in order to configure a norm. Moreover, a norm is not necessarily the expression of a norm-formulation, once the concept of the implicit norm is accepted. More specifically, at least eight different relationships between norms and norm-formulations can easily be singled out (Guastini 1990, p. 243 ff):

1. A norm-formulation expresses only one norm. This is the only case, extremely rare in practice, where there is a bi-univocal relationship or a one-to-one correspondence between a norm and a norm-formulation.
2. A norm-formulation tolerates the disjunctive attribution of a plurality of norms. The one and the same norm-formulation is assumed to express different norms according to different and conflicting interpretations.
3. A norm-formulation tolerates the conjunctive attribution of a plurality of norms. The one and the same norm-formulation is assumed to express not just one norm, but at the same time several norms.
4. Two different norm-formulations are assumed to express the same norm.
5. Two different norm-formulations are partially synonymous. In other words, we could say that they express two partially overlapping sets of norms.
6. A norm-formulation expresses no norm, in the sense that, despite appearing in a normative text, it expresses something different from a norm (e.g., a declaration of will, a political programme, an invocation to gods, etc.).
7. Several norm-formulations express, jointly, a norm. That amounts to saying that, singly considered, each norm-formulation expresses only a fragment of a norm.
8. A norm is not the product of the attribution of meaning to one or more norm-formulations, but the product of an implication (entailment) from other norms, which are expressed by explicitly proffered norm-formulations.

A preliminary distinction is necessary. In the legal domain, "interpretation" designates (at least) two different activities, i.e., (a) "cognitive" interpretation, which amounts to the analysis of a text in view of clarifying its possible (plausible) meanings, and (b) "adjudicative" interpretation, which consists in ascribing a definite meaning to a text (rejecting the others).

[9] Alchourrón (1986, p. 173) puts it this way: "[. . .] when jurists say, for example, that a legal norm has been given different judicial interpretations, it must be understood that they are referring to norm-formulations".

What happens in the ordinary process of attribution of meaning to sources is that lawyers agree on the sources to be interpreted (i.e., the texts that constitute the object of the interpretive activity) and the canons whose use in the process of legal adjudication is admissible. What they frequently disagree about is what canon is the most suitable for resolving the legal issue ingrained in the case at hand. What makes the relationship between norm-formulations and norms not univocal is the presence of several canons that are admitted in the legal system. This is also the reason why you cannot have adjudicative interpretation without carrying out a cognitive one. Drawing on Kelsen, one can think of a framework of legally admitted meanings (which are a function of the several canons at the lawyers' disposal) among which the interpretive solution to the legal issue at hand must or can be selected. This, in turn, implies that the criteria for identifying valid norms within a system normally allow one to detect a disjunction of possible meanings (i.e., of norms) and not just one possible interpretive output. For these reasons it is impossible to have criteria of validity that at the same time would always identify both the norm-formulation and the corresponding norm.

5 The Rule of Recognition, Interpretive Canons and Different Kinds of Legal Positivism

That said, one may ask: what is the theoretical issue underlying the discussion so far? The issue is the following: what is the theoretical aim of introducing interpretive canons into the formulation of the rule of recognition? We think that to affirm that canons necessarily form part of a unique rule of recognition that allows one to identify, at one and the same time, both sources and norms, confuses several issues which, if one wants to reconstruct them more precisely, must be kept separate.

In particular, to introduce canons into the rule of recognition implies that any interpretive disagreement whatsoever necessarily involves a certain dispute about the ultimate foundations of the normative system at hand: which is an exaggeration, if one bears in mind the phenomenology of the disagreements jurists have about the attribution of meaning to sources. In fact, such disagreements often bear on the interpretation of normative documents that are very specific and of a very limited scope. Moreover, such an introduction obscures the differences between different kinds of disagreement, for it does not allow one to trace the fundamental distinction between disagreements about sources and disagreements about their interpretation, since any disagreement whatsoever about the application of canons would be, according to this view, a disagreement about sources.

Conventionalist positivism gets very little from not distinguishing between these two aspects of the rule of recognition: since it assumes a conceptual connection between the rule of recognition and interpretive canons, it cannot reply to Dworkin's critique. It is exactly the possibility of distinguishing between two different rules of recognition (of sources and of norms) that makes the Dworkinian argument philosophically implausible and conceptually mystifying.

Apart from these considerations, there is one further argument that is indeed conclusive. We can agree that the rule of recognition of sources is reasonably easy to identify: determining the sources of a particular legal system is an activity that is normally quite successful, and which consists in identifying, from an extensional point of view, the type-sources of law actually used by the members of a particular social community. By contrast, identifying the rule of recognition of norms seems a much harder task: the factors of a particular social practice of norm identification that need to be considered in order to determine *ex ante* the criteria of legal validity of norms are so numerous and so various[10] that nobody can reasonably claim to have isolated, once and for all, such criteria qua outcome of the mentioned practice. From this it follows that the only plausible way of conceiving the rule of recognition of norms consists in an *ex post* description of the criteria actually used by jurists to identify norms and a prediction of how this practice will evolve in the future.

From what has been said so far, it seems that a more nuanced kind of legal positivism (which, for lack of a better word, could be dubbed "critical positivism"), that accounts for a more elaborate theory of legal interpretation, could easily accommodate a series of circumstances regarded as relevant to the explanation of law: the twofold fact that there is often among lawyers general agreement on "legitimate" sources and at the same time wide disagreement on their interpretation.

However, it has been held that traditional conventionalism and theories aiming at accounting for the presence of several admissible (and sometimes conflicting) canons of interpretation—like the one set out in this paper—have two different (and, under certain aspects, irreconcilable) notions of the rule of recognition. This problem is summed up by Leiter (2007, p. 79) in the following way:

> if the primary rules validated by a society's Rule of Recognition are indeterminate, then they do not really guide judges in deciding cases. In that event, however, the Rule of Recognition is a mere "paper" Rule of Recognition: it sets out the criteria judges *say* they are using, but it does not reflect the *real* criteria, since the primary rules it validates do not determine decisions. But a Rule of Recognition for Hart is a *social* rule, i.e. one constituted by the actual practice of officials in deciding disputes, and thus cannot be a "paper" rule in this way.

To this challenge Leiter (2007, pp. 79–80) replies by arguing that, despite appearances, "primary rules do *guide* most decisions (and thus the Rule of Recognition that validates them is a *social* rule), even if in appellate cases primary rules do not determine the outcomes", and that "the primary rules validated under the Rule of Recognition *guide* decision in some measure for appellate judges (as for other officials of the system), insofar as these primary rules constrain the range of possible decisions". Leiter's reply consists in trying to reconcile the central tenet of traditional conventionalism—i.e., law is based on some kind of consensus among judges and this consensus, in turn, constitutes the foundation of the "normativity" of law

[10]Consider, for instance, only interpretive canons, their ordering, the relations between interpretation and repeal, the choice of the rules of inference, etc.

(Coleman 1982, pp. 156–157)—with the views that law is underdetermined—i.e., it admits different solutions to the same legal issue in virtue of the different interpretive methods that can be used to interpret legal sources—especially in appellate courts.

Two remarks can be made here. On the one hand, Leiter holds a very cautious view about the indeterminacy of law, limiting it to cases debated before appellate and supreme courts. It is, however, not clear why interpretive canons make law indeterminate, and produce interpretive disagreements, only at the highest instance of the judiciary and do not operate likewise at the lower levels of the judicial pyramid. The empirical evidence proposed by Leiter (2009, p. 1226, n. 54) only suggests that, in the US, the cases debated before the lowest courts are not characterized by much disagreement over the canons to be used, but does not prove anything concerning the rational indeterminacy of law, since such disagreement can be explained by referring to social reasons, causal reasons, psychological reasons, etc., without it being necessary to assume widespread interpretive agreement.

On the other hand, the kind of positivism we advocate does not aim so much at delineating the criteria of validity or applicability of norms, in so far as they are, more or less directly, traceable back to the provisions enacted by the legislature. Rather, critical positivism seeks to determine the criteria of effectiveness of the norms actually applied by judges and thus predict, with a reasonable degree of certainty, their future decisions. Within this framework critical positivism is mainly interested in determining: (a) the criteria of validity of legal sources (i.e., what we have called "the rule of recognition of sources"); (b) the interpretive canons allowed within a certain legal community (which are not necessarily included in the rule of recognition) and (c) the norms that can be derived, by means of different interpretive techniques, from validated sources.

Consequently, the main difference between critical positivists and proponents of traditional conventionalism, who defend a one-to-one correspondence between sources and norms, lies not at the level of reconstruction of the rule of recognition of sources, but, for the most part, at the level of the theory of interpretation of the sources validated by means of that rule.

Another difference has to do with the rule of recognition of norms. While according to traditional conventionalists the rule of recognition of norms is a set of definitional criteria applicable *ex ante*, critical positivists tend to regard it as the *ex post* description of the norms actually used by judges in deciding their cases.

This allows us to conclude the following:

(1) often the rule of recognition of norms, as understood by proponents of traditional conventionalism, is actually a "paper rule" since judges do not apply the *prima facie* or "plain" meaning of sources: therefore, such a rule of recognition would, in many cases, identify rules not used by judges and, consequently, does not allow one to properly reconstruct a social practice, of judicial origin, regarding the application of norms;
(2) the application of different canons and the subsequent normative solutions concerning the same class of cases suggests that the rule of recognition of

norms has a disjunctive content, consisting in different norms that depend on the use of different canons, in various instances of application.

(3) critical positivism and traditional conventionalism agree on the fact that the rule of recognition of sources is often conventional in character, although it is not conceptually impossible that such a rule consists in the accidental overlapping of several definitions used within a certain society.

6 Conclusion

The analysis of Hart's theory shows that at least implicitly Hart endorsed the view that at least one canon of interpretation (i.e., the literal or plain-meaning canon) is necessarily a part of the rule of recognition and is thus covered by a consensus or convention among officials. This gave rise to Dworkin's powerful theoretical disagreements objection, based precisely on examples of disagreements about the interpretation of legal sources. However, as pointed out, both Hart's view and Dworkin's attack on conventionalism seem to follow from the fact that their accounts do not appear to stem from a full-fledged theory of legal interpretation, which is necessary to explain interpretive disagreements and the relations between canons and the rule of recognition.

According to one such theory of interpretation as set out in this paper, the concept of the rule of recognition can be divided into two more specific concepts: one bearing on the identification of type-sources of law (the rule of recognition of type-sources), which does not presuppose the use of any canon of interpretation, and the other bearing on the identification of norms (the rule of recognition of norms), which does presuppose the use of canons by law-identifying organs. It is precisely the possibility of distinguishing between these two different rules of recognition (of sources and of norms) that makes the Dworkinian argument philosophically implausible and conceptually mystifying. Such distinction, advocated by a more nuanced kind of legal positivism (which we dubbed "critical positivism"), allows one to account for the twofold fact that there is often among lawyers general agreement on "legitimate" sources and at the same time wide disagreement on their interpretation.

References

Alchourrón CE (1986) Systematization and change in the science of law. In: Eckhoff T, Friedman L, Uusitalo J (eds) Vernunft und Erfahrung im Rechtsdenken der Gegenwart. Rechstheorie, Beiheft 10. Duncker & Humblot, Berlin, pp 195–210

Alchourrón CE (2012) On law and logic. In: Beltrán JF, Ratti GB (eds) The logic of legal requirements. Essays on defeasibility. Oxford University Press, Oxford, pp 39–52

Alchourrón CE, Bulygin E (1979) Sobre la existencia de las normas juridicas. Oficina Latinoamericana de investigaciones jurídicas y sociales, Valencia

Alchourrón CE, Bulygin E (1981) The expressive conception of norms. In: Hilpinen R (ed) New studies in Deontic logic. Reidel, Dordrecht, pp 95–124

Bayón JC (2002) Derecho, convencionalismo y controversia. In: Navarro PE, Redondo MC (eds) La relevancia del derecho: ensayos de filosofía jurídica, moral y política. Gedisa, Barcelona
Beltrán JF, Ratti GB (2013) Theoretical Disagreements: a restatement of legal positivism. In: Canale D, Tuzet G (eds) The planning theory of law. A critical reading. Springer, Dordrecht, pp 169–186
Bulygin E (2015) On the rule of recognition. In: Bulygin E (ed) Essays in legal philosophy. Oxford University Press, New York, pp 117–123
Coleman JL (1982) Negative and positive positivism. J Legal Stud 11(1):139–164
Dolcetti A, Ratti GB (2013) Legal disagreements and the dual nature of law. In: Waluchow W, Sciaraffa S (eds) Philosophical foundations of the nature of law. Oxford University Press, Oxford, pp 301–321
Guastini R (1990) Disposizione vs. Norma. In: AA. VV (ed) Studi in memoria di Giovanni Tarello. Volume II. Saggi teorico-giuridici. Dott. A. Giuffrè Editore, Milano, pp 235–252
Guastini R (1991) Ought-sentences and description of rules. Ratio Juris 4:308–321
Guastini R (2011) Interpretare e argomentare. Dott. A. Giuffrè Editore, Milano
Guastini R (2014) La sintassi del diritto. Giappichelli Editore, Torino
Hart HLA (1994) The concept of law. Oxford University Press, New York
Kelsen H (1960) What is the pure theory of law? Tulane Law Rev 34:269–276
Leiter B (2007) Naturalizing jurisprudence. Oxford University Press, New York
Leiter B (2009) Explaining theoretical disagreement. Univ Chicago Law Rev 76(3):1215–1250
Marmor A (2005) Interpretation and legal theory. Hart Publishing, Oxford
Ratti GB (2012) Diritto, Indeterminatezza, Indecidibilità. Marcial Pons, Madrid
Raz J (1986) Dworkin: a new link in the chain. Calif Law Rev 74(3):1103–1119
Ross A (1962) Review of the concept of law. Yale Law J 71(6):1185–1190
Shapiro S (2011) Legality. The Belknap Press of Harvard University Press, Cambridge

Luka Burazin is associate professor at the University of Zagreb Faculty of Law. His recent publications include Legal Systems, Intentionality, and a Functional Explanation of Law (Jurisprudence 10(2)/2019), Law as an Artifact (Encyclopedia of the Philosophy of Law and Social Philosophy, Mortimer Sellers, Stephan Kirste eds., Springer, 2019), Conflicts Between Fundamental Rights Norms (Proportionality in Law. An Analytical Perspective, David Duarte, Jorge S. Sampaio eds., Springer, 2018), Legal Systems as Abstract Institutional Artifacts (Law as an Artifact, Luka Burazin, Kenneth E. Himma, Corrado Roversi eds., Oxford UP, 2018), The Concept of Law and Efficacy (Encyclopedia of the Philosophy of Law and Social Philosophy, Mortimer Sellers, Stephan Kirste eds., Springer, 2017), Can There Be an Artefact Theory of Law? (Ratio Juris 29/2016).

Giovanni Battista Ratti is Professor of Jurisprudence at the University of Genova School of Law and a permanent fellow of Tarello Institute for Legal Philosophy. His main scientific interests span from general theory of law, deontic logic, legal defeasibility to constitutional democracy and the interpretation of contracts. His main publications include "Lógica de las normas, coherencia y metodología jurídica" (Buenos Aires, 2017), "Diritto, indeterminatezza, indecidibilità" (Madrid, 2012), and the edited collection "The Logic of Legal Requirements. Essays on Defeasibility" (w/ J. Ferrer, Oxford, 2012).

Legal Realism and Legal Doctrine

Dan Priel

Abstract Legal realism is popularly known for its hostility to legal doctrine. In the familiar narrative, the realists showed that legal doctrine does not, and cannot, constrain judges from using existing legal materials to reach virtually any outcome they want. As such, doctrine only serves to hides and obfuscate what is better discussed openly. The purpose of this essay is to complicate this familiar story. I focus on one contemporary take on legal realism that argues that an open discussion of values will give the law greater determinacy. I counter this view, first, by showing that it does not, in fact, fit the views of the legal realists, but reflects a modern view that fits contemporary (American) legal discourse. I also argue that it's very unlikely that such a view would improve the law's determinacy, and that it is likely to have undesirable consequences. I then propose an alternative, which I trace to work by some of the legal realists. This approach gives a clear role to legal doctrine and, so I argue, is normatively more appealing than the view that minimizes the role of doctrine.

1 The Need for a Philosophy of Legal Doctrine

It would seem obvious that legal philosophers should be interested in legal doctrine. To the extent that the philosophy of law is a philosophy of a particular practice, one would expect legal philosophers to be interested in those aspects that distinguish it from other practices. Legal doctrine, as well as its scholarly analysis, is one of them. By and large, however, legal philosophers have shown relatively little interest in doctrine as one of law's unique characteristics. There are several reasons for this lack of interest. One has to do with an exceedingly narrow conception of the proper role

Thanks to Charles Barzun for his comments on an earlier and very different version of this essay, as well as to multiple conversations over the years on some of the issues discussed here.

D. Priel (✉)
Osgoode Hall Law School, York University, Toronto, ON, Canada

P. Chiassoni, B. Spaić (eds.), *Judges and Adjudication in Constitutional Democracies: A View from Legal Realism*, Law and Philosophy Library 135,
https://doi.org/10.1007/978-3-030-58186-2_8

of legal philosophy. According to the proponents of this view, there is something 'anti-philosophical' about thinking about legal philosophy as 'the back-room activity of telling front-line practitioners' what to do (Gardner 2012, p. 24), and more broadly a dismissive attitude toward any philosophical attempt to engage with legal practice (ibid., 183–185). A more substantive reason for avoiding legal doctrine is the view that there is no distinct form of legal reasoning. Larry Alexander presented this view clearly when he said legal reasoning is 'banal'. What is known as 'thinking like a lawyer', he said, is nothing more than moral reasoning, empirical reasoning, and deductive reasoning, applied to the legal domain. All three modes of inference are familiar and are regularly used outside the law, which is why they do not identify anything distinctive about law (Alexander 1998, p. 517; also Raz 1994, pp. 238, 326–327). Legal reasoning is thus just normal reasoning applied to legal premises. It is the content of those premises that's worth discussing, not the modes of inference from them.

This essay takes a different view. In saying this, I do not mean to suggest that lawyers employ esoteric modes of reasoning to which only they are privy, and Alexander is unquestionably correct to deny the existence of legal reasoning in this sense. But that is not what anyone who talks about legal reasoning is talking about. Legal reasoning is concerned with the particular ways lawyers explain conclusions about what is to be done. Central to it is the fact that we expect a legal answer to a practical question to be different, in both explanation (form), and sometimes also in outcome (substance), from the non-legal answer. This relates to the kind of considerations that lawyers employ, and no less significantly, the kind of considerations they think they should not (as lawyers) employ. To speak of legal reasoning is to acknowledge that we can identify ways of answering questions lawyers regularly use which are different from those we find outside the law. That legal reasoning in this sense exists is quite familiar in arguments often couched in institutional terms: 'This is not a matter appropriate for a court to decide on, and it is better left for the legislature'. It indicates that some actions, or some decisions, may be good, perhaps even all-things-considered good, but may still be inappropriate for a court to take. To the extent that it is not nonsensical to say that when faced with a question, a lawyer answering it may answer it differently from a non-lawyer, or even just offer different reasons for the same outcome, one acknowledges the distinctness of legal reasoning. And to the extent that we can identify non-random patterns in which the legal and non-legal answers differ, legal reasoning is worth investigating. This is bound to disappoint those looking for something more exotic, some special ways of reaching conclusions to which lawyers are inducted after learning a secret handshake. Even though no such handshake exists (or, if it does, I have not been introduced to it), the more banal reality can still make for a genuine object of study.

To make this point more palatable, let me add that lawyers are not unique in this respect. There are identifiable patterns or modes of reasoning employed by economists (Morgan 2012, ch. 1), engineers (Madhavan 2015), and others (Crombie 1988). Modeling, for example, is central to economic reasoning today (although not so in the days of Adam Smith and David Ricardo). To say that modeling is central to economic thinking does not mean others don't employ them

(Johnson-Laird 1983), so in this sense economic reasoning is 'banal'. Nevertheless, the centrality of modeling to economic thinking and the kinds of models they typically employ are significant, because it has substantive implications on how questions are framed and what conclusions are reached. Indeed, as philosophers of science have noted, the turn toward modeling, and increasingly mathematical modeling, starting in the late nineteenth century, has had a profound impact on the discipline of economics and on the ideas that gained respect and became orthodoxy (Morgan 2012, pp. 378–379, 400–409). I think something similar is true of law. But just as in economics it is misleading to speak as if there is one mode of reasoning employed by all economists in all times and places, one should not think of 'legal reasoning' reflects a timeless set of techniques or methods. As certain approaches to reaching answers become more prominent, so are the answers they generate. Thus, one can identify legal change in part through changes in modes of legal reasoning. Likewise, one of the ways in which we sensibly talk of legal systems (or legal families) as recognizably different from each other is not just in term of the content of their respective laws (the trust is a common-law concept, abuse of rights is a civilian idea), but in their modes of reasoning. These differences are relative, and they do not make cross-jurisdictional conversation impossible, but they are there and have practical implications.

Even someone who accepts all this may still find it odd to discuss these questions in the context of legal realism, for if there is one thing that both realism's supporters and detractors agree on, it is that the legal realists were dismissive of legal doctrine and legal reasoning more generally. According to received wisdom, both critical (Langbein 1998, p. 61; Birks 1996, p. 4) and sympathetic (Singer 1988, pp. 470, 473), the realists dismissed doctrine as largely irrelevant for understanding why judges decide cases the way they do. The claim is that even though lawyers and judges provide certain 'legal' reasons for their decisions, these are really just covers for other reasons, the real reasons that actually motivated them. It is those (often unmentioned) reasons, that really motivate (and therefore explain) their decisions. If true, this suggests that there is no such thing as legal reasoning, even of the non-exotic form suggested here. What there is, is a more-or-less conscious deception, either of oneself or of others, with respect to what one is doing when engaged with the law. In addition to this descriptive claim, legal realism is also associated with the normative idea that to the extent that lawyers do in fact let legal rules constrain them, they are abdicating their moral responsibilities. When presented with a legal question, lawyers should seek justice, not follow ('mechanically') some pre-existing rules. To those who hold this view, the idea that law implies self-imposed restrictions on the direct pursuit of justice is seen as one of lawyers' worst pathologies, the one to which they reserve their strongest professional epithet. 'Formalism' is what reactionary lawyers practice and what others must resist. This leads quickly to disdain for legal doctrine as, at best, an elaborate deception. Such a view has had considerable influence in the United States, where the anti-doctrinal bent of much American legal scholarship is sometimes considered one of the legacies of legal realism (e.g., Smith 1992, p. 635; Coleman 1995, p. 2585).

I wish to present a somewhat different view of the relationship between legal realism and legal doctrine. I will do so in part view an analysis of Hanoch Dagan's recent work on legal realism (2013, 2015). Dagan develops a particular view about legal doctrine, which he takes to be derived from the works of the realists. As a matter of historical fact, I think Dagan's realism is different from the work of the most famous legal realists in some fundamental respects, and I will spend some time explaining in what ways. By itself, however, this point is of limited force. Dagan's book where he articulates his views is entitled *Reconstructing Legal Realism* and he is free to do so in any way he wishes, taking from their writings the ideas he finds attractive and modifying (and discarding) whatever he is unhappy with. Furthermore, as it is unclear who belonged to the group of legal realists, and since—as we shall see—there were some very significant differences among them, there is an important sense in which any attempt to provide an account of legal real*ism* (as opposed to the views of different legal real*ists*) necessarily involves highlighting the views of some and sidelining those of others.

Nevertheless, Dagan's extended discussion of the relationship between legal realism and legal doctrine is a valuable starting point, which I contrast with an alternative approach to legal doctrine derived from a different strand of realist work. Section 2 presents the contrast between two strands of legal realism and two corresponding strands of legal formalism, and then situates Dagan's realism against them. Section 3 spells out the implications of his views to legal doctrine. Dagan adopts and defends a version of the familiar take on legal realism as largely dismissive of legal doctrine, but Dagan pushes it further by advocating for a more transparent discussion of conflicting values. I argue that the concerns the realists have raised about legal doctrine (which Dagan accepts) are relevant to his view as well. If doctrine is indeterminate and conflicted, Dagan's proposed alternative does not solve these problems, but tends to exacerbate them. However, my criticisms of this view do not lead back to formalism. Rather, in Sect. 4 I present an alternative proposal for a positive role for legal doctrine on the basis of a less familiar aspect of realist thinking, that of engineering and institutional design. I argue there that when properly designed, doctrine can, and does, provide the kind of guidance that minimizes (if not quite eliminates) the problems the realists have identified with adjudication.

2 Setting the Stage

This section is mostly concerned with ground clearing. In Sect. 2.1, I identify the difference between two views often called 'formalism', and which I call 'conceptualism' and 'doctrinalism'. In Sect. 2.2, I introduce a parallel contrast between two versions of legal realism, which I call 'scientific' and 'traditional'. Then, in Sect. 2.3 I present Dagan's realism, and show that though it tries to blend elements of the two types of legal realism, it is much closer to traditional legal realism.

2.1 Two Legal Formalisms

That legal realism and legal formalism are opposing views is a jurisprudential commonplace. It is less clear what it is that they differ about. Tamanaha (2010, p. 162) considered the matter, and concluded that the contrast is empty and the distinction could be given up. I disagree. As I see it, the most illuminating way of understanding formalism is the thesis that law should be closed or autonomous, and realism as the rejection of this view (Priel 2018, 2019). But to say that does not help much, unless we understand what these metaphors mean. Used in this context, these words typically refer to an interconnected set of ideas with respect to the development of legal doctrine, to its justification, to the relationship between law and politics, and to the proper approach to legal scholarship. Proponents of formalism therefore maintain that the study of law and its development should be largely autonomous from other disciplines (Beever and Rickett 2005, pp. 335–336; Burrows 1998, p. 113). This autonomy extends also to political questions: For formalists, law (or at least, private law) is not a tool for achieving any particular goal, and should therefore remain largely the same in all times and places. This implies that law cannot be connected to politics (Beever 2013, pp. 203–205, 301–307). Given that the environment in which law exists radically differs between times and places, this view can only make sense by presupposing, and advocating for, a certain isolation of law from society, something I call ‘closure’.

Beyond this there are two quite different versions of formalism (Priel 2016a, 2019). With respect to legal doctrine, it is common to say, as Pojanowski (2014, p. 1712) puts it, that formalists believe that law must be understood, developed, and justified ‘on its own conceptual terms’. But there are two different ways of articulating this idea. Conceptualists begin with some abstract general principles and derive conclusions to particular cases from them. To give one example, in a recent book Ripstein (2016) seeks to explain much of tort law on the basis of one central idea, that of moral independence. The other approach, I call it ‘doctrinalist’, similarly tends to see law as autonomous and is similarly suspicious of various attempts to explain legal doctrine in non-legal terms, but it is much more attuned to legal practice. Its building blocks are cases, from whose reasons and outcomes doctrinalists construct an account of an area of law. These two approaches are not always kept apart, but they are in principle clearly distinguishable and not infrequently in conflict with each other (Priel 2019).

Conceptualists insist that their approach takes law (and legal doctrine) seriously, that it respects legal concepts and categories, that it seeks to explain law ‘from within’ (Weinrib 2012, pp. 18, 23–24). But in fact, these scholars care little for legal doctrine as such. It is only when doctrine fits their ideas, which are arrived at completely independently of legal doctrine, that they refer to it. When the ideas they favor are not given their due place in doctrinal materials, conceptualists dismiss them as mistaken. For this reason I think that conceptual formalists’ claims to ‘immanence’ are misleading: Answers to particular questions are perhaps immanent in the sense that they can be derived a priori from certain abstract ideas (themselves not derived from positive law), but it is a contingent fact that has no bearing on the justification of conceptualist accounts whether these principles are accepted by legal practitioners (Priel 2015, pp. 360–365).

Doctrinalists are, by contrast, obsessed with positive law. They are the derided 'blackletter lawyers', those who have mastered all the case-law and try to present a general account of the law on the basis of it. For this reason, doctrinalists often look with suspicion not only to instrumental or interdisciplinary approaches to law, but also to the work of conceptualists, whose work they perceive as exceedingly abstract and insufficiently tethered to the law (Waddams 2003, pp. 2–3; Gava 2006, p. 266). For them, the materials used by legal practitioners provide all that is needed for answering legal problems. Though it is common to dismiss this approach as un- or even anti-intellectual, the doctrinalist view presupposes an underlying philosophy of the authority of law and the proper role of lawyers in developing it (Priel 2017, pp. 624–631). In practice, however, proponents of this view tend to shun theoretical interdisciplinary approaches. The law's theory, to the extent that it is needed, is to be constructed from the law's own sources.

2.2 *Traditional and Scientific Legal Realism*

There can be little doubt that conceptualism is at odds with legal realism. Indeed, elsewhere (Priel 2018) I argue that opposition to conceptualism may have been the only idea all legal realists had in common. Perhaps because conceptualism and doctrinalism are not always clearly distinguished, there is often a tendency to think that the legal realists were also opposed to legal doctrine and to doctrinalism, but this is inaccurate. To see why we need to identify two competing versions of legal realism, which are in some ways two mirror images of the two versions of formalism. Just as the two formalist views are quite different, the two realist views present diametrically opposed answers to foundational questions about law and its authority, along with different normative prescriptions.

One realist camp, which I call 'traditional legal realism' and is best exemplified by the work of Karl Llewellyn, was far less radical than is commonly thought. It did not dismiss legal doctrine as empty, it did not think that the law is largely indeterminate, it did not dismiss lawyers' methods, and it was largely sympathetic to the common law. This version of legal realism was oriented toward legal practice, and saw the greatest threat to realism about law coming from the adoption of abstract philosophical theories developed with little input from practice. These realists objected to the tendency to present the law as a coherent scheme derived from general principles. These realists insisted that real law, as found in the cases, was quite different from any theoretical abstractions. It was living law, which like life was often messy and conflicted yet somehow worked for the community in which it grew.

It was not just theoretical abstractions that these realists spurned. Realists of this camp were also often skeptical of the potential contribution of social science to the law. Instead, these legal realists favored a more humanistic approach to the study of society, one that focused on history, cultural anthropology, and anti-naturalistic philosophy. There was also a 'romantic' (of if this word seems too controversial, communitarian) streak in the writings of many realists who belonged to this group, in the sense that they perceived law as emerging from the values of the community.

The second kind of legal realism, which I call 'scientific legal realism', finds its clearest articulation in the writings of Felix Cohen and Walter Wheeler Cook. It had a very different take on virtually all these issues. Its proponents saw law as an activity that belonged to this world, and as such a proper subject for social scientific study, itself ideally conceived of and practiced by extending the methods of natural science. Realists belonging to this camp were thus critical of lawyers' primitive and unscientific methods, which is why these legal realists were often unsympathetic to the common law. For these realists, the methods of science were the right approach to studying how legal practitioners worked but also for improving the law.

The difference between scientific and traditional legal realists was not limited to questions of method, but reflected a fundamentally different view on the basis of law's legitimate authority. Traditional legal realists looked to widely-shared community values as the moral basis for law, and what gave it its normative force. Unlike the traditionalists, scientific legal realists were often quite explicitly utilitarian in orientation, and some of them explicitly stated that questions of value were questions of fact (Cohen 1934; Robinson 1934) and could be tackled using the same methods used to deal with other factual questions. These realists sought to base the law's authority on the authority of science. From this perspective, law reflecting popular opinion had as much legitimacy as physics based on popular opinion.

Taking the two formalisms and two realisms yields four different views. At least in one sense, there is a clear parallel between doctrinalism and traditional legal realism on the one hand, and between conceptualism and scientific legal realism on the other. In the case of the first pair, both are committed to the primacy of actual legal practice and reject attempts to over-intellectualize the law. In the case of the second pair, there is a similar sense that there is room for a more scientific approach to law, something that was thought would help put practice on a firmer foundation. At the same time, in both of these pairs, the realist view is 'open' whereas the formalist view is 'closed': open to society and its influence in the case of traditional legal realism, and to the sciences and the wealth of useful data they provide in the case of scientific legal realism.

2.3 Dagan's Goldilocks Realism

Dagan takes this amalgam of positions and tries to reconstruct out of it a perfectly balanced version of legal realism. On question after question Dagan presents legal realism as a midway position that is not too cold, not too hot, but just right. Dagan begins with presenting us with three 'tensions': between law as science and law as craft (Dagan 2013, pp. 43–44), between law as power and law as reason (ibid.,

28–29, 94), and between law as tradition and law as progress (ibid., 59–60). On each of these, Dagan depicts legal realism as the view that successfully balances the two extremes.

The same attitude carries over to a host of other issues. Dagan tells us that legal realism strikes a 'middle-ground' (ibid., 107, also 92–93) between instrumentalism (ibid., 106) and autonomy (ibid., 107). It gives due recognition to humans' self-interest, but is similarly mindful of their benevolence (ibid., 77–82). It cares a great deal about maintaining the rule of law, but is properly attentive of the need to balance it against other values (ibid., 195). It accords a central place to the view that treats remedies as logically prior to rights (ibid., 148), but recognizes also the place and significance of rights independently of remedies (ibid., 150). It is duly respectful of the past, but is mindful of the future (ibid., 60, 200). It rejects both the 'nominalism' (ibid., 207, 223) and 'particularism' (ibid., 54–55, 206) of case-by-case decision-making, but is also wary of overly broad legal categories (ibid., 55). In this way legal realism balances a concern for stability (ibid., 207) with the need for flexibility (ibid., 211). It cares about the findings of the social sciences, but does not succumb to 'the pretence that a scientific analysis of facts is enough to do the work' (ibid., 47).

Based on this, Dagan provides an account of private law that is neither wholly autonomous nor purely instrumental (ibid., 105), that gives due recognition to the private aspects of private law while reconciling them with public ones (ibid., 113–14). His view promotes 'perfectionism', but, naturally, only a 'moderate' one (ibid., 178). All this fits Dagan's overall picture of private law that 'avoid[s] the dangerous binarism' of 'naïve utopianism or hopeless cynicism' (ibid., 80). On issue after issue, legal realism takes all conflicting considerations into account, and after 'navigat[ing] these unstable middle positions' (ibid., 100), successfully finds the right balance among them. The end result itself is thus 'both inherently self-confident and intrinsically tormented' (ibid., 99; *cf.* Tamanaha 2010, pp. 186–199). It is very difficult to identify any strong commitment in this account, except, perhaps, the fervent dedication to extreme moderation. Those who associate legal realism with a dash of radicalism will be dismayed to learn that Dagan's realism has a clear 'conservative' bent (Dagan 2013, pp. 63, 200). But even these radicals need not be too upset, for Dagan assures them that his realism is 'not limited to the happy middle': after some 'domestication and implementation' his realism will incorporate more radical 'insights' as well (ibid., 98 n. 61). Ironically, this resembles legal realist Thurman Arnold's biting description of jurisprudence, minus the sarcasm.[1]

[1]Arnold (1935, p. 752): 'In the science of Jurisprudence all of the various ideals which are significant to the man on the street must be given a place. It must prove that the law is certain and at the same time elastic; that it is just, yet benevolent, economic; yet morally logical. It must show that the law can be dignified and solemn and at the same time efficient, universal and fundamental, and at the same time a set of particular directions. Jurisprudence must give a place to all of the economic, and also the ethical notions of important competing groups within our society, no matter how far apart these notions may be. In its method it must make gestures of recognition to the techniques of each separate branch of learning which claims to have any relation with the conduct of individuals, no matter how different these techniques may be.'

Following on this general pattern, Dagan attempts to take something from both strands of legal realism. His presentation attempts to smooth the fundamental differences between traditional legal realists like Llewellyn and scientific ones Felix Cohen or Cook.[2] As mentioned, fundamentally different views become, at most, 'tensions' to be (successfully) balanced within a unified legal realism, reflecting Dagan's rejection of any 'one-dimensional account of law [a]s hopelessly deficient' (Dagan 2013, p. 68; cf. Nourse and Shaffer 2009, pp. 127–136). On the question of the place of legal doctrine, Dagan's view 'sanctions the relative stability of the social practice of law' (Dagan 2015, p. 1903), by which he means that it pays due respect to legal categories and recognizes their importance for maintaining legal stability while also balancing them against the need for flexibility.

Despite all this, it is evident where Dagan's sympathies lie with respect to the two strands of legal realism. Dagan does not distinguish between the two views, but he is unquestionably closer to traditional legal realism. It is only with his skepticism about the constraining powers of legal doctrine (2013, p. 21) that Dagan is close to the scientific legal realists. On the question of the source of law's authority, Dagan (e.g., 2015, p. 1903) unambiguously sides with traditional realists, writing, for example, that the 'relative stability' of law comes from 'using the prevalent understandings of the legal community regarding doctrine'. Dagan accepts this conservative stance not just for the pragmatic reason that it is more likely to be accepted, but primarily because 'existing law represents a cumulative judicial and legislative experience that deserves respect' (Dagan 2013, p. 200). The result, he says, clearly echoing traditional legal realists' views, is an attitude of 'legal optimism so typical of the common law tradition' (ibid., 138).

By contrast, Dagan takes from the traditionalists the rejection of attempts to use the methods of science to reduce the messiness of law. He associates this approach with monism, and rejects it as inconsistent with 'autonomy-based pluralism', the view that the law should facilitate humans' autonomy by providing them with a range of options (ibid., 192). Dagan illustrates this with the range and diversity of property institutions that are available in the law and concludes that the extension of these available choices is 'autonomy-enhancing' (ibid., 190). (This makes Dagan an autonomy monist, with autonomy conveniently kept vague enough so as to seem both unified and beyond reproach.) Though not central to my argument, it is worth remarking here that Dagan is wrong to think any of this poses a challenge to monistic theories. The reason is that when Dagan talks of pluralism he has three different kinds of pluralism in mind. One is *methodological* pluralism, the view that different disciplines have irreducibly different methods of inquiry; the second is *value*

---

[2]In the case of Cohen, Dagan (2013, p. 47) quotes him saying that 'Moral judgment will always be necessary "in order to render normative significance to brute facts"'. The quote in question is not found in the work cited, and I did not find it elsewhere. In fact, in the essay cited, Cohen (1934, p. 42) expressed a rather different sentiment: 'Modern ethics seeks to attain moral knowledge through the methods of science. . . .Perceived values are brought into a system, in modern ethics, in the same way that perceived facts of color, weight, size, *etc.*, are brought into a system in the science of physics'.

pluralism, the view that fundamental values are not all reducible to a single value;[3] and the third is *institutional* or *doctrinal* pluralism, the view that (private) law should offer a diversity of legal arrangements and enable individuals to choose among them. There is no simple connection among the three.

Some of the scientific realists (e.g., Cook 1941) explicitly embraced methodological monism as part of a commitment to the larger program of the unity of science, but whether one accepts this idea, it is perfectly consistent with greater doctrinal pluralism. By the same token, a value monist committed to the idea that the law should only be concerned with the promotion of welfare will have no difficulty seeing the importance of diversity and choice. John Stuart Mill (1859/1991) argued on monistic (utilitarian) grounds for the importance of diversity of options as required for people to develop their autonomy.[4] There are similarly familiar arguments (e.g., Demsetz 1967) based on monistic foundations in support of a diversity of property institutions.[5] There is also reason to be skeptical of the link in the other direction. It is not clear that different values are involved in ownership and, say, leasehold, thus making value monism and doctrinal pluralism perfectly consistent.

3 Legal Realism and Legal Doctrine

3.1 Transparency and Opacity

The preceding discussion helps us identify Dagan's realism, as well as its opponents. There is no question Dagan's approach is opposed to the conceptualist version of formalism, but also that his views are also very different from those of the scientific legal realists. What is less obvious is that he should be opposed to doctrinalism.

For one, legal doctrine can hardly be accused of monism of either values or doctrines. To be sure, there have been those who have argued that at the foundation of all law, one can find a single value—liberty, welfare, independence—but such

[3]With respect to value pluralism Dagan (2013, pp. 162–163) makes both the 'descriptive' claim mentioned in the text, but also argues that private law institutions should promote a diversity of values. But one may endorse value pluralism, and still think there are good institutional or political reasons why law (or just private law) should only be concerned with promoting a subset of those values.

[4]Interestingly, with respect to the argument developed in Sect. 3, Mill seems to have endorsed a view that somewhat resembles what I call 'opacity' with respect to the promotion of personal happiness. In his *Autobiography* (1873/1989, p. 117) Mill wrote: 'I never...wavered in the conviction that happiness is the test of all rules of conduct, and the end of life. But I now thought that this end was only to be attained by not making it the direct end....Aiming...at something else, [people] find happiness by the way'.

[5]In fact, welfarist theories have been criticized for wrongly assuming that increasing the number of available options will always promote welfare (Schwartz 2016; cf. Dworkin 1988, ch. 5). This criticism affects Dagan's view as well, for if it is sound—and it is supported by extensive empirical evidence—more choice can actually undermine autonomy.

arguments are unlikely to find favor with doctrinalists considering the number of people who have been involved in the development of the common law. Since legal doctrine, at least in the common law, is complex and develops without special regard to overarching theories, there is little reason to think, and no historical evidence to support the view, that it could be reduced to a single idea (Waddams 2003; Lobban 2014). Other supposed advantages of a realist approach do not seem to set realism apart from more traditional doctrinalism in any clear way: pragmatism, sensitivity to context, flexibility and adaptability to changing circumstances are all familiar attributes of the common law from long before the advent of legal realism (Atiyah 1987, ch. 2; Eisenberg 1988, pp. 70–74, 105–18).

Dagan also favors narrower legal categories (Dagan 2013, pp. 57–58), but this too will not sound particularly controversial to a doctrinalist. The charge may be fairly directed at conceptualists, but doctrinalists are typically at the opposite end of the spectrum on this matter. Indeed, if the conceptualist is right, it implies that the doctrinalists' efforts are rather pointless: Why bother with the writing comprehensive treatises that analyze thousands of cases in minute detail, if most answers to legal questions can be derived from a few general principles? Doctrinal lawyers are the last to need a reminder that law is made up of narrow categories: narrow categories is what they do (contra ibid., 138).

Despite all this, Dagan is generally dismissive of legal doctrine. Of course, in line with his general approach, he does not say doctrine is useless, adopting instead a midway position that purports to give legal doctrine some role in maintaining the law's stability while '*occasionally* us[ing] social developments and new cases as triggers for rethinking the doctrine's conventional understanding' (Dagan 2015, p. 1890). Or as he also puts it, doctrine is valuable while '*pure* Doctrinalism' is impossible. But what is the problem with legal doctrine? The inadequacies of pure doctrine strike Dagan as so overwhelming that in *Reconstructing Legal Realism* he spends only a few sentences to refuting it. He attributes to the realists a fundamental insight that demolished the idea that legal doctrine can be sufficient for legal analysis: 'For (almost) every case…lawyers find opposite doctrinal sources that need to be accommodated.… The availability of such a multiplicity of sources on any given question, all of which can be either expanded or contracted, results in profound and irreducible doctrinal indeterminacy (Dagan 2013, p. 21). There are innumerable cases and even more judicial dicta going in different directions. As a result, any competent lawyer can reconstruct a properly legally-sounding argument for (virtually) any legal conclusion. The implication is that legal doctrine alone can never constrain judge or guide any individual.

This is indeed a familiar realist theme (e.g., Frank 1934, p. 12413), and Dagan credits the legal realists not just with identifying this problem, but also for offering the solution. It is not doctrine alone that constrains judges, but doctrine plus the convergence of lawyers' shared values. Correspondingly, Dagan urges lawyers to discuss the values underlying doctrine more directly. However, in suggesting this Dagan goes beyond traditional legal realists, for he favors not just the attitude I earlier called openness, but also what I will call 'transparency'. To reiterate, a legal theory favors openness to the extent that it does not see a particularly clear division between law and non-law, between legal and non-legal values or ideas; a legal theory favors closure to the extent that it wishes legal discourse, as much as possible, to be closed to or autonomous from such non-legal influences. The choice between openness or closure is thus the major question that divides legal realists (of both strands) from formalists (of both strands). The question of openness is different from the question whether legal decisions should *transparently* discuss those values or opt for opacity. Plainly, the question of transparency does not arise if one opts for closure, but openness does not *imply* transparency. One may favor a relatively open legal system, yet prefer judges not to discuss them directly.

A different way of formulating transparency is in terms of the relationship between rules and the reasons that underlie them. Doctrinalism is premised on the idea that answers to legal questions must be grounded in the rules themselves and that there are no underlying reasons that these legal rules represent. This approach is thus different from the two different open approaches which assume that underpinning the legal rules are non-legal reasons which are the ultimate guides to action. In practice, the more opaque is the view, the more it will tend follow rules even when they conflict with their underlying reasons (roughly, legal rules as exclusionary reasons); a more transparent approach will favor thinking of rules as heuristic approximations (roughly, legal rules as rules of thumb) which ought to give way when they conflict with their underlying reasons.

We can thus distinguish between three distinct positions with respect to legal doctrine: (1) doctrinalism (closed); (2) traditional legal realism (open but opaque); and (3) Dagan's realism (open and transparent). This may seem like excessive hair splitting, but I will try to demonstrate that these three positions are importantly different. A preliminary question with respect to these possibilities is whether opacity is even possible. To some scholars writing today, especially in the United States, it seems the answer to this question is obviously negative. That doctrine could stand in the way of direct engagement with values is, at best, a naïve belief, one from which the legal realists have thankfully liberated us. They look at scholars from other countries who continue to peddle this idea as benighted flat Earthers who refuse to face reality.

It is not obvious, however, that this view is correct, and it is even less obvious that traditional legal realists thought so. Llewellyn (1945, p. 227) distinguished between two styles of adjudication, which he called 'grand style' and the 'formal style'. The mark of the formal style is that 'the rules of law alone—alone—plus our dogmatic techniques of distinguishing, telling the dictum from decision and the like, are enough to decide our cases'. This view implies that Llewellyn thought that following 'pure doctrine' is not just possible, but a historical reality. Based on his own evaluation of the case-law, Llewellyn argued that the formal style was actually the dominant style in American courts in the late nineteenth and early twentieth century (ibid., 227–229). In this period, when judges tended to decide cases on the basis of legal materials alone, Llewellyn did not think that the wealth of sources made them reach whatever decision they wanted. Llewellyn was critical of the formal style, but the critique was not that the law was unpredictable, nor was it that judges failed to articulate the actual grounds for their decisions. Llewellyn's complaint was that the decisions reached were bad. Llewellyn's preference for what he called the 'grand style' was likewise couched in normative terms: 'The formal style of the common law tradition crippled all but its few best men. The grand style of that tradition, on the other hand, stirs many merely average men up into the beginnings of greatness' (Llewellyn 1960, p. 305). The difference is significant. If doctrinal constraint is impossible, then doctrinalism does not even get off the ground; if it is possible, it is open for the doctrinalist to argue that its advantages outweigh its problems.[6]

More intriguingly, traditional realists differed from Dagan also in favoring opacity. The realists clearly recognized the place and influence of values on the law and criticized formalists (of both stripes) for denying it or wishing it away. However, what one rarely finds in the work of Llewellyn and most other traditional realists is the explicit, conscious weighing of values that Dagan favors. Most of Llewellyn's articles on contract and commercial law are thoroughly doctrinal and replete with citations to cases. What one does not find in them is any transparent discussion of values of the kind Dagan associates with legal realism. Llewellyn's teaching, both in his contract and commercial law courses and in his more jurisprudential courses was almost devoid of discussions of values like liberty or equality. For example, Llewellyn taught a course an introductory course called 'Elements of the Law' at the University of Chicago. Unlike another instructor's use of 'materials [that] included numerous excerpts from classical philosophy... Llewellyn included no philosophy, only cases' (Hutchinson 2003, p. 156).

Here is how Llewellyn (1960, p. 307) explained his approach: 'What the legal system does is to provide materials which have behind them cumulated experience easy otherwise to overlook, and which also assure adequate steadiness in movement; and the *well-built* portions of the received legal system give guidance in the lines and manner of sound movement.' To be sure, as Llewellyn immediately stressed, 'the test [for the law] remains living reason, explicit; and whether a reason is living must be determined from current life and from without.' But note that here too, the 'test' for the law does not come from any philosophical theory, but from 'current life'. Jerome Frank too had occasion to consider whether lawyers should engage in a more transparent analysis of 'values and policies'. He replied that '[i]n a legal system, social values, ideals, policies, find their expression in legal rules, standards and principles....[W]hatever otherwise may be the effect of [legal] rules on the community's mores, yet, *so far as the courts are concerned*, those policies and ideals become operative chiefly in one direct way—through specific decisions in specific law suits' (Frank 1947, p. 1324 (emphasis in original)). Leon Green noted 'the elasticity of legal theories as well as their wealth' as the reason why they cannot provide determinate answers (Green 1930, p. 791). In the famous *Palsgraf* (1928) case, he said, the competing theories underlying the majority and dissent could have been relied upon to reach the opposite outcome (ibid., 791–92). But this did not lead

[6]If Dagan were to argue that this view is a form of realism, only one that favors certain values (stability or certainty) over others, he would in effect be arguing that doctrinalism is also a form of realism (albeit perhaps a normatively unappealing one), not that it is impossible.

him to skeptical conclusions about the integrity of law, nor did he think that climbing to even loftier planes of theory would make the law more determinate. He railed against an approach that had one 'fantastic generalization' clashing with another 'equally fantastic generalization... in an atmosphere wholly removed from the cases, and in phrases which have no integrity of their own'. His advice for avoiding such conflicts, one that will surprise those familiar only with second- or third-hand accounts of legal realism, was 'to stick by the cases' (ibid. 796).

Finally, in Cardozo's writings, both in his judicial capacity and in his reflections on adjudication, what one finds is discussion of the way the judicial process and the common law method are means for getting to legal answers. This is true for the vast majority of cases, where the judge 'compare[s] the case before him with the precedents', but also for those in which the judge has to 'fashion law for the litigants before him' by 'extract[ing] from the precedents the underlying principle, the *ratio decidendi*' and 'then determine the path or direction along which the principle is to move and develop' (Cardozo 1921, pp. 19, 21, 28).[7] Cardozo freely admitted that in the gaps judges make law, and that when this happens, this is done 'in the recognition of the need that law shall conform itself to an end'. However, even when this is the case, 'the end [is] best served by disregarding it and thinking only of the means' (ibid., 116).

In contrast to all that, Dagan wants lawyers to transparently discuss the value questions at stake. Dagan thus repurposes 'legal theory' (Dagan 2013, p. 85) as the solution to the indeterminacy of doctrine. Properly conceived, legal theory is not applied economics or applied moral philosophy, but the place for adopting and adapting ideas coming from all other disciplines into a unique blend suited for law. It is this mélange that is somehow capable of 'compensat[ing] for the limitations of both external and internal analyses of law' (ibid., 93). Where traditional legal realists like Llewellyn, Cardozo, and (to a lesser extent) Frank looked to practice and legal doctrine as the place where unphilosophical but civic-minded practitioners will develop 'working' solutions to legal problems, Dagan wants lawyers to become versed in theory.

For anyone familiar with contemporary (American) legal discourse, this will sound familiar (Gjerdingen 1986, pp. 398–408). But this is a surprising claim for someone who thinks that legal doctrine contains conflicting materials that cannot constrain judges, for the same, only worse, is true of discussions of value. Though this is a crucial point for his position, Dagan's argument in support for his view is brief and rather offhand: 'At least relative to the hopeless indeterminacy of pure doctrinal analysis, a contextual normative inquiry can secure a much more stable, and thus predictable, legal equilibrium' (Dagan 2013, p. 134, n. 22). It is hard to see how this could be true. Doctrine is undoubtedly often vague, but the values Dagan invokes are vaguer. Doctrine often is contradictory; but so are values. More

[7]Whether Cardozo was a realist is sometimes contested. I think he was an exponent of traditional legal realism. Dagan (2013, p. 3) mentions him as one of the proponents of his version of legal realism.

accurately, whether values conflict is a contested question among moral philosophers; but those who deny this—those who think that with proper analysis one can show that values do not conflict—are those who are likely to hold a similar view with respect to legal doctrine. The best-known exponent of such ideas is Ronald Dworkin, and he famously acknowledged that in both law and morality demonstrating coherence this is a Herculean task.

It is here that Dagan's espousal of value pluralism comes back to haunt him. Dagan's claim that transparency is less vague and indeterminate than legal doctrine might have had some plausibility if he had been a value monist,[8] but it is unconvincing coming from a value pluralist. At one point he lists 'autonomy, personhood, utility, labor, community, and distributive justice' (Dagan 2013, p. 164) as *some* of the relevant values underlying our property law regime, and as such relevant for deciding property cases. It is hard to see how determinacy could be borne of such a list. If one were to seek some clarity and precision on any of the values he listed in the available literature, one would find a range of conflicting opinions that would put any case of doctrinal indeterminacy to shame. And as values conflict, decisions based on them will inevitably call for some kind of 'balancing' that is amenable to numerous possible resolutions that reflect subjective preferences.

Thus, the possibility of formulating legal doctrine in different ways to justify different outcomes can be recreated at least as easily with respect to values. Based on competing conceptualizations of values like equality or liberty, based on the ability to give different weights to different values, one may deduce different outcomes to particular cases. In fact, some of the scientific legal realists (Oliphant and Hewitt 1929, pp. xv–xvi) made exactly this point:

> [I]t must be clear that, for any case wherein there is a clash of two groups having conflicting interests, two conflicting major premises can always be formulated, one embodying one set of interests, the other embodying the other. . . . That two such conflicting major premises can always be found is but the result of the fundamental futility of this approach as a method of determining how cases should be decided.

This is, in essence, the same argument Dagan found convincing about the indeterminacy of legal doctrine, only made at the level of values. If successful in the former context, it is a fortiori successful in the latter.

Here is a concrete example. At one point Dagan considers the question of whether a court should have invalidated restrictive covenants, as the United States Supreme Court did in *Shelley v. Kramer* (1948). '[V]alue pluralism', Dagan says, 'not only allows but also *requires* the invalidation of such interpersonal practices as the racially restrictive covenants discussed in *Shelley v. Kraemer*' (2013, p. 180, emphasis added). I have no quarrel with Dagan's claim that such considerations are internal to the law of property (ibid., 180 n. 69, 220) and therefore it is easy to accept that value pluralism *permits* the outcome of *Shelley*. But nothing he says compels his

[8]Indeed, I speculate that one of the reasons why monistic economic theories of law attracted so many American academic lawyers was the perception (justified or not) that they could help regain the lost determinacy of law.

conclusion that this concrete outcome (or, for that matter, any other) is required by it. Let us assume for simplicity's sake that this case only involves the values of autonomy and distributive justice. Each of these values has widely, even wildly, divergent interpretations. And even if we settled on one for each of these values, they still have to be balanced against each other. Pushing autonomy up a notch or two, taking distributive justice down a bit, leads to the conclusion that people should be allowed to do with their property as they wish, even if their actions are racially motivated. In short, if transparency is to make a difference to legal practice, it is likely to increase indeterminacy, not decrease it.

3.2 The Problems with Transparency

The problem identified in the example of *Shelley v. Kramer* is generalizable, and it forces us to try and evaluate the costs and benefits of value transparency. For context, consider the following words:

> Any man who knows how to handle the professional apparatus of reference can find, with moderate industry, something like a show of authority for almost anything: and it is the delight of a certain class of advocates to snatch an advantage (though it is apt to be a fleeting one) by this method. But the law is not made by casual and hasty decisions in courts of first instance. Its guiding principles and the harmony of its controlling ideas must be sought in the considered judgments of the higher tribunals which command universal respect; and whatever is contrary to the general consent of leading authorities ought to be frankly discarded as erroneous.

This is a quote from Pollock (1912, p. 114), not a name frequently associated with legal realism. Pollock identifies here the exact same problem with legal doctrine the 'discovery' of which is usually attributed to the legal realists: Any competent lawyer familiar with existing legal materials and the techniques of case analysis can construct a 'valid' legal argument leading to virtually any outcome. Pollock then proceeds to offer a similar solution to Dagan's. It is true, he says, that there are many logically possible outcomes one can reach by using the tools of the lawyer's trade, but that does not undermine the law's predictability and determinacy when one takes into account that 'the law' is not *just* what one finds in the legal materials. The law consists of *accepted* interpretations by the legal community. When there is a single appellate court that eventually decides the cases, adherence to legal doctrine could explain which uses of past legal materials are 'correct' and which are 'incorrect'. Pollock, in other words, suggests that if the constraints on doctrine imposed not by logical or conceptual analysis but by the standards of community acceptability, the problem of indeterminacy can often be abated. Importantly, this solution *depends* on, rather than being thwarted by, opacity (or closeness). After Pollock, many defenders of closeness or opacity have given roughly similar answers. Birks (2003, p. 159), for example, has stated that adhering strictly to doctrine 'is the only way to keep extremism at bay and to enable people from different value-systems to sit on the same bench'.[9] There is thus an argument *for* opacity *from* recognition and respect for value pluralism.

Whether closure or opacity can have these beneficial effects of maintaining stability in a pluralistic society is an empirical hypothesis—it may be that rules will only allow for consensus when there is agreement on the outcome, but will not be able to overcome disagreements when the conflicting underlying reasons lead to different conclusions—but it is not implausible on its face. There is empirical evidence suggesting that partisan (i.e., transparent) political discussion often leads to intensification of political disagreement Sunsein (2009, ch. 2). Thus, it may be that maintaining discussion at the 'technical' level of legal doctrine can reduce some legal indeterminacy. If this is the case, there is a value-based, design-based, argument for opacity (and perhaps even some degree of closure).

This point comes out particularly clearly in the context of the rule of law. Dagan (2013, p. 195) distinguishes between two senses of the rule of law—rule of law as guidance and rule of law as constraint—but there is another sense of the rule of law, which he does not discuss, and which might be called, 'the rule of law as impersonality'. This is the sense in which we can sensibly talk of 'the rule of law and not of men', despite the fact that the law is administered by men (and women). We can say that it is the law that rules a case and not the particular person deciding it when changing the person deciding the case is unlikely to change its resolution. When this is the case, it is 'the law' that decides the case, and it does not matter that it is 'channeled' through a human being, because the person in question is only, to use Montesquieu's (1748/1989, p. 163) old phrase, 'the mouthpiece' of the law. This sense of the rule of law is particularly important to some doctrinal lawyers. Birks explained that '[a] judge must be able to say: "It is not me who does this to you, it is the law. Look, I will show you".' Any other view, he said, is 'antithetical to the rule of law' (Birks 1999, pp. 21, 22).

The suggestion mentioned above is that closure or opacity are important guarantees of the rule of law in the sense of impersonality. But, of course, if this is the case, they are also relevant to the senses of the rule of law Dagan does talk about: If the outcome of a case depends on the judge assigned to hear it, then law's guidance is undermined. If a transparent discussion of values is even less determinate than legal doctrine, then the conception of law Dagan favors is even less constraining on those required to decide cases. This is true even if one believes in the possibility of rational

[9]I consider Peter Birks a defender of closeness, but these words also support opacity. Similar arguments come from rather different corners. Sunstein (2018, p. 123): 'A great virtue of rules is that they limit permissible grounds for both action and argument. . . .[I]n a heterogeneous society, containing people of limited time and capacities, this is an enormous advantage. It saves effort, time, and expense. By truncating the sorts of value-disputes that can arise in law, it also ensures that disagreements will occur along a narrowly restricted range.' Raz (1986, p. 58): 'the practice [of reliance on opaque rules] allows the creation of a pluralistic culture. For it enables people to unite in support of some "low or medium level" generalizations despite profound disagreements concerning their ultimate foundations, which some seek in religion, others in Marxism, or in Liberalism etc.'

argument and the possibility of persuasion on questions of value when conducted in ideal settings. But when taking into account the effect of time constraints, insufficient information, and cognitive biases, there is a real risk that calling on judges to discuss values transparently will result in impressive-sounding window dressing behind which there are only ad hoc, intuitive judgments. Dagan comes close to admitting this when he writes that his approach 'will generally rely on pragmatic judgments as to the optimal degree of suspension from the practice of law and as to the optimal mix of sociohistorical and normative perspectives that should be called in for its analysis' (Dagan 2013, p. 100).[10]

Dagan's response to such concerns over the indeterminacy of value is that 'the convergence of lawyers' background understandings at a given time and place generates a significant measure of stability' (ibid., 210–11). It is unclear whether a similar background can guarantee a convergence in views: William Brennan and Antonin Scalia were both Catholics from New Jersey who attended Harvard Law School, and if such similar backgrounds did not result in similar views, there is little reason to expect any convergence in lawyers' background understandings. Lawyers come from all backgrounds and their views are as divergent as anyone else's. Convergence among lawyers can be generated, if at all, only by creating a homogeneous but unrepresentative legal elite.[11]

By contrast, opacity does not require us to think that there are no values behind legal doctrine, only that judges should not directly address them. It is the view that when faced with a novel legal question, they should try to solve it by grappling with legal doctrine rather than by thinking of themselves as amateur philosophers or social theorists. On this view doctrine is not a stumbling block that stands in the way of the 'real' questions. It is there because of doubts over judges' ability to resolve conflicts by transparent appeal to values, it is the view that given judges' limitations they are more likely to reach overall better outcomes (including a more certain and stable law) when they find legal doctrine binding. So understood doctrine is not a nefarious device for judges to hide behind; it is a means—obviously imperfect—for discouraging or minimizing some bad tendencies that judges, like all other humans, are prone to.

---

[10]Appeal to intuition is of course a familiar part of *traditional* legal realism (Hutcheson 1928; Frank 1930, pp. 102–104). This appeal is understandable, for given the likely identity of judges, their intuitions will typically broadly match mainstream community values. By contrast, scientific legal realists were much less enamored of the idea. Cohen (1934, pp. 45–46) is illustrative: 'From the standpoint of modern ethics conscience cannot be viewed as a final source of moral wisdom. Lawyers do not need to be told that conscience varies among men no less than the size of the human foot'.

[11]Frank (1930, p. 143) also appealed to shared community values as a means for generating uniformity, but he noticed its dark side: 'it is perhaps just possible that we could get stereotyped [i.e., similar, certain] results from our judges by picking stereotyped men for the judicial office'.

4 A Different Legal Realism: Legal Doctrine and Institutional Design

4.1 An Engineering Outlook on Law

The updated version of legal realism offered by Dagan and others before him who put 'legal theory' at the center are premised on great confidence that law, or the great judge, or, nowadays the great legal academic, will have the answers to society's problems. I don't. When reading cases, I often see well-meaning but rather jejune attempts by judges who are intelligent but with have little relevant training. They are armed with little more than vague verbal formulas and appeals to open ended values, backed up by speculations rather than empirical evidence, to provide answers to policy questions. Opacity is obviously an imperfect solution, but it should be understood as part of a wider set of 'devices' with a similar aim. In this section I wish to turn the critical comments of the previous section into more constructive suggestions by examining those devices on the basis of other strands of realist thinking. As already mentioned, alongside the more traditional realist view, there existed a fundamentally different one that was more scientific in orientation. Here, I want to add to it the idea of addressing the question of the value of legal doctrine by looking at it in terms of comparative institutional analysis. This perspective is more often associated with legal process rather than legal realism, but I think it's an important theme in realist writing as well. (I cannot explore the issue here, but I note in passing that I see legal process as an important version of legal realism rather than as a reaction to it.) Llewellyn's support for adjudication in the 'grand style' is a typical example. As quoted above, Llewellyn thought that the grand style helped mediocre judges achieve greatness (1960, p. 305; also 1962, p. 38). Along similar lines, the Uniform Commercial Code was conceived in such a way that would push judges toward the grand style (Wiseman 1987, p. 497), thereby improving the quality of their decisions. Llewellyn's view depended on the idea that law gets its authority from corresponding to a particular political community's values. He thus sought to create the institutional setting that will push judges to be informed by these values.

The argument in this section tries to develop an institutional perspective on legal doctrine and legal reasoning, but on the basis of the scientific strand of legal realism. A key aspect of it is that legal doctrine often reflects not an attempt to craft a first-order 'best' rule that directs the judge to the normatively best answer; instead, it attempts to direct certain questions to certain bodies, or to exclude certain matters from consideration, because of a wholesale perception that some bodies are more likely to decide them better, especially in circumstances in which the ability to provide direct guidance on the first-order best answer is limited. This approach often starts from the assumption that 'pragmatic' judgment on the basis of all potentially relevant considerations is precisely the kind most prone to the influence of cognitive biases and subjective preferences (cf. Schauer 2006). Such an approach thus involves choices that have costs that cannot be avoided by balancing values in tension.

The alternative that seems to me far more promising is captured in what Richard Posner (1997; also Priel 2016b) provocatively called 'the path away from the law'. This is not a reference to the Marxist idea of the withering away of law and state when communist utopia finally arrives, nor is it a reference to the libertarian view that sees most legal regulation as an unjustified intrusion into human freedom. By some measures there is more law today than ever before, and this is unlikely to change. Instead, it is the idea that with respect to much of the law the kind of skills that law-school-law develops and celebrates, the alleged virtues of the common law tradition, are of relatively little significance. What is needed is not the practical wisdom or common sense we use for dealing with everyday interactions with others, but the skills for addressing systemic problems.

Such an approach enjoys a poor reputation due to the perception that it favors cold 'managerialism' over justice, but I believe this criticism is often misplaced. While speedy resolution is obviously an important goal, and highly relevant also for achieving justice, the motivation for this approach is different. I will mention three interrelated points: First, solutions that look commonsensical ('reasonable', 'fair') in addressing a particular case can have bad consequences at a systemic level. By contrast, 'counterintuitive' solutions may prove superior when adopting a wider perspective. Solutions to such problems require expertise based in part on knowledge of the complex implications of individual actions. Judges have partially recognized this point and have developed various techniques aimed at limiting their intervention in matters they don't really understand. Deference in administrative law, reliance on experts (both directly as expert witnesses trials, and indirectly when relying on their judgment as reflected in legislative standards), are examples. So understood, however, such doctrines are confined to a narrow area: It is widely accepted that judges have no idea what the right concentration of certain particles in the atmosphere, so on such questions they defer to scientists. My point is that even when the question is at the 'core' of setting of legal standards (e.g., the appropriate scope of liability, the appropriate remedy for breach of contract), even in core 'lawyer's law' areas like contract, tort, or criminal law, counterintuitive answers may be superior at the systemic level than the ones that appear fair. For example, many find retributive justice—the idea that offenders 'deserve' the punishment they receive and that the punishment should be proportionate to their blameworthiness—very natural. There is no question that people often feel elation at the hardships that befall those they consider bad (including, remarkably, fictional characters). The same rationale also underlies accounts of personal responsibility as the basis for tort liability. Some scholars have argued that retributive punishment may have evolutionary origins, as it can explain the evolution of human sociality (Richerson and Boyd 2005, pp. 200–201). But this natural response, one that may work well for individual cases and small-scale societies, can have undesirable effects in other contexts. It is why in practice no legal system adheres to such ideas in anything close to pure form in either criminal or tort law. The American criminal justice system, which came closer than most in recent decades to adopting this approach, can hardly be called a success story.

The second concern revolves around the role of appellate litigation as a means for creating general rules in a precedent-based system. Because of the way appellate litigation is conducted, its focus is often on the way a case resolves within the pattern of existing law, and also tends to focus on the litigants at the expense of the effects of the decision on the wider population. Even if they want to consider the broader effects of their decision, judges often do not have sufficient information on the likely consequences of their decisions and have to rely on conjecture. Courts have attempted to address the problems of lack of information, mainly by expanding participation in the legal proceedings to those who can bring useful information on the wider impact of a court decision. So-called 'friends of the court' are one way of addressing this problem. However, without adequate ability to assess the veracity of this information or adequately analyze it (Larsen 2014), courts' ability to make good use of this mechanism is limited.

Third, courts have responded to the lack of information by making extensive use of vague standards. Terms such as 'reasonable,' 'foreseeable' or 'fair' are a staple of judicial lawmaking, and they are a way of postponing an answer to problems when one does not have the means to address it in an informed way. To a body entrusted with making law on the basis of little relevant information, this may be the only realistic approach to lawmaking. When at a later time the court is forced to decide the matter, it often relies on little more than an intuitive sense of the case at hand. While the later case presumably does add some valuable information for making an informed decision, the specifics of the case and the lack of information about the decision's potential impact, may result in a poor decision.

There is no doubt that vague terms appear also in legislation, but legislation has also employed other law-crafting techniques, and those can better address indeterminacy and provide more refined legal responses to different factual scenarios. Faced with the need to provide a contextual answer that treats different people differently, income tax legislation does not demand of them a 'reasonable' amount of taxes (with the amount to be determined in an ad hoc fashion), nor does it adopt a simple rule (e.g., 25% of income). Instead, most countries adopt a complex array of rules, including variable marginal tax rates based on income, that adjust the level of taxation to the particular circumstances of different individuals. Judge-made law cannot realistically achieve this degree of precision.

These problems point to the limitations of traditional legal realism with its appeal to pragmatic balancing. These problems are in no way solved by the theory-based approach Dagan proposed. The alternative approach outlined here recognizes more consciously the need for an 'engineering' perspective, one that makes central the need to provide evidence-based, empirically-tested solutions to social problems (Howarth 2013). Such an approach can be seen in the work of some of the legal realists (Robinson 1934; cf. Llewellyn 1942, p. 802; Llewellyn 1960, pp. 170, 190). What follows is an attempt to sketch some of its implications for legal doctrine.

4.2 How to Think About Legal Doctrine

The problem with any attempt to apply an engineering approach like the one suggested here to legal doctrine is that it is hard to implement it at the level of the individual case. This is, I think, one of the main reasons why economic analysis of law, despite its enormous influence on the American legal academy, has not had a more profound impact on common law adjudication. To be sure, economic concepts and ideas now roll easily on the tongues of legal academics and some judges, and there is no question that they have influenced legal doctrine at the wholesale level. But when judges need to actually apply economic ideas to particular cases, the seemingly precise mathematical formulas become not very different from the vague verbal expressions that economic analysis has sought to displace. Even when a case comes before a judge sympathetic to the application of economics, he is bound to admit that the data needed to apply the 'Hand formula' to a particular case is just not there (*McCarty v. Pheasant Run, Inc.*, 1557). At this stage judges will have to continue to rely on intuition, practical wisdom, pragmatic judgment (or any similar expression) to decide the case. Legal theory is unlikely to have a significant effect on the quality of adjudication at this stage.

The approach suggested here seeks to respond to the problem of the indeterminacy by thinking about legal doctrine as a means for simplifying controversy, often by simplifying the number of cases in which judges feel the need to rely on legal theory. Central to thinking about law in this way is spending more time on design values such as simplicity and ease of use, precision, cost effectiveness, and robustness against the influence of interpersonal differences, rather than the values Dagan talks about (for instance, autonomy, equality, and community). Behind this approach is the idea that courts are not a neutral medium that pure law passes through, but a 'distorting' element that must be taken into account when thinking about the right laws to adopt. The fact that judges are human of limited time and ability, that they are prone to the same cognitive biases that affect all humans, must be taken into account when designing laws for them and by them.

Of course, all legal realists, just like everyone before them, recognized that law is administered by human judges. The remainder of this subsection considers three ways of implementing this idea in practice that reflect the scientific realist view on legal doctrine. Since such a view is often associated with 'social engineering' of humans, let me emphasize that my emphasis is on thinking about *law* in engineering terms, as a device that should be designed with humans' limitations in mind. I consider three ideas: giving a more prominent role to legislation; using what I call 'doctrinal devices' for the sake of minimizing the effects of biases and subjective forces on judges; and assessing substantive doctrines (in part) by their ability to minimize the biasing effects of adjudication.

4.2.1 Legislation

Traditional legal realists have a romantic attachment to common law adjudication as a method of solving disputes, one that is sensitive to the particular facts of the case while representing a kind of human (or humane) justice absent from legislation. The relative indifference to legal doctrine in contemporary incarnations of legal realism is part of this view, reflecting the view that doctrine stands in the way of doing justice. The revamped common-law method as practiced in (American) law schools' seminar rooms is seen as the solution. Legislation does not figure much in this discourse, because it does not readily lend itself to it. Judge-made law fits this discourse because it relies on vague standards, which judges then try to further specify with the aid of multipart 'tests'. Such tests have some value in making sure that the decision maker does not fail to take the relevant considerations into account, in giving some structure to otherwise loose thinking, but they are limited in their ability to guide and constrain judges. Because they involve the verbal balancing of competing considerations, they are easy to 'hack', i.e. it is easy to use them to justify opposite conclusions. By contrast, statutes make for a far duller reading, but they are usually a superior form of lawmaking, because they allow for a far more sophisticated forms of regulation. Legislation can be far more specific in its demands, and its prescriptions can be based more directly on experts with specialized knowledge on the matter at hand.[12]

To get a clearer sense of this view it may help to distinguish it from a related but different one. Preference for legislation is nowadays sometimes known as 'ethical positivism' and is traced by its proponents to Jeremy Bentham (Campbell 1999). This is no coincidence, as Bentham has a good claim to being the first scientific legal realist, which for him meant, among other things, rejecting the common law in favor of legislation (e.g., Bentham 1827, p. 291). However, while defenders of this view typically support it with political arguments, especially pertaining to legislation's superior democratic legitimacy (Campbell 1999, pp. 81, 85), I focus here on its potential for being more factually informed—more evidence based, as one might say today—than judge-made law, and for the capacity of the legislative form for superior legislative design.

By far, most law these days is public regulation that governs the quality and safety of aspects of the environment, as well as the specific regulation of different products (cars, drugs) and services (banking, insurance, air travel). Even in areas in which the common law is still dominant, it is in practice almost a sideshow to public regulation. Medical malpractice litigation is superficially governed by common-law negligence, but this forms only a relatively small part of a much larger body of regulation of health services, which includes setting physicians' professional standards and

---

[12]This point should not be overstated: This argument depends on comparing the institutional strengths and weaknesses of judges against those of other lawmakers, something that cannot be determined a priori, and on which the circumstances of different countries may yield different answers. In a country with a corrupt legislature, judge-made law may be superior.

licensing requirements. Even negligence litigation is heavily dependent on the medical profession for determining what counts as a 'reasonable doctor'. Traffic accidents, the type of event for which tort law is, by numbers, most in use, are now largely controlled by car safety regulation, road traffic regulation, and driver licensing laws. In many places, the 'fault' regime has been replaced by a complex scheme of no-fault and compulsory insurance. Even where negligence ostensibly remains the governing legal standard, there is in reality a wholly bureaucratized practice controlled by insurance companies that deals with the vast majority of such accidents in ways that are often quite different from what one finds in tort textbooks (Lewis 2005). One important reason for this change is the inadequacies and limitations of private-law regulation (*cf.* Schauer 2004). As a result, the common law approach, either in its doctrinal, 'traditional' form, or in the more theory-heavy version that Dagan envisions, plays a relatively small role in all this.

This is not meant to say that private *ordering* in the form contracting is unimportant; but even when an aspect of life is left to private ordering, its legislative regulation is often far more significant than the common law. The vast majority of contractual transactions are consumer contracts which are typically quite heavily regulated by legislation. Employment contracts, possibly the most significant contracts for most people's lives, are so heavily regulated that the subject has been cut off from contract law and is now considered a separate legal area, whose focus is the many ways in which government regulation restricts private ordering and departs from general contract-law doctrine. In common law jurisdictions no less than civil law jurisdictions, this is the age of statutes.

Of course, all the values Dagan talks about are found in the statutes no less than in the common law. This point helps identify the difference between our respective views: Despite the similarity in underlying values, legislation presents a different attitude to the *design* of legal solutions, a different approach to information gathering and to the practice of law-making itself. In some areas, such as the protection of the environment, the vague phraseology of the common-law tort of nuisance has given way to detailed laws based on scientific expertise. The effect of this is often to reduce the need for judges to engage in transparent discussion of values.

As is well documented, legislation has its own significant drawbacks. It is more likely to be captured by private interests, and it seems plausible to give courts an important role in protecting against such abuses. However, it is worth remembering that this abuse of legislation is the result of the fact that legislatures engage in transparent political debate. To introduce such debates to the judiciary risks undermining one of the most significant institutional advantages courts have over legislatures, and limits their ability to perform their supervisory role over legislative bodies.

4.2.2 The Institutional Role of Doctrinal Devices

The point just made may be summarized as follows: An important way to reduce the impact of judges' personality and political outlook effect on adjudication is to reduce judges' opportunities to develop the law, because they are likely to develop it in ways that make such negative influences more likely to occur. Even with that, it is fair to say that eliminating judges from the process of lawmaking altogether is unlikely to happen, and there are good reasons why it should not happen. Therefore, it is important to design the laws in such a way as to minimize the impact of judges' personality on the instances in which judges make law. This should be particularly central aim for those who think, following some legal realists, that legal doctrine cannot constrain judges. This approach provides a different lens through which to analyze legal rules (Komesar 1981).

Much of legal doctrine consists of substantive rules that pertain to certain factual scenarios. But doctrine also consists of different kind of rules, which I call 'doctrinal devices'. These are not substantive rules, but methods for dealing with substantive rules. Originalism, for example, is a doctrinal device meant to constrain judges by forcing them to base their decisions on some external standard, one that is supposed to be relatively objectively verifiable. (Whether any version of originalism can do that is not a question I consider here.) Legal rights, understood as trumps, are another such device, one designed to give special weight to considerations that are otherwise difficult to quantify and therefore tend to be given insufficient weight. Still other devices include the choice between rules and standards, justiciability and standing doctrines, precedent (itself a label that covers several quite different possible institutional devices), and the canons of interpretation.[13] From an institutional perspective these doctrinal devices should be seen as attempts to control judges' reasoning process in order to improve their decision making. They do so by, in the first place, taking certain disputes away from judges; at a second stage, by limiting the kind of considerations a judge may entertain in the disputes they do hear; and, finally, by giving special prominence to certain considerations (often designated as 'rights') over others.

The realists are sometimes taken to have shown that just like substantive doctrines, doctrinal devices are thoroughly manipulable and therefore equally incapable of constraining judges. They are just more-or-less sophisticated covers by which judges deciding cases hide their subjective preference behind a veneer of constraint. There is no doubt that such manipulation is possible and that it takes place. But that such manipulation exists does not yet show that doctrinal devices have no force. After all, if that had been the case, we could not talk about individual judges, or legal systems, being more or less 'formalistic'. And if precedent had no constraining force, we could not say, for example, that same-sex marriage is currently legal across the United States but was not so in 2010.

The approach proposed here would focus on how effective such devices are and whether there are ways of making them more effective in constraining judges.

[13]No less relevant for a complete institutional analysis, although perhaps less naturally classified as doctrinal devices, are rules regarding panel size and majority rules, judicial opinion technique (single opinion, seriatim, opinion of the court), judicial appointment procedures, norms regulating judicial impartiality, and other ways that shape the environment in which judges work.

4.2.3 Institutional Analysis of Substantive Doctrines

Less obvious, but no less important, is the influence of institutional considerations on substantive legal doctrine. Even if doctrinal devices may be understood in the way just described, substantive doctrines themselves look like they aim at fitting or promoting a certain moral value or goal that it serves. Non-instrumental accounts say that the law just manifests a certain moral tenet or value (e.g., moral responsibility); instrumental accounts look at law as a means for promoting some values. (Dagan, for instance, makes various normative suggestions with respect to the reform of property law because he thinks they will promote autonomy.) But such debates miss out on many of the questions that are actually found within legal doctrine, and which are motivated by institutional concerns.

Such considerations have long played a central role in the shaping of substantive doctrines. Summarizing his review of cases on duty of care in negligence, Leon Green (1928, pp. 1014, 1044, 1045), a leading legal realist tort scholar, wrote: 'administrative difficulties have always been the first to present themselves to common law courts. . . .Duties must await the court's finding a workable method by which they can be given meaning'. The idea that no duties will be found (and consequently no liability be imposed) because courts have difficulties dealing with them is but one example of the way substantive doctrines, supposedly concerned with the interpersonal relations (what duties we owe to each other), have been shaped by courts' worries over their institutional limits (Henderson Jr. 1982).

The legal limits on recovery for certain kind of losses are an obvious example. If one looks at legal doctrine as a conduit for the promotion of some value, such limitations appear unfair, and so suggest some kind of hidden bias. Psychiatric injury is no less real than physical injury; its impact on one's ability to lead a successful life is often more severe than that of a physical harm, and recovery from it can be more fraught. Add to it the fact that from a scientific perspective, the very difference between physical and mental injury is dubious, and the law's treating the two differently looks, at best, suspect. All this is true, and an institutional perspective on doctrine need not deny it, but it can still help make some sense of the law. From this perspective, the law on these matters looks like an attempt, albeit sometimes clumsy, to address the real problem of identifying genuine cases of psychiatric harm, rather than an arbitrary distinction. Second, if the institutional problem is real, then it suggests that simply changing the doctrine (in the example: removing all limitations on liability for psychiatric injury) will not be without costs. Such a view therefore implies that to solve the problem will require not just a simple change in a legal rule, but also some institutional adjustment. On the other hand, such an approach also provides a sound basis for changing the doctrine if the grounds for the distinction (e.g., judges' limited ability to separate real from fake cases of pure psychiatric injury) no longer hold, for example because advances in technology makes correct diagnosis more reliable.

With both doctrinal devices (e.g., rules about justiciability) and substantive doctrines like duty of care, doctrine makes a real practical difference. Contrary to the view that legal doctrine is thoroughly manipulable and therefore has no practical effect, such institutional decisions have real practical consequences. A precedent that, for example, determines that there is no duty of care with respect to a kind of activity or relationship, or a precedent that says that there will be no compensation for a certain kind of harm, will have real consequences for the ability of certain individuals to sue for damages. Such cases are unlikely to get litigated, and if they are, will usually result in a summary judgment for the defendant. Perhaps even more than vague verbal formulas, multi-step 'tests', or the normative basis of certain doctrines (e.g., whether a particular defense is a justification or excuse, and the implications that follow from that), matters on which 'pragmatic judgment' can be influenced by subjective judgment, rules on the scope of liability based on institutional concerns have the potential to have significant effect in practice.

5 Conclusion

Let me tie the threads of the argument. The main goal of this essay has been to explain why it makes sense to speak of legal reasoning without having to assume that lawyers engage in some esoteric ways of thinking. I have attempted to answer this question by considering the work of the legal realists, often credited with demystifying the law and legal reasoning by forcefully arguing that behind the odd jargon and outdated ritual, there is nothing special about law. If true, it suggests that law and legal reasoning are just normal reasoning about moral or political questions conducted in a stylized language one learns at law school. An enticing conclusion to draw from this view is that the best way to treat legal doctrine is ignore it.

Dagan's legal realism is a good illustration of this view. He is largely dismissive of legal doctrine and urges lawyers to address directly—transparently—the real value questions underlying the doctrine. As I have tried to show, this reflects a familiar but historically inaccurate reading of one strand of realist thought that matches present-day American academic legal discourse, one that prizes a vague discussion of values as the key to solving society's problems.

If one takes seriously the idea of testing ideas against reality, then this version of legal realism must itself be taken as a testable hypothesis about the right shape for a legal system, one that has to be tested by its effects. Though American legal practice is more doctrinal than its academic counterpart, I think it is fair to say that it is generally more 'realistic' than the legal practice in most other jurisdictions. (In this regard, it is notable that Dagan's complaint is not that American law and the American legal academy are too realistic, but that they are not realistic enough (2013, p. 13).)

Even if one is certain that American law is overall superior to the law of other countries, one must acknowledge that some of its strengths are inseparable from some of its weaknesses. It will not do to identify its problems and promise to balance them out so that we will be able to capture all of the good and avoid all of the bad. It is impossible to adopt the favored balanced, midway position on *all* questions. Consequently, it is inevitable that in some respects a more legal realistic legal system will fare worse than a less realistic one.

It would be presumptuous to suggest that all the ills of the American law are the product of the fact that it is closer to the realist end of the spectrum than most other legal system, but there is a good case to be made that some of them are, especially those having to do with the corrupting influence of politics on American law and the role given in it to low-evidence ‘legal theory’. Both phenomena are arguably connected and seem to me to be a direct result of the greater transparency of American legal discourse. Though he does not use this terminology, one of the distinctive features of what Kagan (2001) called ‘adversarial legalism’ (his label for ‘the American way of law’) is the politicization of law and the involvement of lawyers in what elsewhere is decided by experts.

Given the less than stellar record of American law on many issues, and especially the perception that this record has partly to do with its underlying ideology about the relationship between law and political ideas, the proposal to push legal realism further by urging lawyers to adopt a more transparent approach deserves to be tested not in seminar rooms, but in the real world. While I know of no conclusive evidence either way, here is a sort of hypothetical thought experiment that may shed some light on the matter: If there existed a way of avoiding the costs of realism, there is reason to believe that all legal systems would converge toward it. But reality is quite different. American law is the closest to Dagan’s realism, and yet in remains exceptional. People from other legal systems, including ones that are historically quite close to it, look to American law and often recoil from what they see. Perhaps because the relative costs and benefits are difficult to measure, and perhaps because the determination whether something is a cost or a benefit is itself, in part, a product of a particular political tradition, different legal systems have largely remained more formalistic. But this is enough to show that the benefits of a realist (transparent) approach are not unambiguous and evident.

This is not to say that the issues American lawyers discuss need not be discussed; it is that it is unclear that it should be lawyers, armed with legal theory, who should be deciding them. And it is not clear that having law as a domain of constant political disputation is the basis for an effective legal system. This is the background for an alternative way for thinking about legal doctrine, one that can be traced to a less familiar strand of legal realist thinking. This approach more openly embraces science and engineering as its model, and seeks to explain the role doctrine plays in such terms. Rather than dismissing legal reasoning as an illusion, it provides an unmysterious answer to what makes it unique without: It is concerned with institutional constraints in a way that does not figure in first-order moral discussion. This view explains why there may be good reasons for less transparent discussion of values within legal discourse, as well as why the legal response to a given factual scenario may be justifiably different from the first-order moral answer. How much of a change such constraints make, and whether it is overall for the good are very difficult questions to test empirically, but comparative work like Kagan’s (2001) shows that there is some empirical evidence that a different approach is possible, that it makes a practical difference, and that it is not without its virtues.

References

Alexander L (1998) The banality of legal reasoning. Notre Dame Law Rev 73:517–533

Arnold TW (1935) Apologia for jurisprudence. Yale Law J 44:729–753

Atiyah PS (1987) Pragmatism and theory in English law. Stevens, London

Beever A (2013) Forgotten justice: the forms of justice in the history of legal and political theory. Oxford University Press, Oxford

Beever A, Rickett C (2005) Interpretive legal theory and the academic lawyer. Modern Law Rev 68:320–337

Bentham J (1827) Rationale of judicial evidence, vol iv. Hunt and Clarke, London

Birks P (1996) Equity in the modern law: an exercise in taxonomy. Univ Western Australia Law Rev 26:1–99

Birks P (1999) Equity, conscience, and unjust enrichment. Melbourne Univ Law Rev 23:1–29

Birks P (2003) Book review. Law Q Rev 119:156–161

Burrows A (1998) Understanding the law of obligations: essays on contract, tort and restitution. Hart, Oxford

Campbell T (1999) The point of legal positivism. King's College Law J 9:63–87

Cardozo BN (1921) The nature of the judicial process. Yale University Press, New Haven

Cohen FS (1934) Modern ethics and the law. Brooklyn Law Rev 4:33–50

Coleman JL (1995) Legal theory and practice. Georgetown Law J 83:2579–2617

Cook WW (1941) My philosophy of law. In: My philosophy of law: Credos of sixteen American scholars. Boston Book Law, Boston, pp 51–66

Crombie AC (1988) Designed in the mind: Western visions of science, nature and humankind. Hist Sci 26:1–12

Dagan H (2013) Reconstructing American legal realism & rethinking private law theory. Oxford University Press, New York

Dagan H (2015) Doctrinal categories, legal realism, and the rule of law. Univ Pa Law Rev 163:1889–1917

Demsetz H (1967) Toward a theory of property rights. Am Econ Rev Papers Proc 57:347–359

Dworkin G (1988) The theory and practice of autonomy. Cambridge University Press, Cambridge

Eisenberg MA (1988) The nature of the common law. Harvard University Press, Cambridge

Frank J (1930) Law and the modern mind. Brentano's, New York

Frank J (1934) Experimental jurisprudence and the new deal. Congressional Record 78:12412–12414

Frank J (1947) A plea for lawyer-schools. Yale Law J 56:1303–1344

Gardner J (2012) Law as a leap of faith: essays on law in general. Oxford University Press, Oxford

Gava J (2006) Can contract law be justified on economic grounds? Univ Queensland Law J 25:253–269

Gjerdingen DH (1986) The future of legal scholarship and the search for a modern theory of law. Buffalo Law Rev 35:381–477

Green L (1928) The duty problem in negligence cases (part 1). Columb Law Rev 28:1014–1045

Green L (1930) The Plasgraf case. Columb Law Rev 30:789–801

Henderson JA Jr (1982) Process constraints in tort. Cornell Law Rev 67:901–948

Howarth D (2013) Law as engineering: thinking about what lawyers do. Edward Elgar, Cheltenham

Hutcheson JC (1928) The judgment intuitive: the function of the "hunch" in judicial decision. Cornell Law Q 14:274–288

Hutchinson DJ (2003) Elements of the law. Univ Chicago Law Rev 70:141–158

Johnson-Laird PJ (1983) Mental models: towards a cognitive science of language, inference, and consciousness. Harvard University Press, Cambridge
Kagan RA (2001) Adversarial legalism: the American way of law. Harvard University Press, Cambridge
Komesar N (1981) In search of a general approach to legal analysis: a comparative institutional alternative. Mich Law Rev 79:1350–1392
Langbein JH (1998) The later history of restitution. In: Cornish WR et al (eds) Restitution past, present, and future: essays in honour of Gareth Jones. Oxford University Press, Oxford, pp 57–62
Larsen AO (2014) The trouble with amicus facts. Va Law Rev 100:1757–1818
Lewis R (2005) Insurance and the tort system. Legal Stud 25:85–116
Llewellyn KN (1942) The crafts of law re-valued. Am Bar Assoc J 28(801–803):844
Llewellyn KN (1945) How appellate courts decide cases (part 1). Pa Bar Assoc Q 16:220–248
Llewellyn KN (1960) Jurisprudence: realism in theory and practice. University of Chicago Press, Chicago
Llewellyn KN (1962) The common law tradition: deciding appeals. Little, Brown, Boston
Lobban M (2014) Mapping the common law: some lessons from history. New Zealand Law Rev 2014:21–67
Madhavan G (2015) Applied minds: how engineers think. W.W. Norton, New York
Mill JS (1859/1991) On liberty. In: On liberty and other essays. Oxford University Press, Oxford
Mill JS (1873/1989) Autobiography. Penguin, London
Montesquieu (1748/1989) The spirit of the laws (trans: Cohler AM et al.). Cambridge University Press, Cambridge
Morgan MS (2012) The world in the model: how economists work and think. Cambridge University Press, New York
Nourse V, Shaffer G (2009) Varieties of new legal realism: can a new world order prompt a new legal theory. Cornell Law Rev 95:61–135
Oliphant H, Hewitt A (1929) Introduction. In: Rueff J (ed) From the physical to the social sciences: introduction to a study of economic and ethical theory. John Hopkins Press, Baltimore, pp ix–xxxii, 1940
Pojanowski JA (2014) Private law in the gaps. Fordham Law Rev 82:1689–1750
Pollock F (1912) The genius of the common law. Columbia University Press, New York
Posner RA (1997) The path away from the law. Harv Law Rev 110:1039–1043
Priel D (2015) Land-use priorities and the law of nuisance. Melb Univ Law Rev 39:346–383
Priel D (2016a) The philosophies of the common law and their implications: common law divergences, public authority liability, and the future of a common law world. In: Robertson A, Tilbury M (eds) The common law of obligations: divergence and unity. Hart, Oxford, pp 233–258
Priel D (2016b) Holmes's 'path of the law' as non-analytic jurisprudence. Univ Queensland Law J 35:57–73
Priel D (2017) Conceptions of authority and the Anglo-American common law divide. Am J Comp Law 65:609–657
Priel D (2018) The return of legal realism. In: Dubber MD, Tomlins C (eds) The Oxford handbook of legal history. Oxford University Press, Oxford
Priel D (2019) Two forms of formalism. In: Robertson A, Goudkamp J (eds) Form and substance in the law of obligations. Hart, Oxford
Raz J (1986) The morality of freedom. Clarendon Press, Oxford
Raz J (1994) Ethics in the public domain: essays on the morality of law and politics, rev. edn. Clarendon Press, Oxford
Richerson PJ, Boyd R (2005) Not by genes alone: how culture transformed human evolution. University of Chicago Press, Chicago
Ripstein A (2016) Private wrongs. Harvard University Press, Cambridge
Robinson ES (1934) Law—an unscientific science. Yale Law J 44:235–267

Schauer F (2004) The failure of the common law. Arizona State Law J 36:765–782
Schauer F (2006) Do cases make bad law? Univ Chicago Law Rev 73:883–918
Schwartz B (2016) The paradox of choice: why less is more, rev. edn. HarperCollins, New York
Singer JW (1988) Legal realism now. Calif Law Rev 76:465–544
Smith SD (1992) In defense of traditional legal scholarship: a comment on Schlegel, Weisberg, and Dan-Cohen. Univ Colorado Law Rev 63:627–640
Sunsein CR (2009) Going to extremes: how like minds unite and divide. Oxford University Press, New York
Sunstein CR (2018) Legal reasoning and political conflict, 2nd edn. Oxford University Press, New York
Tamanaha BZ (2010) Beyond the formalist–realist divide: the role of politics in judging. Princeton University Press, Princeton
Waddams S (2003) Dimensions of private law: categories and concepts in Angl0-American legal reasoning. Cambridge University Press, Cambridge
Weinrib EJ (2012) The idea of private law, rev. edn. Oxford University Press, Oxford
Wiseman ZB (1987) The limits of vision: Karl Llewellyn and the merchant rules. Harv Law Rev 100:465–545

Cases

McCarty v. Pheasant Run, Inc. (1987) 826 F.2d 1554 (7th Circuit)
Palsgraf v. Long Island Railroad Co. (1928) 162 N.E. 99 (N.Y.)
Shelley v. Kramer (1948) 344 U.S. 1

Dan Priel is professor of law at Osgoode Hall Law School, York University.

Epistemic Authority and Legal Interpretation

Bojan Spaić

Abstract The relations between epistemic authority and legal interpretation have been widely neglected in contemporary legal theory. In this paper I'll lay out the grounds for the discussion about the sociological and philosophical conceptions of power and authority in order to access their relevance for the theory of legal interpretation. The main hypothesis is that the problems of the practice of legal interpretations in contemporary legal systems are by and large solved not by resorting to philosophies of language nor by doctrines of legal interpretation, but by relying on various kinds of authorities. The paper will present (1) an analysis of authority that will lead to the kinds of authority that are relevant for legal interpretation and argue that (2) the proper way to understand these authorities is by employing the concept of institutional control of legal interpretation. The analysis substantiates the conclusion that authority is a key component of understanding judicial interpretation as a volitive or stipulative enterprise, without implications of arbitrariness.

I'm grateful to Ken Himma and Miodrag Jovanović for insightful and detailed comments on the first draft of the paper, as well as to participants in the following workshops of the XXVIII World Congress of the International Association for the Philosophy of Law and Social Philosophy (IVR), organized in Lisbon, from July 17 to July 21, 2017: Potential of Precedent in the Statutory Legal Order. Context of Political and Legal Discourse (organized by Leszek Leszczyński and Adam Szot) and Continental and Anglo-American Approaches to Hermeneutics (organized by Andreas Funk, Teixeira Martins, and Péter Sólyom). The opportunity of engaging the topic of the paper was provided by the Alexander von Humboldt Foundation scholarship for research on the Institute for public law, constitutional law and philosophy of law under the supervision of Martin Borowski. An shorter, earlier version of this paper, discussing only the general problems of justified epistemic authority was published in Belgrade Law Review (Spaić 2018).

B. Spaić (✉)
University of Belgrade, Belgrade, Serbia
e-mail: bojan.spaic@ius.bg.ac.rs

P. Chiassoni, B. Spaić (eds.), *Judges and Adjudication in Constitutional Democracies: A View from Legal Realism*, Law and Philosophy Library 135, https://doi.org/10.1007/978-3-030-58186-2_9

1 Introduction

In theory and philosophy of legal interpretation we tend to analyze this elusive enterprise as a solitary endeavor.[1] In the majority of treatises, comments and analysis the tacit premise seems to be that the interpretative work in law is done by a single person, to a significant degree isolated from the community in which he does his work, with little or no contact with others in that community and with others from other communities. This simple relation in which interpretation is the non-mediated, direct contact of a person with the text is a rare one; it is the position of the first interpreter of the text. Yet, theoretical and philosophical inquiries into interpretation are often conceived in ways that entail our model interpreter is just this interpreter—a person ascribing the meaning to a text without much regard to previous ascriptions of meaning, and without strong ties to the community in which interpretation occurs. On the one hand, the talk of influences on legal interpretation often encounters a strong skeptical response, stemming perhaps from a core assumption that one authoritative interpreter, the legal text and the case at hand are not only useful as an object of explanation, but also represent the normative ideal of the knowing subject in law. One of our main requirements for judges, the model interpreters that we tend to confound with authoritative interpreters of law in general (administrative bodies, legislative bodies, independent state agencies), is that they are formally independent from the political process in virtue of their lifetime appointments and the lack of regular political accountability to the electorate. On the other hand, if we venture into characterizing interpretation as dependent in significant ways on legal and general community to which an authoritative interpreter belongs, we tend to either stray into mostly uncharted territory of social legal studies (or sociology of law in other traditions) or we just leave this idea of community empty of most contents, a mysterious but important entity, that doesn't allow for further analysis.

My initial assumption in this paper will be that particular instances of interpretation in law (i.e. the very process of interpreting and its results)[2] are influenced in significant ways by other interpreters of law as members of a community of jurists. Interpretative statements of the kind "A means B" are not just a product of the relation between the interpreter, the interpreted object (commonly a text) and the author of that object. The context of interpretation is a complicated context in which a great variety of different, if not conflicting interpretations of the same text exist, in which those interpretations influence new individual ascriptions of meaning in various ways. This position of the authoritative interpreter of legal texts has mostly

[1]Writing about judges in a multimember court Eric Posner and Adrian Vermeule talk about this solipsism as a possibility of judicial behavior, but this in fact is the way in which we tend to analyze judicial interpretation (Posner and Vermeule 2016, pp. 158–190).

[2]The ambiguity between those two meanings of the word interpretation is often not emphasized enough. This can lead to quite a bit of terminological confusions. Ricardo Guastini does a good job distinguishing between: (1) interpretation as a process and interpretation as a product, (2) interpretation in abstracto and interpretation in concreto, (3) interpretation as cognition and interpretation as decision, and finally (4) interpretation and interpretative construction (Guastini 2014, pp. 375–385).

been identified and discussed in the tradition of American legal realism,[3] but attempts to describe this very position of the interpreter from an ontological and epistemological standpoint have been made in continental hermeneutics, by employing complicated and often obscure notions of prejudice, historicity, application and so on.[4] I'll argue that some of those notions can be fruitfully analyzed for the purpose of better understanding the nature of interpretation.

My argument relies on four principle claims. First, I introduce the idea that interpretation is to a significant degree influenced by various kinds of authorities. Second, I explicate the notion of epistemic authority, distinguishing it from practical authority, in terms of the kind of reasons each provide. Third, I identify the conditions for justified deference to utterances of epistemic authorities. Fourth, I apply the conditions for justified deference to utterances of epistemic authorities to authoritative legal interpretation (i.e. the interpretation of legal officials, mainly courts). Accordingly, I conclude that in matters of legal interpretation it can be rationally justified to defer to the ascriptions of meaning of epistemic authorities under certain conditions. In the final part of the paper I discuss the import of an analysis of epistemic authority for discussions about legal interpretation in theoretical jurisprudence.

[3]This is at least the case with the interpretation of the realist tradition proposed by Brian Leiter. According to Leiter, the core claim of legal realism has been widely misunderstood in Anglo-American jurisprudential tradition. In the classical and conventional interpretation, realism is a descriptive theory about adjudication claiming that judges exercise unlimited discretion in deciding cases according to their tastes and values, that are ex post facto rationalized with "appropriate legal rules and reasons" (Leiter 2007, p. 16). Leiter convincingly shows that this received wisdom about legal realism is bunk, and that one core claim that could be attributed to legal realists is in fact that the claim that in deciding cases "judges respond primarily to the stimulus of facts" (ibid., p. 21). In contrasting this view with the view of legal formalists, Leiter arises to the conclusion that according to formalist accounts of legal reasoning judges respond primarily to legal reasons, while on a realist account the judges respond primarily to non-legal reasons (ibid., p. 24). This creates an epistemological problem for legal realism—how are we to predict the decisions of judges if interpretation and adjudication are idiosyncratic? Leiter puts it this way: "choice of decisions must, in fact be sufficiently fettered so that prediction is possible," and more importantly the choice of decision "must be of sufficient generality or commonality to be both accessible and to admit of sorts of lawful generalizations that make predictions possible." The realist view is in fact that "given the actual existence of regular patterns of decision, the best explanation of such regularities must be that judges share certain features that channel their decisions into these patterns" (ibid., p. 27). The realist picture of legal interpretation fundamental poses the problem of the position of the authoritative interpreter of legal texts, that influences his interpretation in such a way that it makes it predictable.

[4]The most prominent figure being Hans-Georg Gadamer whose magnum opus is focused on providing a description of the hermeneutical experience, i.e. the description of the necessary influences on process of interpretation that are operational no matter the method of interpretation we choose (Gadamer 2006, p. 268).

2 Epistemic Dependence and Interpretation

Theorizing about legal interpretation entails talking about the meanings of texts or actions. The meaning of words and the meaning of legal texts are to a degree stable in virtue of the ability of persons to use the same words in different societal contexts and in different linguistic contexts. In this sense meaning is public; it entails that the persons who use the word share beliefs about what something means with other persons within a community (Marmor 2017, p. 581). If interpreting is ascribing meaning, the process itself consists in the formation of belief about the meaning of a word or text, at least one of the results of the process of interpretation are beliefs about the meanings of texts.[5] Legal interpretation is no different. When we interpret a legal provision, we form a belief about its meaning, and ascribe that meaning to the provision. For all intents and purposes this belief about the deontic content of a legal text held by the authoritative interpreter becomes the meaning of the interpreted text in virtue the act of authoritative ascription of meaning in a reasoned judicial decision.

The starting epistemological point of most doctrines or interpretation is epistemic individualism—the view that we are to be entirely epistemically self-reliant in the sense that we are to disregard, refuse or personally examine every reason that we were given to believe something (Zagzebski 2012, p. 52). This sketch of belief formation in regard to the meanings of legal texts is arguably an over-idealized picture of an imaginary privileged position that no one holds. A single individual belief about a meaning of the word can be constitutive of the meaning of the word only in a private language. In all other cases, "collectively held beliefs about what the word stands for, what it signifies, are *constitutive* of the word's meaning" (Marmor 2017, p. 582). On a more general note, insofar as "the demands of everyday life require us to make many more decisions and hold many more opinions than we could ever base on personally examined reasons," (Pierson 1994, p. 398) the same demands of contemporary legal systems generally require authoritative legal interpreters to rely on reasons that are not personally examined.

Interpreting law is a technical matter, and the very possibility of interpreting law authoritatively is dependent on an entire range of more or less strict requirements prescribed by contemporary legal systems ranging from legal education, practice of law, a certain age, and so on. Before engaging in a method of interpretation, or following any normative guideline on how to ascribe or disambiguate meaning, individuals within every interpretative community operate with "normal intellectual inertia" within "paradigms" or "quasi-paradigms of the day" (Dworkin 1986, p. 89).

[5]The very word interpretation is ironically a source of much controversy. If we follow Kelsen and we take interpretation to include cognitive interpretation—that ascertains the possible meanings of a legal text—and adjudicative interpretation—that decides on one meaning of the legal text, than we could say that overt or uttered results of the process of interpretation are either statements about the possible meanings of texts, or authoritative ascriptions of meaning to the legal text. My primary interest here is the process in which the authoritative interpreters form beliefs about meanings of a legal text; or, to put it in terms of traditional legal hermeneutics, I'm in this case more interested in *subtilitas inteligendi* than in *subtilitas explicandi* or *subtilitas aplicandi*.

Decisions in law, along with interpretative decisions—ascriptions of meaning—are often "chosen out of habit, out of respect for the (. . .) practices and traditions." (Raz 2009, p. 328).

The interpretative task of adjudication starts from the practices within a community, it is "dependent on understanding already being in place" (Patterson 2005, p. 696). The general terms in which the law is expressed are undetermined or underdetermined, and we constantly define and redefine our beliefs about meanings of legal texts to the best of our knowledge. Most, if not all, of our initial beliefs about the meanings of legal texts will be based on testimony.[6] In this sense, we are necessarily epistemically dependent on other members of the legal community, even before becoming a part of that community. This, of course, is not specific to law. Epistemic dependence on testimony, understood as a way of conveying information, opinions and knowledge is the predicament of the entirety of human knowledge (Fricker 2017, p. 227). Relying on one's autonomy in reasoning whenever an interpretative issue arises would not only be unreasonable but also "wasteful" (Shapiro 2014, p. 338). The contents of interpretive utterances as well as the "material rightness" of results of interpretative act are ultimately influenced and even determined by the level of acceptability that an interpretive utterance has in a legal community (Aarnio 2011, p. 135).

The issue of epistemic dependence was, in fact, analyzed in the theory of legal interpretation, but it's today neglected. One of the main points in the continental tradition of ontological hermeneutics, or more precisely in Hans-Georg Gadamer's analysis of understanding and interpretation is, in fact, the problem of prejudices that are always operational in interpretation in such a way that understanding itself wouldn't be possible without them. One of those prejudices is a specific mode of reliance on others when it comes to interpreting texts and actions. One of those prejudices, namely the prejudice of authority is understood as a source of error in reasoning[7] fundamentally opposed to unrestricted use of one's reason. This very prejudice was to Gadamer's mind crucial in our identification of meaning of a text. Reliance on authority makes understanding possible, without excluding critical thinking, reason and deliberation (Gadamer 2006, pp. 278–279).[8] Even though authority has received much attention in mainstream legal philosophy in recent

---

[6]The term *testimony* is used exclusively in the epistemological and not in a legal sense in this paper. In other words, it denotes cases in which *X* says something to *Y* and the *Y* believes the assertion at least in part because it was told so.

[7]Gadamer blames the Enlightenment for the understanding of reason as fundamentally opposed to authority. In this tradition, the two main sources of prejudices that lead to errors in reasoning are hastiness and authority. And while hastiness impedes the methodological use of reason, authority impedes the use of reason in general (Gadamer 2006, p. 281). The move from the claim that authority sometimes leads to false beliefs to the claim that authority is fundamentally opposed to truth is according to Gadamer not warranted, because it disregards the importance of authority in reasoning, and its aptness to give true reasons for action or belief.

[8]According to Gadamer, authority is based "on an act of acknowledgment and knowledge—the knowledge, namely, that the other is superior to oneself in judgment and insight and that for this reason his judgment takes precedence—i.e., it has priority over one's own" (Gadamer 2006, p. 281).

decades, the implications of differing conceptions of authority on legal interpretation have never been subject to theoretical scrutiny.[9]

3 Authority and Its Kinds

My intention here is to review the import of authority on authoritative legal interpretation and to pinpoint the kinds of authority that play significant roles in legal interpretation. Before we engage with those modes in which authority has baring on authoritative legal interpretation, it is necessary to explain the concept of authority that is presently of interest.

From the dominant sociological perspective, authority is a kind of social power. According to most influential accounts of power, this essentially contested concept has at least one core element—that of *affection*. Where there is talk of power, there is talk of one subject affecting another subject. Now, not all affection is power, but only the one that affects the subject(s) in a non-trivial or significant manner (Lukes 2005, p. 30).[10] Furthermore, an affection can be termed a power iff it conflicts with the interests of the person who is affected (Lukes 2005, p. 37). In the same sociological and empirical vein, within power one can distinguish between *coercion*, in which compliance is assured by threat of deprivation; *influence*, a change of action without the explicit or overt threat of deprivation; and *authority*, implying compliance with a deontic proposition of the authority for reasons of accepting an affection as

[9]The lack of discussions on the relation between authority and interpretation is somewhat understandable. Both legal interpretation and authority are highly contested concepts. As a topic of jurisprudence authority was promoted to one of the predominant issues by Josef Raz. A long line of thinking has been rooted in the position between authority on one side and reason and autonomy on the other (Zagzebski 2012, pp. 4–8). In his *The Authority of Law* Raz explains this line of reasoning in the following way: "To be subjected to authority, it is argued, is incompatible with reason, for reason requires that one should always act on the balance of reasons of which one is aware. It is of the nature of authority that it requires submission even when one thinks that what is required is against reason. Therefore, submission to authority is irrational. Similarly, the principle of autonomy entails action on one's own judgment on all moral questions. Since authority sometimes requires action against one's own judgment, it requires abandoning one's moral autonomy. Since all practical questions may involve moral considerations, all practical authority denies moral autonomy and is consequently immoral" (Raz 1979, p. 3).

[10]Precisely, Lukes states that "A exercises power over B when A affects B in a manner contrary to B's interests" (Lukes 2005, p. 37). There is a lot to be said about this definition, since it doesn't seem evident that the exercise of power necessarily involves affection contrary to one's interests. Compelling a relative to apply for a scholarship that is in his best interest seems to imply an exercise of power, despite the fact that that this exercise is in the best interest of your relative. Lukes is aware of this possibility and tends to interpret it by stating that the relative isn't aware of his own interests, and that the power relation ends when he gets to his real interests.

legitimate or reasonable from the perspective of its content or procedures that brought forward the decision (Lukes 2005, pp. 21–22).[11]

According to Joseph Raz, since authority has a bearing on what we ought to do, or what we ought to believe, the best account of authority should be able to explain its role in our practical reasoning (Raz 1979, p. 10). From the perspective of practical reasoning, authority can be defined as a property of an entity *X* that enables (mostly verbal) behaviors of *X* to act as reasons[12] for a person *Y* (Raz 1979, p. 12). We say that *X* has authority over *Y* if *X* is able with dominantly verbal utterances to change *Y*'s reasons for doing or believing something (Raz 1979, p. 19). Authority is, then, the ability to give rise to new reasons for action or belief or the ability to change reasons for action or belief (Raz 1979, p. 16).

On one plausible account shared by a large number of contemporary writers there is at least one necessary feature to authority—*content independence.*[13] A proclamation or directive is authoritative not in light of its content, but in light of its source (Schauer 2008, p. 1935). We are inclined to say that something or someone is an authority if its expression is able to change our reasons for acting or believing, not in virtue of the content of the expression but in virtue of the source of the expression.[14] We could therefore state that *X* has authority over Y if *X*'s utterance of *p* can gives *Y* new reasons or changes his existing reasons for acting or believing, not in virtue of the content of *p* but in virtue of *p* being uttered by *X*.

To have authority is not just the ability to affect other persons' actions or beliefs. This would conflate any exercise of power with authority, which is certainly not the way we normally use the concept. The power of any kind of authority is conscious or rational in the sense that it gives reasons for persons about what to believe or how to act, and in the sense that it is exercised just by expressing what is to be believed or what our actions should be. While authority in some cases involves power, this power must claim authority and/or must be followed the belief of the subjects of authority that someone is in fact an authority (Raz 1981, pp. 106–107). According to this, we are in principle able to distinguish between *de facto* and *de jure* authority (Raz 1979, p. 4; Raz 1994, p. 211), even if *de facto* authority has to "either claims to be legitimate or is believed to be so" (Green 1988, p. 60).

---

[11]The concept of power is by no means uncontroversial in sociology. Steven Lukes important book revolves around the idea that there are three different conceptions of power which differ in a significant manner one from another. Moreover, given the empirical underlining and empirical expectations of theories in sociology, there are more problems than in other disciplines concerned with power. Lukes himself declares power to be an essentially contested concept.

[12]Reasons being facts that "count in favor" of doing or believing something (Marmor 2009, p. 5).

[13]See: Himma (2017).

[14]An important difference that Raz makes in this regard is the difference between having authority and being an authority. I could have the authority to use the scanner in my Institute without being an authority for anyone. The central case of authority is for Raz the authority over persons (Raz 1979, pp. 20–21).

3.1 Epistemic and Practical

The distinction between various types of reasons in our practical reasoning, like reasons for emotions, attitudes, norms and institutions and so on, can in principle be condensed to two fundamental types—*reasons for action* and *reasons for belief* (Raz 1999, p. 15). This leads us the second crucial distinction is routinely made in contemporary epistemology and jurisprudence (Hurd 1999, pp. 62–63)—the distinction between epistemic (or theoretical) and practical authority.[15] As Raz points out "there are practical authorities whose authority is based entirely on their being theoretical authorities" (Raz 1979, p. 8), but argues against the idea that all practical authorities can be reduced to theoretical authorities (Raz 1988, pp. 28–29). According to him, theoretical and practical reasons have "the same basic structure", but that the main difference is that "they provide reasons for different things" (Raz 1988, p. 53) and most of his discussions are, in his words, pertinent to both practical and theoretical authority (Raz 1994, p. 212).[16] Be this as it may, one core difference between epistemic and practical authority is always emphasized: the two kinds of authority give reasons for different things. While practical authority is thought of as giving reasons for action, epistemic authority is understood as giving reasons for belief.[17]

[15]The literature on the authority of other persons and their opinions over oneself and his opinions varies significantly when it comes to naming the kind of authority that the authors analyze. Heidi Hurd takes epistemic authority to be a general term that includes advisory authority, influential authority and theoretical authority (Hurd 1999, p. 63). Richard Foley tends to call this kind of authority intellectual authority (Foley 2001, p. 83). Raz is inclined to call it theoretical authority (Raz 1979, p. 8; Raz 1988, p. 29), and Zagzebski uses the term epistemic authority (Zagzebski 2012). The possible terminological confusions and subsequent or antecedent conceptual confusions will be made clearer in the remainder of the paper.

[16]One kind of authority that is often mentioned but won't be a topic in this paper is called persuasive authority. H. Patrick Glenu in a paper from 1987 notes that the concept lacks formal definition (Glenu 1987, p. 264), but still states metaphorically that it is "the authority which attracts adherence as opposed to obliging it" (ibid., p. 263). Glenu's primary motive behind this "definition" of persuasive authority is to analyze the sources of law and to contrast sources of law that poses persuasive authority to those that have binding authority.

But persuasive authority obviously has a problem. If an authority is conceptually characterized by the fact that it purports to provide content independent reasons for action, persuasion in this sense can never really be authoritative. A partial solution to this problem is proposed by Oran Doyle who claims that persuasive authority is essentially a theoretical authority (Doyle 2016, p. 90).

[17]Even though there is significant agreement in legal literature on this subject, the exact differences between theoretical and practical authority are not uncontroversial. Heidi Herd believes that all kinds of epistemic authority function evidentially, the give us "reasons to think that there are other reasons to act as recommended" (Hurd 1999, p. 63). What follows is that the utterances of an epistemic authority are content dependent reasons for action, or, more rigorously formulated: "X has epistemic authority for Y if and only if, as a result of X's stating that Y ought to do act A, Y has a reason to believe that the balance of (content-dependent) reasons dictates that Y ought to do A." On this account, an utterance of an epistemic authority merely makes more probable that we should act in accordance accordingly, since it only points us to other antecedently existing reasons to act in a certain manner. This applies of course only on deontic propositions, and not on beliefs in general,

3.1.1 Practical Authority

In order to explain both theoretical and practical authority we have to dive into an analysis of reasons, given that our reasoning with authority is crucially determined by the kinds of reasons that utterances of authorities give rise to. A particularly important kind of reasons that figures prominently in explanations of practical authority is called *exclusionary reasons*. Normally, an utterance of another person that is meant as an advice or just a transmission of someone's knowledge gives the person to whom it is directed a reason to act in a certain way or to believe a certain thing. When my friend tells me that I should listen to the new album by *The National* the utterance of my friend purports to give me two separate reasons to listen: (a) a reason to believe that the album is of a certain quality;[18] and (b) a reason to listen to the album. Let us concentrate on the second one of those reasons. Needless to say, the utterance of my friend is not intended to give me an absolute reason that trumps all other reasons for doing something at that same moment. Normally, I'll weigh the reason that I was given by my friend's utterance with other reasons, decide if I should listen to the album right away or not, and act on the balance of reasons. Arguably, no matter its exact formulation, the utterance of my friend is advice, and advice is meant to be taken as a first order reason for action or belief, to be weighed with other preexisting reasons to listen to the new album of a music band I like. A similar thing happens when a request is issued. According to Raz, when we issue requests we in fact intend to give the hearer a particularly weighty reason to act according to the request (Raz 1979, p. 14).

The characteristic way in which practical authority affects reasons is not the same as the way advice and requests affect reasons. Practical authorities issue orders, and orders are qualitatively different from both advice and request. The main intention of an order issuing authority is not to impact the balance of reasons by giving us weighty reasons for action, but to give us a reason for acting that excludes all the other reasons against acting in a certain way (Raz 1979, p. 18). In order to understand practical authority issuing orders we, thus, have to employ not just first-order reasons but also *second-order reasons*. The role of second-order reasons in practical reasoning is to simply give us reasons to act for other reasons (positive second-order reasons), or reasons not to act on other reasons (negative second-order reasons or

---

and may be sound in situations in which an epistemic authority utters deontic propositions. Still, even in those cases it is not clear what makes a person who tells us what to do an authority, even an epistemic authority, if he doesn't give us new reasons for belief, and the reasons for belief that he gives us are content dependent. If we can call something or someone an authority it seems necessary that it's utterances are authoritative in virtue of their source and not in virtue of their content. Influential authority and practical authority would, in this line of thought, provide for new reasons to act. Those reasons would be content independent (ibid., p. 65). While it could be that theoretical authorities can give us content dependent reasons for action by giving us content independent reasons for belief, this is certainly not a core feature of epistemic authorities.

[18]Not necessarily good or great. It may well be that it gives me reason to believe that it is the worst album by the band in question.

exclusionary reasons).[19] In the unlikely occurrence that my friend was to issue an order for me to listen to that new album, he would, according to Raz, in fact be addressing me with the intention to give me a reason to listen that excludes all reasons that I might have not to listen. His order for me would act as a first-order reason to listen to the album, and as a second-order reason not to act on reasons that I might have not to listen to the album. In this exact situation, the exclusionary reason gives a reason to act as ordered, and a reason not to act in a different manner. A combination of first order reasons and second order exclusionary reasons is called by Raz a *protected reason*. The ability to give rise or to change protected reasons is *normative power*, and practical authority is one kind of normative power. In the most general sense, we could therefore say that someone or something has practical authority iff its utterances are protected reasons for action (Raz 1979, p. 29).

For present purposes, I won't dwell on the issue of justification of practical authority. *De facto* authority is, according to Raz, dependent on *de jure* authority, and utterances of practical authorities give rise to reasons that are exclusionary in character, justification is a necessary part of every account of authority. According to his normal justification thesis, *X* having authority over *Y* and correlatively *Y* having the duty to obey *X* is justified if Y is more likely to act in accordance with the reasons that antecedently apply to Y by doing what X says than by acting on Y's own assessment of the reasons (Raz 1988, p. 53). Raz's justification of authority within the service conception, based on the normal justification thesis and preemption thesis, is subject to much controversy.[20] I'll divert my attention to the kind of authority that is supposedly helpful in understanding the ascription of meaning to legal texts.

3.1.2 Epistemic Authority

Epistemic authority has been widely neglected in favor of discussions about practical authority. This is understandable. It seems that practical authority, followed regularly by the possibility of using coercive mechanisms in order to make the subjects of authority comply with its commands, demands justification. As it turns out, a justification is not so easy to come by, and the concept of authority itself is contested. As for the lack of discussion on theoretical authority, the main reason seems to be the

---

[19]Heidi Hurd notices that it is pretty hard to come up with every day examples in which someone gives us exclusionary reasons for action (Hurd 1999, pp. 73–75).

[20]The list of literature is seemingly endless. Helpful overviews and counterarguments to Razes positions can be found in: Darwall (2010), pp. 257–278; Shapiro (2014); Christiano (2004); Rodriguez-Blanco (2014); Hershovitz (2003), pp. 201–220; Ehrenberg (2011), pp. 884–894. The account of practical authority based on second-personal reasons given by Stephen Darwall seems is an especially important challenge to Razes views on two grounds: (1) the concept of authority necessarily involves accountability (Darwall 2010, p. 267), and (2) the fact that one has reason to regard some directives as creating exclusionary reasons doesn't actually mean that directives actually create exclusionary reasons (ibid., 270).

dominance of epistemic individualism or egoism in epistemology (Foley 1994, p. 57), the perceived conflict between authority, autonomy and egalitarianism (Zagzebski 2012, p. 6),[21] as well as the prevalence of certain convictions about our ability to form beliefs and the taken-for-granted separation between conceptual and non-conceptual inquiries in philosophy and consequently philosophy of law.

Fundamental Epistemic Authority

It makes little sense to deny that we are fundamentally social beings when it comes to acquiring beliefs and knowledge. Our beliefs are formed in socialization; they are formed and reinforced by socialization. Most if not all that is known to us is a result of the fact that someone else has previously said or written it. In situations in which we lack knowledge, the testimony of others is readily available to us via recent technological advancements that we came to regard as basic necessities of contemporary life. We are, it seems, inescapably epistemically dependent in a degree that even warrants the question about whether we are able to have any knowledge if we exclude what others have taught us (Fricker 2006, p. 592). Since there can't be any real debate about whether our beliefs are, in as a contingent matter of fact, influenced by others, the main question is whether we are justified in holding beliefs in virtue of someone else having those same beliefs and sharing them with us. To explain epistemic authority is to do the same thing that Raz expects from an explanation of theoretical authority—namely, to explain the role of authority in our inferences explained (Raz 1979, p. 10).

Despite the fact that every belief has a social aspect, it is commonly thought that the social aspects of belief formation cannot answer the question of whether our beliefs are reliable or justified. Social aspects of knowledge are unable to tell us if the practice of forming our beliefs (doxastic practice) is reliable (if it has verific propensity) (Alston 1994, pp. 33–34). Doxastic practices that are reliable produce evidence, and the evidence in turn gives justified reasons for belief. The fact that another person and a group of persons have a shared opinion are not in themselves evidence (Hardwig 1985, p. 337). It thus seems that the opinion of another person or a group of persons can never substitute a belief-forming practice with verific propensity. If this is so, the most that can be stated regarding beliefs formed by means of epistemic authority is: *Y* sometimes can have good reasons to believe that *X* has good evidential reasons to believe *p*. On this account, the knowledge that Y gains from an utterance of another person, *X*, is always secondhand, since it implies that *Y* has a commitment to believe that *X* is expressing knowledge (Fricker 2006, p. 592), which entails that the knowledge transmitted by another person that we trust

[21]Zagzebski describes the general attitude towards authority in epistemology and elsewhere by stating two general ideas: (1) adult human beings are "roughly" equal in their epistemic capacities, (2) autonomy in the epistemic domain means the complete self-reliance in belief-formation (Zagzebski 2012, pp. 6–7).

can, or could be checked, verified in some other way that doesn't imply utterances of other persons and "say-so" in general (Fricker 2006, p. 608).

Some distinctions are necessary. When we talk about any kind of authority, we have in mind something more than sheer influence. Another person could spell out for me the procedure to arrive to a belief, and the belief itself in which case I could say that he influenced me to undertake the procedure that leads me to a belief, but the procedure and the belief are the result of my own faculties. The issue of authority is posed when I trust the other persons opinion either because it comes from another person, of because there is some other reason to trust the opinion of the other person (Foley 1994, p. 53). Epistemic authority can thus be twofold—fundamental and derivative. *X* has fundamental epistemic authority over *Y* iff *p* is believed by *Y* in virtue of it being uttered/believed by *X*. *X* has derivative epistemic authority over *Y* if *p* is believed by *Y* in virtue of other independent reasons for thinking that *X* is reliable when uttering something. In the case of fundamental authority, we believe *p* because it was uttered/believed (excluding cases of insincerity) by *X*; in the case of derivative authority we believe *p* because of some properties of *X* that make us believe that *X* is reliable in claiming *p* (Foley 1994, p. 54).

An important question that will be discussed only briefly here concerns the possibility of justifiably conferring fundamental epistemic authority to anyone, without regard for whether her knowledge about the subject that she is talking about. After all, it seems highly unusual to place prima facie trust in utterances of random persons. When someone tells us that there is a roadblock around the corner, our belief in his proposition is dependent on contingent factors at best. It seems that there is a case, advanced by Richard Foley and Linda Trinkaus Zagzebski, that fundamental epistemic authority is sometimes justified.[22] Be this as it may, for our

[22]Given my innate trust in my own faculties and the fact that our human environmental conditions and upbringing are, by and large, similar it can seem rational to assign fundamental authority to other persons (Foley 1994, p. 63). On this account, it seems necessary to accept that there is at least some minimal sense in which the reliability of our belief-forming practices is social: (a) As a minimum, even idiosyncratic doxastic practices have to rely on one's upbringing and education in socially established practices. (b) Moreover, the reliability of doxastic practices is evaluated socially in the sense that the reliability represents the ability of those practices to result in true propositions (Alston 1994, pp. 35–36), or to give evidence for beliefs. Finally, (c) there are good reasons to think that a doxastic practice is reliable if it is entrenched in a society over a long period of time, even though this doesn't have to be necessarily the case (ibid., 47). Even if the argument in favor of fundamental epistemic authority fails, belief acquired by an epistemic authority can still reach the status of knowledge under the condition that "there is or there was someone who knows that P in some other way - not in virtue of having been told that P and trusting the teller." (Fricker 2006, p. 604). It should be noted that my primary interest here is not in testimony as a means of transferring knowledge between persons. It seems plausible that at least a certain percentage of opinions that we hold in virtue of getting them from another person can be transformed to personally examined reasons. In simple cases persons can acquire evidence about the assertion of an expert and thus substitute the opinion of the expert with an opinion based on evidence. If someone who has epistemic authority tells me that outside is raining, in most situations I have no problem to acquire knowledge about the weather conditions by myself, and thus base my knowledge on perceptual evidence (Fricker 2017, pp. 225–226). These two positions have been framed in

present purposes the differences between belief and knowledge are not crucial, as will be shown in the discussion about some salient properties of legal interpretation and its context.

Derivative Epistemic Authority

If we put temporarily aside some of the fundamental questions about the social character of doxastic practices, like questions about whether social relations determine the reliability of belief-forming procedures, we are left with the fact that our knowledge about things is dependent on other persons, groups of persons, and the society at large. Our reliance on the opinions of others in all areas is ubiquitous. In other words, we are often inclined to take the opinions of other persons as reasons for holding those same opinions just because they are held by persons that possess some qualities that make their opinion trustworthy.

The possibility of justifying derivative epistemic authority seems intuitively quite unproblematic, even if not universally so, so a brief *reductio ad absurdum* of the idea that our beliefs are justified only if they are based on personally examined reasons should suffice for our present purposes. Imagine that person *Y* cannot in any way reach an evidence based, personally examined opinion on the issue either because he lacks the possibility of repeating the steps necessary, or he lacks the competence to inquire in the issue, or he simply doesn't have the faculties needed to be able to validate the opinion of *X*. If we think that under these conditions the belief of *Y* cannot be justified on the grounds that *X* has the same belief, we are compelled to admit that a large percentage of beliefs that persons rely on within a society are simply completely irrational (Hardwig 1985, p. 339). This is to say that at least certain beliefs from the entire range of beliefs acquired by listening or reading, are justified. In the remainder of this part of the paper I'll rely on a moderate position, that doesn't exclude a majority of our beliefs from the domain of rationality.

In short, we tend to treat the opinions of other persons that possess relevant knowledge or skills as reasons for belief.[23] The most common way of thinking about

---

recent debates on epistemology of testimony as *non-reductionism* and *reductionism*. According to reductionists, accounts testimony is one of the sources of justification of belief or knowledge equivalent with perception, memory, and inferences. It goes without saying that belief held as a result of testimony can be defeated as any other kind of belief. Reductionism claims that there a belief based on testimony has to be justified by other sufficient positive reasons like perception, memory, or inferences in order to qualify as knowledge. Detailed accounts by contemporary epistemologists from both camps can be found in: Lackey and Sosa (2006). It should be noted that not all epistemic authority has to be testimonial, for belief is not coextensive with telling. Also, testimony needn't be epistemically authoritative if there is no special reason to think that another person could form better beliefs in one domain than I could (Zagzebski 2012, p. 134).

[23]From the perspective of contemporary epistemology and social epistemology epistemic authority could be treated as a subsection of testimony and testimonials based belief. This would however depend on the definition of testimonial belief. One of the prominent positions on testimony is the claim by Elizabeth Fricker that testimony is connected with telling in general see: Lackey (2017),

an epistemic authority is to view it as a kind of expertise; we say that a practicing lawyer has epistemic authority in the domain of litigation in civil or criminal suites, or that a medical doctor has epistemic authority when it comes to common illnesses.[24] The word "expert" should be understood as relative to the person that believes something in virtue of the expert telling her that it's so. In this thin definition, an expert is simply a person that is epistemically in a better position that the other person to "have, or make a judgement to form a conscious belief" regarding something (Fricker 2017, p. 233). It seems uncontroversial enough that it justified to confer derivative epistemic authority to an MD when it comes to your health or to a lawyer when it comes to court proceedings. If I have no idea what is causing pain in my abdomen, the only reasonable thing to do is to defer to a medical doctor; if I'm completely oblivious about the functioning of civil litigation in Serbia (in most cases), it is perfectly reasonable for me to confer derivative epistemic authority in these matters to my lawyer. Still, justifying the deference to epistemic authorities will depend on the knowledge that we possess about the issue at hand. From a justificatory standpoint, we can distinguish at least three types of situations:

(1) When *Y* has no opinion about *p*, it is rational for *Y* to defer to the opinion of *X* if there are reasons to think that *X* is more knowledgeable about *p* than *Y*. *Y* "has good reasons to believe that" *X* "has good reasons to believe" *p* (Hardwig 1985, p. 338). Consequently, *Y* is justified in holding the opinion that *X* holds. In situations in which we have no knowledge whatsoever about an issue it can be rational to defer to opinions of other persons about the issue, even if we don't have particularly good grounds to believe that they are particularly knowledgeable on the issue. If we have good reasons to believe that another person is more knowledgeable about the issue than the first person we trusted, we can justifiably defer to the other person's opinion. This is for the most part in line with our intuitions and our practices of forming beliefs. A news report on an accident that we haven't witnessed will lead us to form a provisional but justified belief about the information provided to us by the person reporting about the incident. Since we don't have any knowledge about the situation it is rational to give *prima facie* derivative epistemic authority to the person reporting. A testimonial of eyewitnesses that might contradict the statements of the reporter will justifiably make us change our opinion about the matter, since it is reasonable to assume that the eyewitnesses have more knowledge about the accident than the reporter. These are situations that are important for our belief formation; as a normative matter of

p. 2. The basic characteristics of authority and epistemic authority could be enough to delimitate it in the field of testimony in general, as we are not interested in any inquiry into knowledge based on what other people tell us, but only insofar as it gives us content independent reasons for belief.

[24]Hans-Georg Gadamer devotes most of his discussion about authority to derivative epistemic authority and writes: "It is primarily persons that have authority; but the authority of persons is ultimately based not on the subjection and abdication of reason but on an act of acknowledgment and knowledge—the knowledge, namely, that the other is superior to oneself in judgment and insight and that for this reason his judgment takes precedence—i.e., it has priority over one's own" (Gadamer 2006, p. 281).

epistemic justification though, we are more interested in the relations between persons with a substantial amount of knowledge or skill in a certain filed (experts) and a layman. A layman is in many situations rationally required to trust the knowledge and training of a certified MD, and the same goes for ordinary knowledge about the workings of a legal system. For the most part, we have reasons for accepting the authority of an MD or a lawyer since we rarely have consciously formed opinions about matters in which we have little knowledge, skills or training. As much as we would like to think about our beliefs in terms of personal examined reasons, and as much as we would like to believe that our opinions are grounded in evidence or even more in fact, a great part, if not the majority of our opinions are formed by taking someone's word for it; we believe evolution or climate change even if we have no personal examined reasons to back our belief.

(2) The reliance on the opinions of others is often not justified on the grounds that I can't get some beliefs directly at all, but on the grounds that I can get them directly but in a less trustworthy manner (Zagzebski 2012, p. 12). When *Y* has beliefs about *p*, it can still be rational for him to substitute some or all of his beliefs about *p* for beliefs about *p* that *X holds*. If one of my perceptual abilities is worse than the perceptual ability of another person, it is reasonable to defer to the opinion of that person. In an example borrowed from Elizabet Fricker, my shortsightedness can make a person that I'm with an "expert" in matters that require good vision (Fricker 2017, p. 234). If we have formed justified opinions about certain matters about our health or about the legal system, one could say that, in principle, we would be able to arrive to a justified belief by finding the evidence ourselves. The reasons that we have for believing the opinion of somebody else may well be derivative, but they can't simply be substituted for personal examined reasons. Even if one conducts the same inquiry that the MD or a lawyer conducted before giving a diagnosis or advice, he would still lack the training and experience required for evaluating the results of the inquiry. Conversely, a person determined to go to law school in order to gain knowledge about a case might lack the means to conduct the inquiry necessary to reach an evidence based belief. Evidence obtaining practices in contemporary sciences are often financially, geographically or in other ways out of reach of most people. (Hardwig 1985, pp. 338–339). So, having our own independently formed opinions that are in conflict with the opinions of others, doesn't by itself delegitimize conferring epistemic authority to others on various grounds, the main one being the fact that the other person has more knowledge, training, has devoted more time to investigating the issue or has just put more effort into it (Foley 1994, p. 65). In this stronger sense, an expert is a person with "specific differentiating characteristics" related to her skills, training or knowledge, be it derived from "genetic endowment" or "special training and education" (Fricker 2017, p. 235).

In both (1) and (2) a problem arises from the fact that if I'm not able to judge the merit of an expert opinion, I'm, in most cases, not able to judge on their expertise.

Deference to the opinion of another person seems rationally justified as a matter of derivative authority in both of those cases, even if the person who is trusted is only contingently an expert. In these cases, nothing prevents us from shifting from opinions of others to personal examined opinions if we manage to gain the skill, training or knowledge required to form a belief for ourselves.[25] Even if we can, at times, rely on our own knowledge and expertise in order to ascertain if a person is really an expert, most of the time we are rationally bound to defer to either other persons who have more knowledge about experts in the field or to other experts, lists of experts etc. This issue leads us to the third possibility to explore in relation to epistemic authority.

(3) While it may be that ordinarily epistemic or theoretical authority is associated with an expert in relation to a layman it would be very wrong to think that this is the only relation of epistemic authority.[26] The situation in which we have epistemic peers seems to be completely devoid of relations of epistemic authority. But ideal peer disagreement in which two persons are experts in the exact same domain is more of an exception than it is a rule. An example from the domain of legal interpretation would be the example of a judge compared to a scholar. Both could be very proficient in law in general terms, but it could still be justified for the judge to defer to the scholar. The scholar is usually highly specialized in a particular field, and the judge is often a "generalist jurist" that doesn't know the nuances of a particular field of study. In the sense of knowledge about the relevant subject matter the judge and the scholar are in fact not peers, even though their relative position makes it seem so.[27] The derivative epistemic authority of the scholar is in this case justified by the fact that the knowledge of the judge is not detailed nor granular enough in a specific field of research that the scholar has devoted his career to studying.

(4) Finally, we can easily imagine a situation in which a layman isn't sure about which expert opinion to follow; indeed, we don't even have to imagine the situation in which the opinions of experts in a certain field contradict one another (Lehrer 1977, p. 476). From a layman's perspective, the disagreement of experts doesn't change much in regards of the basic rationality of him deferring to an expert opinion. Even if the opinion of an expert is not as good as the opinion of

[25]Elizabeth Fricker differentiates between week and strong deference to another's opinion. Weak deference is appropriate when someone is contingently an expert on an issue. This is often the case when someone heard something that we were not able to hear simply because our hearing is worse. In cases of week deference, the evidence for a belief wasn't even available to me. In cases in which I do possess the entirety of available evidence the condition for justifiably deferring to the opinion of another person who has the same evidence is stricter. Strong deference is according to Fricker justified iff the other person has superior expertise (Fricker 2017, p. 236).

[26]It would seem that Tom Christiano conceives of theoretical authority in this way. He writes: "Theoretical authorities operate primarily by giving advice to the layman, which advice the layman is free to take or not... Theoretical authorities do not normally impose duties on others, although they might give advice on what a person's duty is." (Christiano 2004).

[27]This point is made in another context by Sunstein and Vermeule (2002).

another expert, it is still rationally justified to defer to the lesser opinion and to grant the lesser expert derivative epistemic authority. The option might as well be a result of contingent factors like the availability of experts, the general quality of experts in a certain area, and so forth. But the contingent matter of the quality of expert opinion doesn't change the main thesis—namely, that derivative epistemic authority is justified under those conditions.

If one is in a position to choose between different experts or groups of experts with conflicting opinions, it can be quite hard to determine on which basis should she make a decision. Other expert opinions in this regard are quite common (Lehrer 1977, p. 477), but they just move our problem one step up. It is quite common that experts have irreconcilable opinions about other experts and their expertise. In order for the choice of the layman to be justified it is necessary to introduce the category of relative weight that an expert is given to within a group of experts (Lehrer 1977, p. 478). Some models of aggregating the social information about the comparative merits of experts have been proposed, but their empirical soundness is dubious. But if the weighing of expert opinions has a rational character, certain opinions within a group of experts should be accepted because they are in fact accepted by members of the community that are the most well regarded and respected (Lehrer 1977, p. 481). For present purposes, the topics of peer disagreement and relations to conflicting epistemic authorities will be put on hold, in order to focus on the basic question of the importance of epistemic authority in the ascription of meaning to legal texts.[28]

General Conclusions About the Nature of Epistemic Authority

Having in mind the analysis of epistemic authority, we could, in principle, identify some of its basic features. It seems clear enough that not every power over behavior amounts to practical authority. Forcing or threatening someone to perform a certain action can be highly effective as a means of inducing behavior, but it doesn't imply the right to rule over that person. When it comes to epistemic authority things are quite different, as the problem of distinguishing it from power becomes simple. It is impossible to force a belief in the way that it is possible to force a behavior. The issue of coercive mechanisms backing the authority dissipate. Utterances of an epistemic authority do not require compliance, but are believed by subjects to the authority in question (Green 1988, p. 29).[29] Other general thesis about authority, however apply in quite a similar manner.

[28]During the writing of this paper the idea of disagreement between epistemic peers has received some attention in legal philosophy. Baude and Doerfler noticed that the epistemological analysis of peer disagreement can aid us in explaining disagreement between judges in multimember courts, and in justifying their decisions (Baude and Doerfler 2017).

[29]It would seem that Tom Christiano conceives of theoretical authority in this way. He writes: "Theoretical authorities operate primarily by giving advice to the layman, which advice the layman

In order for someone or something to have epistemic authority it's utterances have to be able to give *content-independent reasons for belief.* Still, epistemic authority is quite different from practical authority in various ways. First, it is rare and difficult, if not impossible, to order a belief.[30] Epistemic authorities do not give reasons by giving orders, and the utterances of epistemic authorities are not intended as exclusionary reasons for belief. It would seem that from a Razian standpoint this should be enough to exclude the possibility that epistemic authorities give preemptive reasons for belief.[31]

Practical authority involves "power, whether it be the power to command another or act for him." (De George 1970, p. 199). This is not the case with epistemic authority. We say that *X* has epistemic authority over *Y* if *Y* believes *p* in virtue of the fact that *X* uttered it. As we have seen accepting the epistemic authority of another person is, for the most part, justified by the fact that Y has superior knowledge. For there to be *de facto* epistemic authority, the bar is much lower. In fact, the proposition "X has superior knowledge" doesn't have to be true; it is enough that Y believes that X possesses superior knowledge for X to have authority over Y. The expertise of the only MD in a small village might as well be in a rather narrow subfield of medicine, he would still exercise epistemic authority over the villagers, based on the belief of the villagers that the MD has superior knowledge in the domain of health in general.[32] For authority to be justified, this, of course, doesn't suffice. Any account of legitimate epistemic authority has to incorporate the fact that

is free to take or not... Theoretical authorities do not normally impose duties on others, although they might give advice on what a person's duty is": Christiano (2004).

[30]At least not in a literal fashion. Robert Nozick though claims that we can be coerced to believe, at least in philosophy (Nozick 1981, p. 4; Zagzebski 2012, p. 24).

[31]Raz himself disagrees and claims that theoretical advice pre-empts the other reasons for belief that I would otherwise have, and in this way, it resembles practical authority (Raz 2009, p. 155). Some contemporary authors like Linda Zagzebski defend the claim that epistemic authority gives exclusionary reasons for action by relying on Raz's analysis of practical authority. The preemption thesis can be reformulated to include epistemic authorities in this way: "The fact that the authority has a belief p is a reason for me to believe p that replaces my other reasons relevant to believing p and is not simply added to them" (Zagzebski 2012, p. 107). This is not the place to discuss in detail this complicated issue. Most of the discussions are based on the supposition that epistemic authority is in fact practical authority based on expertise. This is the case with discussions of Darwall and Hurd (Darwall 2010, p. 274; Hurd 1999). In this vein Darwall for example writes that expertise alone doesn't give anyone "the standing to issue authoritative directives that create preemptive reasons".

[32]The most interesting thing from a non-conceptual standpoint is certainly our usual tendency to dilate epistemic authority in a specific field to completely unrelated domains of knowledge. Factually, authority proliferates from one field to another quite easily. The mentioned only MD in the village would usually be trusted in various other matters, not just those related to health. The opinion of a law professor about an issue in international relations or anything for that matter often is taken as a opinion with crucial weight, even if the person in question doesn't know anything about international relations. Or, to use a more common example, the commentators on TV shows are often complete ignoramus when it comes to the issues they are asked about. That still doesn't stop persons who consider them authorities in certain fields, to regard them as authorities in completely unrelated fields.

epistemic authority is confined to one or a couple of doxastic domains (Jäger 2016, p. 170). Needless to say, *X* doesn't have to be a person, but can also be "a text or other written work or document", "a fund of knowledge of a discipline accepted by *Y*" and even "ones conscience". Since epistemic authority is not a kind of normative power in the Razian sense and in this way, it is *powerless*. There are however some situations in which someone who has theoretical authority exercises power, but this doesn't necessarily have to be in virtue of him being a theoretical authority. A MD who utters deontic propositions that are obeyed, during a epidemic outbreak is not acting in virtue of being a theoretical authority, but in virtue of being a practical authority. The utterance of a doctor ordering a quarantine for a patient are not intended, nor they are understood as giving reasons for belief, but reasons for action. The fact that he has the power to exercise practical authority is only contingently connected to the fact that he is regarded as an epistemic authority. But the right to issue deontic propositions and the duties of other persons to obey those propositions are not based on his superior knowledge, because "there are no epistemic laws, epistemic courts, or epistemic punishments" that would enforce compliance with an utterance of an epistemic authority (Zagzebski 2012, p. 138).

An important feature of epistemic authority is that it exists iff Y explicitly or tacitly *acknowledges* that authority of X (De George 1970, p. 200). De George gives interesting examples of acknowledgement to prove a point that "no-one can be forced to acknowledge another as an epistemic authority". Faculty members may well legitimately ask of someone else to consider them an epistemic authority, but they cannot one force someone else to consider them an epistemic authority (De George 1970, p. 203). These characterizations of epistemic authority, even with the side note that students "may be predisposed" to consider a teacher as an epistemic authority, seem to be lacking in at least one important way: genealogically, epistemic authority precedes acknowledgement in many cases. Epistemic authorities do seem to be settled as authorities before we reach the point in which we can rationally deny or acknowledge their status as authorities for us. This will be the case with canonical texts in literature or theology, historical data, and even many theoretical positions within most domains of science and philosophy.

Another characteristic of epistemic authority is that it is *substitutional*—"its purpose is to substitute the knowledge of one person in a certain field for the lack of knowledge of another" (De George 1970, p. 201).[33] It should be noted that the former analysis shows that while substitution is in principle possible, it is often unattainable. John Hardwig is certainly right when he emphasizes the importance of our time constraints and constraints in talents, resources and knowledge for personal examining every belief that we hold. Still, substitutionality is an important trait of

[33] A closely related characteristic is that epistemic authority is often *time-relative* in the sense that an authority can be justified at one time and not justified at another because of the permanent possibility of substituting the beliefs acquired by means of epistemic authority with personally examined beliefs (Jäger 2016, p. 170).

epistemic authority in narrow domains of knowledge, and can therefore be important for interpretation in law.

The relations of epistemic authority are often *formalized, or institutionalized* within a society. Richard T. De George stresses that an epistemic authority is formally produced in as society by being certified as such by peers; he then acts as an epistemic authority for subjects of epistemic authority only if it accepted by them (Jäger 2016, p. 202). This characteristic of epistemic authority is almost completely neglected in epistemic literature, which can be explained by its primary interests, and the intentions behind the analysis of epistemic authority.

4 Import of Various Authorities on Legal Interpretation

As much as I was trying to remain neutral in terms of various kinds of beliefs, and to avoid talking about knowledge as evidence-based belief, it could be argued that most of the discussion about epistemic authority relates in fact to empirical knowledge. This is the case only to the extent that we believe that only opinions worth having are simple opinions formed on perceptual data or a priori knowledge. Deferring to opinions of other persons in on this account justified iff the opinions in question can also be verified *ex post facto* by an objective procedure that can be undertaken by every individual. The expert is in this sense at least provisionally in a better position to form the opinion according to those very standards for knowledge. It seems quite clear, though, that even without holding a strong realist account of objectivity, the above said applies to experts in other areas as well. If it is common to have experts in aesthetic matters, even in moral matters, then it shouldn't be a problem accepting that there are experts in legal matters.

Even if the standards on which the opinions of those experts are not as set in stone as some philosophical realists think about perceptual knowledge, it can still be, and often is the case, that my personal belief-forming process is completely out of tune with the topic on which an opinion should be formed.[34] The other reason for not conflating epistemic authority as a replacement of perceptual belief is that epistemic authorities do not testify about perceptual data, but form entire conclusions about various kinds of data and present them (Raz 2009, p. 155).

This is especially true of law since legal interpretation and our understanding of law are not always settled by invoking truth (Marmor 2017, p. 584). Law relies on much more than the simple truth of propositions in order to regulate behavior. In fact, for reasons of legal certainty, coordination, protection of interests, and various other, the meanings of words in law often overtly deviate in a significant manner from meanings shared within a community or even meanings established by contemporary natural sciences. It thus seems perfectly justified to consider belief

[34]For Elizabeth Fricker moral and aesthetic judgements are a special additional problem in the topic of testimony: Fricker (2017, p. 237).

formation about the meanings of legal texts as a special case of belief formation in general, and to test the explanatory force of this account of justified epistemic authority in the domain of legal interpretation.

Some of the cases of epistemic authority that we considered involved law, but they were mostly concerned with the relation between the layman and the expert lawyer. For the most part, the most reasonable course of action for a layman when it comes to law is to follow the advice of an expert lawyer. The enterprise of justifying such an attitude, as interesting as it may be for legal doctrine and legal science, doesn't cover much ground in the domain of epistemology and philosophy of law. Relations of practical and epistemic authority in regard to legal interpretation become much more interesting when it comes to its workings within the community of lawyers, especially within the smaller community of those exemplary authoritative interpreters of legal texts—judges.

4.1 Practical Authority and Legal Interpretation

I finally turn to the issue of how the former analysis of authority along with an analysis of specific traits of legal interpretation is relevant for legal interpretation. To address this, it is necessary to pinpoint the authorities that provide content-independent reasons for beliefs or actions of authoritative interpreters of law, and to show in what ways do these kinds of authority have an import on the activity of ascribing meaning to legal texts and behaviors that we call legal interpretation. Even though epistemic authority is a topic of this paper, it should be noted that communities of shared beliefs often include epistemic and practical authority, with a special role of epistemic authority in fields that require training, teaching or cooperative epistemic efforts (Zagzebski 2012, p. 144). The community of legal interpreters is one such case.

For one legal interpretation is, at times, the object of statutory regulation. If we conceive of law as possessing practical authority, or necessarily claiming legitimate authority, a legal provision mandating a certain ascription of meaning to a legal term or a legal text gives protected reasons for action (assuming Raz's account of practical authority is correct, of course) to officials that are interpreting legal texts in three respects: (a) Contemporary modes of writing laws often encompass a part with definitions of crucial terms. An authoritative legal interpreter in these cases is given content-independent reasons to ascribe a certain meaning to the terms used in the statute. (b) Some systems of national and some international laws prescribe methods of legal interpretation, giving some doctrines of legal interpretation absolute weight when it comes to the ascription of meaning to legal texts. (c) In jurisdictions in which precedents or general opinions of highest courts are binding as a matter of law, those legal acts give reasons for interpreters to ascribe a meaning to a legal text that conforms to a precedent or to a general legal opinion.[35]

A common problem with statutory definitions, interpretative rules, and formal binding precedents acting as reasons for action is that they are still expressed in terms that are either natural language terms, although, hopefully, made less vague and ambiguous by legislative or judiciary action. This is not always the case. To use just one example: "Secret data" is defined by the Serbian Code of Criminal Procedure as "secret data and foreign secret data", so that the first part of the definition goes exactly like this: "secret data is secret data and foreign secret data..." Fortunately the second part of the definition gives something that can conceivably be helpful in the ascription of meaning: "...determined in accordance to the law that regulates the secrecy of data". I don't possess enough reliable empirical data to state if this definition was of any help in disambiguating the usage of the term in Serbian legal practice. If it was, this wasn't in virtue of the formulation of this definition. The wording of rules that are supposed to minimize or solve interpretative problems are also the subject of interpretation.

There is still one important sense in which practical authority is at work in the ascription of meaning to legal texts, even if one interpretation is not formally binding as a matter of law. If there is a review system in place, the opinions of the highest courts will have authority on prudential grounds. Decisions of higher administrative courts in Germany are not formally binding for lower administrative courts. The conflicting opinions of two courts in 1986 about the right to asylum of the Tamil minority from Sri Lanka lead to the Federal Administrative court reversing 160 decisions which were in line with the opinion of the Higher Administrative Court. Finally, the Higher Administrative Court deferred to the opinion of the Federal Administrative Court, arguing that it was a requirement of "uniformity of adjudication" (OVG NW decision of 27 June 1986—file number 19A 10005/85, p. 18) (Alexy and Dreier 1997, p. 37). This kind of influence is rarely exercised as overtly as in this case. More often than not, the lower courts conform to the opinion of higher courts in order to avoid the situation in which a decision is overturned on the basis of a certain interpretation.[36]

On a more general note: A court or judge *X* is legally or prudentially justified in deferring to the ascription of meaning *p* to an utterance q by the legislator *Y* or another court *Z* in virtue of *X's* institutional position in the legal system. The reasons

---

[35]In the analysis of practical authority, in this occasion I follow Raz in order to draw some possible conclusions about the import of his idea of practical authority on legal interpretation, for the main purpose of the paper is to dwell on the connection between epistemic authority in interpretation. This is not to say that the practice of legal interpretation raises some issues about Razes conception of practical authority. Some of those issues are motioned in the remainder of this section.

[36]Some of the most extreme cases in which nothing but the law is cited in the decision are the judgements of the French *Cour de Cassation*. This court doesn't even mention previous judgments in its decisions. Of course, this is mostly a matter of style intended to show (arguably needlessly and to an extreme) that the decision follows from statutes as a matter of logical necessity (Taruffo et al. 1997, p. 454).

for deferring to the ascription of meaning might be of a legal nature—when the legal system prescribes that the courts have to follow the ascriptions of meaning of other courts or the legislator, or simply prudential—when the institutional arrangements in the judiciary make it possible for a court's decision to be directly or indirectly invalidated by another court.

4.2 *Epistemic Authority and Legal Interpretation*

Practical authority can do the trick in helping us disentangle the relation between authority and interpretation only partially. To authoritative interpreters of law, the must-sources of law[37] are a source of practical authority in the interpretation of law. Given that the law is for the most part written, and that legal provisions are, as a rule, in virtue of their generality and indeterminacy, inapt to provide precise guidelines for the ascription of meaning to legal texts, practical authority can't account for the entirety of procedures and results of legal interpretation. If it were otherwise, our interpretative debates could, in principle, be canceled pre-empted by a well-drafted statute regulating legal interpretation.

The statutory rules are not nearly enough to explain all of the influences that condition an individual act of interpretation. When a judge faces something, he perceives as an interpretative problem, the activity of ascribing meaning to the legal text is, in many ways, dependent on various epistemic authorities. In much the same way, it can be reasonable to a layman to defer to an opinion of an expert, it is often justified for an official to defer to an opinion of another official or an opinion of a prominent scholar.[38] This dynamic can be compared to the dynamic of proliferation of precedent and an increase of its importance in civil law countries. The dynamics of contemporary common law legal systems has led to a wide adoption of precedents as sources of law with various degrees of bindingness depending on the country, legal areas in which precedent is used, and the legal tradition.[39] This reliance on precedent is, more often than not, based in statutory or constitutional obligation to follow previous decisions; it has come about as a matter of legal necessity to conform judicial decisions to standards of legal certainty, coherence, and equality before the law (MacCormick and Summers 1997a, b, p. 535). Epistemic authority

[37]I rely here on the distinction between must, should and may sources of law proposed by Aleksander Peczenik (Peczenik 2005, p. 15).

[38]Sunstein and Vermeule show quite convincingly that some of the contemporary doctrines of legal interpretation heavily premise unsubstantiated trust in institutional and epistemic capacities of judges: "It is reasonable to believe that judges are not well-equipped to engage in theoretically ambitious tasks" (Sunstein and Vermeule 2002, pp. 40–43).

[39]The best study in this regard is most certainly Interpreting precedents edited by Neil MacCormick and Summers. The work of various important contemporary theorists of law shows in great detail the amount in which precedent is used especially in those systems in which precedent is not a formal source of law (MacCormick and Summers 1997a, b).

allows us to understand the cognitive processes operational in many cases of legal interpretation in which we don't have overt regulation of interpretation by the law or by higher ranking officials. Let me briefly sketch a couple of cases in which the employment of the notion of theoretical authority helps us understand the behavior of authoritative legal interpreters.

The most obvious examples of the fact that the determination of meaning of a legal text is based on utterances of epistemic authorities are the situations in which the meaning of a word or an utterance in law is entirely unrelated to the meaning of this word or utterance in the corresponding natural language.[40] A frequent example used in the literature is the First Amendment to the U.S. Constitution, which states "Congress shall make no law ... abridging the freedom of speech." This fairly simple statement is taken to include the "prior restraint doctrine, the rules that define the freedom of speech doctrine governing expressions via billboards, and the distinction between content-based regulations and content neutral time, place, and manner restrictions" (Solum 2012, p. 99). One needn't be a legal expert to notice that none of those crucial elements of meaning of the provision are present in the formulation of the provision, but that they are still crucial for the interpretation of the provision. The ascription of meaning is dependent on a doctrine formulated by courts and scholars on various occasion and with regard to various cases. The meaning of the provision is shared by authoritative interpreters in virtue of the epistemic authority of representatives of practical or theoretical jurisprudence.

A still more simple case is the meaning of the word "hold" in the context of Serbian criminal provisions banning the "unauthorized holding of weapons and ammunition," as well as the "unauthorized holding a small amount of substances that are designed as narcotic drugs." In this case, the criminal courts defer to the definition of "holding" by civil law courts that encompasses the idea that one holds a thing if he is acting as the owner of that thing, and has the opportunity to dispose of the thing. Now even if the deference is not helpful, it certainly is not based on the ordinary meaning of the expression but on the authoritative inferences of practical and theoretical jurisprudence. Disregarding the problems that this causes for certain contemporary doctrines of legal interpretation, it seems straightforward that if we were to ask about the meaning of the word "hold" in Serbian law, it would be plainly incorrect to specify the meaning of the word without reference to its specific legal meaning established in legal doctrine or legal practice. Theoretical authority of other national courts and of national legal doctrine has been the subject of much attention; and the influence it exercises on legal interpretation, according to many legal theorists, warrants its status as a source of law in national legal orders.[41]

---

[40]This is characteristically the case with legal presuppositions and legal fictions, which seem to deny claims that meaning in law is determined by the literal meaning of the words or utterances that are used in law (Schauer 2015, pp. 501–513). Fictions are often influential on legal interpreters as a matter of practical authority, since they are most of the time to be found in formal sources of law.

[41]The works of Aleksander Peczenik and Fabio Shecaira analyze this issue in detail: Peczenik (2005) and Shecaira (2013). The most detailed research and analysis of judicial decisions as sources of law can be found in: MacCormick and Summers (1997a, b).

The influences of epistemic authority have become obvious in the form of courts interpreting domestic law according to legal decisions made either by international courts or courts from other countries. In a decision from 2012 (IESC 10), the Irish Supreme Court upholds the constitutionality of provisions of the Irish Criminal Code that discriminates between males and females by excluding criminal liability for females that engage in intercourse before the age of 17, in spite of the fact that it bans similar activities for both males and females. The reasoning of the Court was based entirely on the reasoning of the US Supreme Court in a similar case (Michael M. v. Superior Ct., 450 U.S. 464 1981), up to the point that disregarded important differences between the respective codes in US and in Ireland.[42] Leaving aside for a moment the justification of this interpretative stipulation, the Irish Court relied on the opinion of another court without any formal obligation to do so. Arguably, the court would have done better to access the authoritative texts that were available to it fully and thoroughly. But even if the justification for deferring to a foreign court in such a significant manner is lacking, the fact is that theoretical authority of the US Supreme Court explains the interpretive behavior of the Irish Supreme Court. The interpretative opinion of the US Supreme Court about the meaning of a legal provision was, in fact, a content-independent reason for the Irish Supreme Court to believe that the corresponding legal provision means exactly what the US Supreme Court states that it means.

On a more general note: A court or judge *Y* is rationally justified to defer to the ascription of meaning (interpretation) p to a legal text *q* of the person *X*, if the court or judge *Y* has good reasons to believe that that *X* has more knowledge, skills, experience or training in ascribing meaning to (interpreting) *q*.

5 Moving Forward

Ricardo Guastini notes, in his contribution to the present volume, that one of the shortcomings of the standard picture of interpretation is that it completely disregards juristic interpretation—interpretation of law done by legal scholars. In his view, this is especially important because the juristic interpretation "equip judges with concepts, doctrines, interpretive tools, forms of reasoning – as a matter of fact, the interpretive and dogmatic practice of legal scholarship conditions the very *forma mentis* of judges.". Brian Leiter, in his contribution to the present volume, argues that the norms of interpretation evolve and vary with the nature of the judiciary and interpretive practices, in such a way that there are not many interesting things that can generally be said about viable norms of interpretation.

[42]I'm taking this example from, who in fact analyses this and other cases from the perspective of theoretical authority, insisting that the idea of persuasion doesn't suffice to provide an account of judicial dialogue (Doyle 2016, pp. 100–101).

In interpreting texts contained in sources of law, officials are not only influenced by the content of those sources. Their beliefs about the meaning of the texts, their interpretative practice that is for the most part shared by other members of a community of jurists. In at least some cases that were discussed, namely cases of overt reliance on the opinions of others, the beliefs are not based on personally examined reasons. A sizable amount of those beliefs about meaning is in fact based on testimony. Among the beliefs that are shared within a community of jurists, utterances of epistemic authorities play an important role in ascription of meaning to legal texts. In cases ranging from the meanings of single words of legal provisions to entire fields of regulation, the utterances of epistemic authorities in significant ways determine the ascription of meaning to legal texts. The amount and ubiquity of this influence is of course an empirical question, but it's necessity and justification in authoritative interpretation in law are not. The third perspective is of course a philosophical one—and this last analysis is the one that I tried to develop on previous pages. In all of the cases in which the reasons for one authoritative interpretation of the legal text are not based on autonomous detached non-contextual ascription of meaning (if there is such a thing), the enterprise of interpretation occurs within boundaries set by different authorities. Frank Kermode would state it like this: "No person can go about the work of interpretation without some awareness of forces which limit, or try to limit, what he may say, and the ways in which he may say it" (Kermode 1979, p. 72). It was shown previously that in some instances deference to opinions of others is rationally justified. In this last part of the paper, I'll try to advance some tentative conclusions by sketching the path of further research on this topic.

Within a community of legal interpreters, the distribution of power in the form of authority is of significant import for the determination of meaning of legal texts; and some instances of that influence are justified. The analysis of these influences on belief forming practices of authoritative legal interpreters, having in mind the amount of our beliefs that rely on testimony and epistemic authority, does some work in explaining the regularity of interpretative ascriptions of meaning in law. Even if we don't have the formalist criterion of semantic determinacy, relations of epistemic authority within a community of jurists have justifiably enough pull to make the interpretation process and the interpretative results overall predictable and reasonably certain. In other words, conceiving of interpretation as a procedure in which one always chooses one of the multiple meanings of legal texts doesn't endanger legal certainty and predictability as core values in the basis of contemporary legal systems, and doesn't lead to erratic interpretative behavior. The exemplified analysis of practical and theoretical influences on legal interpretation brings us, it seems, closer to an explanation of legal practice whose centerpiece is not the imaginary individual official and her effort to interpret the given legal text in order to decide the case at hand. An account of the community and the relations within that community based on the concept(s) of authority (1) grounds individual interpretative enterprises in knowledge about our belief forming practices, (2) establishes their peculiarities in the domain of law, and (3) inquires if they are justified both generally and on a case by case basis.[43]

Thus, the importance of an analysis of authority in the context of legal interpretation seems manifold: (1) it can provide us with a clearer picture of belief formation in legal interpretation, and can therefore explain the ascription of meaning more broadly than is possible with theories of meaning or theories of the nature of legal interpretation; (2) it provides for a philosophical ramification of various practices broadly used in interpretative ascription of meaning by authoritative legal interpreters and lawyers in general; (3) it explains the formation of specifically legal meaning as a function of the relations within an institutionally defined community; (4) it accounts for those ascriptions of meaning that cannot be covered by most theories of meaning, especially realist ones, in which law confers a new meaning to words of natural languages, in order to achieve a certain legal value.

References

Aarnio A (2011) Essays on the doctrinal study of law, vol 96. Springer, Dordrecht

Alexy R, Dreier R (1997) Precedent in the Federal Republic of Germany. In: MacCormick N, Summers RS (eds) Interpreting precedents. Routledge, Abingdon, pp 17–64

Alston WP (1994) Belief-forming practices and the social. In: Schmitt FF (ed) Socializing epistemology. Rowman & Littlefield Publishers, Lanham, pp 29–51

Baude W, Doerfler RD (12 June 2017) "Arguing with Friends"

Chiassoni P (19 March 2006) A nice derangement of literal-meaning freaks. Analisi E Diritto

Christiano T (2 July 2004) "Authority"

Darwall S (2010) Authority and reasons: exclusionary and second-personal. Ethics 120(2):257–278

De George RT (1970) The function and limits of epistemic authority. Southern J Philos 8 (2–3):199–204

Doyle O (2016) Constitutional cases, foreign law and theoretical authority. Global Constitutionalism 5(01):85–108

Dworkin R (1986) Law's Empire. Harvard University Press, Cambridge

Ehrenberg KM (2011) Joseph Raz's theory of authority. Philos Compass 6(12):884–894

Foley R (1994) Egoism in epistemology. In: Schmitt FF (ed) Socializing epistemology. Rowman & Littlefield Publishers, Lanham, pp 53–73

Foley R (2001) Intellectual trust in oneself and others. Cambridge University Press, Cambridge

Fricker E (2006) Second-hand knowledge. Philos Phenomenol Res LXXIII(3):592–618

Fricker E (2017) Testimony and epistemic autonomy. In: Lackey J, Sosa E (eds) The epistemology of testimony. Oxford University Press, Oxford, pp 225–250

Gadamer H-G (2006) Truth and method (trans: Weinsheimer J, Marshall DG). Continuum, New York

[43]A restatement of this issue could be that authority plays an important role in the view about legal interpretation termed by Pierluigi Chiassoni "pragmatic non-cognitivism." One of the main tenants of this view is that interpretation works by using various resources like linguistic meaning, speakers' intention, or whatever else the interpreter decides to base his interpretation on (Chiassoni 2006, p. 118). The reliance of the interpreter on an "interpretative code" or a doctrine of legal interpretation is, according to the views endorsed in this paper, influenced in important ways by relations of epistemic authority.

Glenu HP (1987) Persuasive authority. McGill Law J 32(2):1–38
Green L (1988) The authority of the state. Clarendon Press, Oxford
Guastini R (2014) La Sintassi Del Diritto, 2nd edn. G. Giappichelli Editore, Turin
Hardwig J (1985) Epistemic dependence. J Philos 82(7):334–349
Hershovitz S (2003) Legitimacy, democracy, and Razian authority. Legal Theory 9(03):1–21
Himma KE (23 April 2017) Practical authority. Forthcoming In: Bongioivanni G, Postema G, Rotolo A, Sartor G, Walton D (eds) Handbook of Legal Reasoning and Legal Argumentation). Springer, 2018. Available at SSRN: https://ssrn.com/abstract=2957215
Hurd HM (1999) Moral Combat. Cambridge University Press, Cambridge
Jäger C (2016) Epistemic authority, preemptive reasons, and understanding. Episteme 13 (2):166–185
Kermode F (1979) Institutional control of interpretation. Salmagundi 43:72–86
Lackey J (2017) Introduction. In: Lackey J, Sosa E (eds) The epistemology of testimony. Oxford University Press, Oxford, pp 1–21
Lackey J, Sosa E (eds) (2006) The epistemology of testimony. Oxford University Press, Oxford
Lehrer K (1977) Social information. The Monist 60(4):473–487
Leiter B (2007) Naturalizing jurisprudence. Oxford University Press, Oxford
Lukes S (2005) Power. Palgrave Macmillan, London
MacCormick N, Summers RS (1997a) Further general reflections and conclusions. In: MacCormick N, Summers RS (eds) Interpreting precedents. Routledge, Abingdon, pp 531–550
MacCormick N, Summers RS (eds) (1997b) Interpreting precedents. Routledge, Abingdon
Marmor A (2009) Social conventions. Princeton University Press, Princeton
Marmor A (2017) Meaning and belief in constitutional interpretation. Fordham Law Rev 82 (2):576–596
Nozick R (1981) Philosophical explanations. Harvard University Press, Cambridge
Patterson D (2005) Interpretation in law. San Diego Law Rev 42:685–710
Peczenik A (2005) Scientia Juris: legal doctrine as knowledge of law and as a source of law, vol 4. Springer, Berlin
Pierson R (1994) The epistemic authority of expertise. Proc Biennial Meeting Philos Sci Assoc 1994:398–405
Posner EA, Vermeule A (2016) The votes of other judges. Georgetown Law J 105:158–190
Raz J (1979) The authority of law. Oxford University Press, Oxford
Raz J (1981) Authority and consent. Va Law Rev 67:103–131
Raz J (1988) The morality of freedom. Oxford University Press, Oxford
Raz J (1994) Ethics in the public domain. Oxford University Press, Oxford
Raz J (1999) Practical reason and norms, 3rd edn. Oxford University Press, Oxford
Raz J (2009) Between authority and interpretation. Oxford University Press, Oxford
Rodriguez-Blanco V (2014) Law and authority under the guise of the good. Hart Publishing, Oxford
Schauer F (2008) Authority and authorities. Va Law Rev 94:1193–1196
Schauer F (2015) Is law a technical language? San Diego Law Rev 52:501–513
Shapiro SJ (2014) Authority. In: Coleman JL, Himma KE, Shapiro SJ (eds) The Oxford handbook of jurisprudence and philosophy of law. Oxford University Press, Oxford, pp 382–439
Shecaira FP (2013) Legal scholarship as a source of law. Springer, Berlin
Solum LB (24 January 2012) "Interpretation-Construction Distinction". 1–24
Sunstein CR, Vermeule A (2002) Interpretation and institutions. SSRN Electronic J. Last modified July 24, 2002. Accessed July 28, 2015. http://papers.ssrn.com/sol3/cf_dev/AbsByAuth.cfm?per_id=231075
Taruffo M (1997) Institutional factors influencing precedents. In: MacCormick N, Summers RS (eds) Interpreting precedents. Routledge, Abingdon, pp 437–460
Zagzebski LT (2012) Epistemic authority. Oxford University Press, Oxford

Bojan Spaić is assistant professor of Jurisprudence at the University of Belgrade Faculty of Law and Alexander von Humboldt Research Fellow on the Institute for Public Law, Constitutional Law and Legal Philosophy of the University of Heidelberg. Spaić has edited multiple books in English and in Serbian including: Jurisprudence and Political Philosophy in the twenty-first Century: Reassessing Legacies (with Miodrag Jovanović, published by Peter Lang, 2012), Fundamental Rights: Justification and Interpretation (with Kenneth Einar Himma, published by Eleven international Publishing, 2016), Unpacking Normativity: Conceptual, Normative and Descriptive Issues (with Kenneth Einar Himma and Miodrag Jovanović, Hart Publishing, forthcoming in 2018), Savremeni problemi pravne i političke filozofije (with Damir Banović, published by Šahinpašić, 2016). He published two books in Serbian and multiple papers in Serbian and English regarding legal interpretation, ontological and methodological hermeneutics, pragmatism.

The manufacturer's authorised representative in the EU is Springer Nature Customer Service Centre GmbH, Europaplatz 3, 69115 Heidelberg, Germany. If you have any concerns regarding our products, please contact ProductSafety@springernature.com

Printed and bound by CPI Group (UK) Ltd, Croydon, CR0 4YY
30/09/2026
02225505-0003